Leading Your Business *into the* Future

with the

Internet

DISCARD

Leading Your Business
into the Future
with the
Internet

Danielle Vallée

$$S^t_L$$

St. Lucie Press
Boca Raton   London   New York   Washington, D.C.

Library of Congress Cataloging-in-Publication Data

Catalog information may be obtained from the Library of Congress

© 1999 by CRC Press LLC
St. Lucie Press is an imprint of CRC Press LLC

No claim to original U.S. Government works
International Standard Book Number 1-57444-252-X
Printed in the United States of America 1 2 3 4 5 6 7 8 9 0
Printed on acid-free paper

Table of Contents

Introduction

If this book is in your hands, you are probably a busy person who is interested in using the Internet for business purposes but do not have much time to delve into the zillion sources of information available on the market. You have chosen the right book.

There is a lot of talk about the Internet. Some people are completely addicted to it, and others think it's only a fad. You probably have been told more than once that you should "be on it." You may have been asked for your e-mail address or your Web site address. You may have been told that you should be doing business on the Internet and even that you can quickly become very rich doing so.

Businesspeople who want to use the Internet face myriad possibilities. Some people may be accustomed to some Internet services and others may not. However, there is a huge gap between using the Internet for one's personal needs and using it effectively in doing business. The Internet offers an incredible range of services and possibilities which start at the simplest level and move on to very technically complex setups.

One can start very modestly and gradually increase one's level of expertise. This medium is as available to small businesses as it is to large companies. However, it is important for a businessperson to properly gather the necessary information in order to make the best decisions and get the most out of this amazing medium. Failure to do so can devour tremendous amounts of money while producing only mediocre results.

As examples of the possibilities, faxes, letters, memos, messages (written and voice), documents, images and sounds can be sent all over the world without any additional cost. The Internet can be used to advertise products and services for a lot less money than traditional advertising media. Orders can be taken via a Web site, and the whole process can be automated and performed for a fraction of your existing costs. The Internet allows telephone conversations and video-conferencing, thus dramatically decreasing long-distance and travel expenses. It contains virtual stores and chat rooms. It contains millions and millions of pages of information where just about anything you can dream of can be found. It can be used for research, testing and focus groups. Newsletters and bulletins can be sent simultaneously and instantly to all of a company's locations around the world as well as to thousands of customers. The list is endless. Furthermore, the medium itself is evolving at a mind-boggling pace, both technologically and in the new potential it offers.

It is estimated that over 145 million people were using the Internet worldwide as of 1998. That is an incredible market for the business-person who has enough savvy to tap into it.

Although this new medium has its own rules, requirements and specifications, it offers a dimension no other medium can: interaction with customers. This new dimension brings new challenges in using it effectively.

If you have not used the Internet yet, the process is probably still a mystery to you and you may not know where to start. If you already personally use the Internet, you may have encountered one or more services you would like to know more about or would like to apply to your business operations. Even if you are a regular user, implementing the Internet in your business requires good planning and preparation in order to minimize costs and maximize opportunities and profitability. It will definitely have an impact on your day-to-day operations.

The Internet has a lot to offer. To use it efficiently, you have to master some basic technical aspects as well as creative elements. If you are serious about doing business on the Internet, you need a minimum of knowledge, some good ideas and a good plan. Your strategies should be based on hard facts and data in relation to your business.

There are also several myths about the Internet. Some people say it is a revolutionary communication tool, and others pretend that you can make a fortune overnight with it. Some think it can be controlled, and others say it will soon control the world. Some think it is the part-time responsibility of a company's technical department, and others think that just about anyone can set up and maintain a Web site. Some say it is simply an experiment, and others are convinced it is a money pit.

The speed at which the Internet is evolving, both on the technical side and in the potential it offers, can be intimidating at times. New business opportunities are emerging at an incredible pace and are the direct result of new technologies developed at an equally fast pace. In order to be able to follow this evolution, one has to remain involved and follow it on practically a daily basis. Most of the information offered by magazines assumes that you have familiarized yourself with the developments from early on. Thus, it is easy to get lost in the technobabble if you have not yet assimilated the basics.

The Internet is a very effective and interesting medium for a business to use in order to make its operations more efficient and to expand into new markets. However, the technical aspects are numerous and not always easy to understand all at once, especially if one lacks crucial basic knowledge. Finding one's way through the maze of services, software offers, hardware options, and so on can be a real challenge because a lot of the information is spread out in numerous places and tends to be very technical. There are magazines, books, computer software and Web sites that contain diverse information and very often promote one product or another. Furthermore, using the Internet for personal purposes is quite different from implementing it in a business and using it for commercial purposes. As a reference, the following table provides a comparison between basic/personal use and business/commercial use.

Parallel Between Personal Use and Business Use

Basic/Personal Use	*Business/Commercial Use*
■ Send and receive electronic mail	■ Distribute electronic mail (on a more or less regular basis)
■ Surf the World Wide Web	■ Put up a World Wide Web site
■ Buy goods and services	■ Sell goods and services
■ Place orders and purchase merchandise	■ Sell merchandise, receive and process orders

Basic/Personal Use	Business/Commercial Use
■ Read news	■ Produce and publish news
■ Do research	■ Offer and provide information
■ Receive information through push channels	■ Send information through push channels
■ Listen to audio broadcasts	■ Produce audio broadcasts
■ View and be seen through video	■ Organize videoconferences and produce video broadcasts
■ Register with distance learning programs	■ Produce and implement distance learning programs
■ Subscribe to electronic newsletters	■ Produce and distribute electronic newsletters
■ Read electronic magazines	■ Publish electronic magazines
■ Read PDF documents	■ Publish PDF documents
■ Obtain information about specific products	■ Advertise and promote your products (goods and services)
■ Obtain customer service	■ Set up customer service
■ Find new suppliers	■ Find and serve new markets

Without proper planning, you can spend a lot of money just to learn about and experiment with the basic aspects: technical issues, administration, management and marketing. That is why you need to be well informed and well prepared in order to start using the Internet to the advantage of your business.

A business's Internet operation either can be organized in a very simple manner without incurring too many costs or can call for a sophisticated and expensive setup. A lot of free tools are available on the Internet, and you can choose to do it either way. The main thing is good planning and deciding how much you can spend and how you want to proceed. But doing that requires complete information.

In addition to basic technical knowledge, a good marketing strategy must be designed. It would be preposterous to think that being on the Internet will automatically bring in a lot of new business and make you rich instantly. The Internet is an effective tool only when used properly, and it must be integrated into the overall marketing strategy of a business.

Both Internet and business specialists agree that having well-planned and strong strategies is as important as their efficient execution in determining success. Sensible use of the Internet in a business may very well be what differentiates the winners from the losers in the coming years of globalization.

The Internet offers the same opportunities to small businesses as it does to large businesses. However, depending on the kind of business you are in and the size of your business, the implementation will be different. This means that it does not make any difference to the Internet customer whether you have a small or a large business, but it will make a difference for your business operations and your Internet setup.

This book provides a complete range of information from a business point of view, from basic to more advanced. Even if you are not yet familiar with the Internet, it will be easy for you to understand. The last thing a businessperson needs is to waste a lot of time searching for basic information. Time is a precious resource, and a businessperson needs accurate information and needs it fast. *Leading Your Business into the Future with the Internet* is a comprehensive guide to help the businessperson understand the implications of the Internet for his or her business, including both implementation as well as potential profits. A decision maker does not need the same level of expertise as a technical expert but does need a minimum of technical knowledge in order to use the Internet effectively and to ask the right questions when it is time to make sound business decisions. This book offers a step-by-step method to start using this new medium effectively and to lead your company into the future. I hope it will provide you with a global appreciation of what this wonderful and amazing medium can do within and for your business.

Acknowledgment

I would like to thank my good friend Germain Decelles, Vice-President Research and Development, Hypertec Systems, who has so patiently answered many of my questions and provided unfailing encouragement all along the preparation of this book.

About the Author

Danielle Vallée is a North American Specialist in Business Development, Marketing Communication and Training. She has over 20 years of experience in management, technical and marketing activities in large corporations and as an independent business consultant to large, medium and small companies. Her strong interest in new technologies is focused on telecommunications and the Internet.

Ms. Vallée has pioneered the use of the Internet for small and medium businesses and has managed the development of major Web sites. She has given numerous seminars and lectures on how to use the Internet in businesses and organizations. She is the author of several books and magazine articles about the Internet and business topics. This is her second book published in the U.S. market. Ms. Vallée also has experience as a host and television producer for the business sector and has been a regular guest on the national TV News Network of Radio-Canada. She has prepared and delivered numerous lectures on business topics in English and well as French. She has also developed several training programs, including distance learning programs, for various levels of management and entrepreneurs and for businesses of all sizes.

Her diversified experience working with major corporations as well as smaller businesses has allowed her to develop a broad understanding of needs, problem resolution, business opportunities, planning challenges and marketing strategies for small, medium and large businesses. Her latest project is a Virtual Business Network for Teenager Entrepreneurs.

She can be reached at dvallee@point-net.com or through http://www.whizteens.com or http://membres.point-net.com/~dvallee.

1 What Is the Internet?

1 The Network

To understand the potential the Internet has to offer, one has to understand what it is and how it works. Let's look at what the Internet is and is not.

The Origins of the Internet

There has been a lot of talk and hype in recent years about the Internet, but, surprisingly, the Internet network is over 20 years old. However, in the beginning, it was far from the network we know today. The commercial aspects that have made it so popular have been developed only recently. Originally, it started in 1969 as a project to link four computers from several university computer departments and a few private companies with the U.S. Department of Defense's Advanced Project Agency, and it gradually evolved from that cluster of computers linked together to several million today. Just remember what computers were like in those days: They were far from the small and efficient computers we are now very fortunate to have.

This small network evolved gradually throughout the 1970s and 1980s as more research organizations were encouraged to link up to the existing network. The advantage of such a structure was that the information was not concentrated in a unique location but rather was spread throughout a wide geographical area. This offered additional safety in that whatever destruction might happen, the totality of the information was never completely lost, and most likely a duplicate would exist in another location. It was even built to withstand a nuclear attack.

In the mid-1980s, a high-speed network was established by the National Science Foundation and then added to the existing network (called ARPANET) which produced the Internet. The Internet went from a few computers to over 20,000 in 1990. There are over 4.5 million World Wide Web domain registrations today, and that number grows by over 65,000 per week. The growth is phenomenal. We must also consider the growth of electronic commerce: It is estimated that e-commerce will reach $300 billion in the year 2002.

The Physical Network

The physical network, which in reality is a complex setup, is described here in a very simple manner in order to facilitate understanding of the concept.

When you connect to the Internet, you do so with your own computer, which must be equipped with a modem. A **modem** is a small piece of equipment that acts as a telephone for your computer, allowing you to call another computer. Modems transfer data at various speeds, which are measured in baud. The current measurement is in kilobaud per second (Kbps); 1 kilobaud is equal to 1,000 baud. A few years ago, most modems transferred data at rates of 3,600 and

Figure 1   Modems transfer data at various speeds, which are measured in baud.

9,300 baud (3.6 and 9.3 kilobaud or Kbps, respectively). Then, a couple of years ago, their speed increased to 14.4 Kbps, then 28.8 Kbps. Current modem speeds range from 33.6 to 56 Kbps. Some can even attain 128.8 Kbps and more. The faster the modem, the faster one will have access to the information on the Internet, although this is not an absolute truth because there are other limitations imposed by hardware and telecommunication lines (discussed in Chapter 15).

When you want to log onto the Internet, your computer calls an information system which is composed of several devices, the central part of which is a server. A **server** is a higher capacity computer dedicated to serving other computers. It acts as a central computer, linking a multitude of other smaller computers just like yours (Figure 2). It is also linked to other servers throughout the Internet network. In fact, the Internet is a network of networks (Figure 3). Remember that this is a simplified explanation!

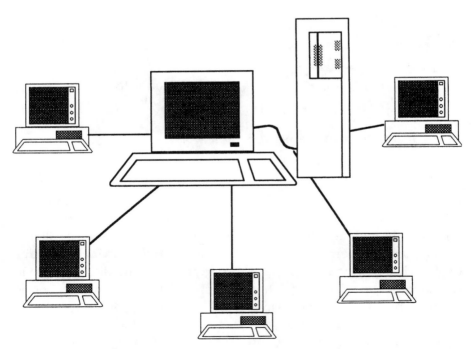

Figure 2   A server acts as a central computer, linking a multitude of other smaller computers.

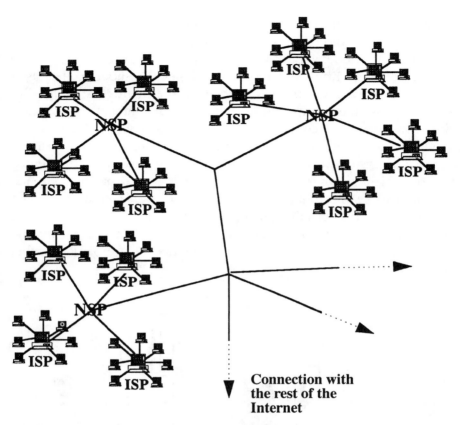

Connection with
the rest of the
Internet

Figure 3   The Internet is a network of networks.

The Internet is composed of a multitude of these servers that are linked to one another through a network of special cables and connections, throughout the world. A group of servers is then connected together through a larger central Internet provider, sort of like a wholesaler of Internet access, called a **network service provider** (NSP). That is why it is not necessary to make a long-distance phone call in order to connect to the Internet and talk to any number of people anywhere on the planet. In other words, you connect to a local server which allows you to access any other server in the network, anywhere in the world. The local server either belongs to your **Internet service provider** (ISP), sort of a retailer of Internet services, or can be your own server if you decide to have your own setup and connect directly to the Internet network.

Of course, in reality, the connection structure of the network is more complex than described here, and there are several pieces of equipment that come into play between servers and on various parts of the network. The model has been simplified here for the purpose of convenience.

Suffice it to say that you connect to your local ISP with a local phone number, therefore incurring no long-distance charge, and from there, you have access to the whole network. Why? Because your ISP is connected to an NSP. NSPs may run local or national networks. NSPs connect to one another at various locations usually called network access points. When you connect to your ISP, you are therefore connected to all of the above and your queries travel throughout the whole network.

In order to communicate, all these different computers must use a common language to be able to talk to one another. There are, however, many types of computers on the market, and they are not always compatible with one another. There are different kinds of servers, different kinds of personal computers and different kinds of operating systems on various servers and computers. The various operating systems are called **platforms**. When all those computers connect to the Internet, they have to become compatible to a certain extent in order to be able to communicate with one another. They must therefore use standard protocols. A **protocol** is a code for transferring data and for communicating.

Several software programs are required in order to accomplish various tasks while using the Internet. There is software for the servers, for instance, for connection purposes, for administration purposes and for security purposes. There is also a variety of software for the personal computers to allow them to connect to the network and accomplish various things.

For basic services, as far as you are concerned, you need a connection and communication program to allow your computer to connect to the server and to make your modem work with your computer. Then you will need electronic mail software, World Wide Web surfing software and so on, according to what you want to do. These types of software are explored further in the next chapters. For the moment, let's just say that it doesn't matter what kind of computer you have. As long as you use the proper software, it will allow your computer to speak a common language with all other computers on the Internet. Presently, different versions of the same software exist for various platforms: mainframes, servers and client stations, as well as types of mainframe (VM, MVS, VMS); types of server, such as NT, UNIX (Sun Solaris, HP-UX, AIX, SCO, Linux) and Novell; and types of client station (Macintosh, Windows, NT Station, DOS, UNIX). This allows practically anyone to get on the Internet. The interesting thing is that whatever your computer's capacity, you will be able to find appropriate software that allows you to access the Internet. However, the capacity of your computer (the random access memory or **RAM** capacity, which manages the flow of information on your computer during a given session) may limit what you can do. Some of the software has become quite sophisticated, integrating several functions such as electronic mail, World Wide Web browsing, audio, chat and so on. The downside is that the software is RAM hungry.

There are currently over 6.5 million servers accessible worldwide. These servers are located everywhere, and although all are linked together, each acts independently from the rest of the network. How can they communicate together effectively? The answer is that the only constraints imposed by the Internet are the communication protocol and the identification of the server and its users.

What Countries Have Access to the Internet?

Today, the Internet is present in about 60 countries. However, the Internet service level is not the same everywhere. Some countries have access to full Internet services, while others have access to partial services. Some have full-time access, and others have only part-time access. In some countries, there are many servers, and in others they are more scarce.

For example, in some African countries, Internet services are provided by a few university servers that are connected to the network only some of the time. Often, they only provide subscribers with basic e-mail services. Some countries do not allow their populations to have full access to the World Wide Web for fear of "propaganda," corruption and exposure to values that are not in accordance with their own belief systems. There is a whole range of Internet service arrangements throughout the world. However, the network is constantly improving, and international organizations are making efforts to widen Internet access as much as possible worldwide.

In most industrialized countries, Internet services are widely available, although some subscribers may be subjected to particular financial constraints. For instance, in some European countries, the basic telephone service is charged on a per-minute basis, which makes endless hours of Web surfing impractical and increases the cost of it. Furthermore, access is not priced equally everywhere. For example, a basic Internet account can cost up to $100 per month in certain South American countries. When doing business on the Internet, one has to keep these facts in mind.

The following is a list of countries that have access to Internet services. Each country has its own identification code (according to ISO 3166) which is used to identify it on the Internet. This country identification code is sometimes, but not always, in the URL address, depending on the type of address. A **URL**, an acronym for Uniform Resource Locator, is the address of a World Wide Web site. Just as you have an address for your residence, the URL address is the place where a Web site is located.

Afghanistan	af	Bahrain	bh
Albania	al	Bangladesh	bd
Algeria	dz	Barbados	bb
American Samoa	as	Belarus	by
Andorra	ad	Belgium	be
Anguilla	ai	Belize	bz
Antarctica	aq	Bermuda	bm
Antigua and Barbuda	ag	Bhutan	bt
Argentina	ar	Bolivia	bo
Armenia	am	Bosnia and Herzegovina	ba
Aruba	aw	Botswana	bw
Ascension Island	ac	Bouvet Island	bv
Australia	au	Brazil	br
Austria	at	British Indian Ocean Territory	io
Azerbaijan	az	British Virgin Islands	vg
Bahamas	bs	Brunei Darussalam	bn

Bulgaria	bg	Gabon	ga
Burkina Faso	bf	Gambia	gm
Burundi	bi	Georgia	ge
Cambodia	kh	Germany	de
Cameroon	cm	Ghana	gh
Canada	ca	Gibraltar	gi
Cape Verde	cv	Great Britain	gb
Cayman Islands	ky	Greece	gr
Central African Republic	cf	Greenland	gl
Chad	td	Grenada	gd
Chile	cl	Guadeloupe	gp
China	cn	Guam	gu
Christmas Island	cx	Guatemala	gt
Cocos Islands	cc	Guernsey	gg
Colombia	co	Guinea	gn
Comoros	km	Guinea-Bissau	gw
Cook Islands	ck	Guyana	gy
Costa Rica	cr	Haiti	ht
Croatia	hr	Heard and McDonald Islands	hm
Cuba	cu	Honduras	hn
Cyprus	cy	Hong Kong	hk
Czech Republic	cz	Hungary	hu
Democratic Republic of Congo	cg	Iceland	is
Denmark	dk	India	in
Djibouti	dj	Indonesia	id
Dominica	dm	Iran	ir
Dominican Republic	do	Iraq	iq
East Timor	tp	Ireland	ie
Ecuador	ec	Isle of Man	im
Egypt	eg	Israel	il
El Salvador	sv	Italy	it
Equatorial Guinea	gq	Ivory Coast (Côte d'Ivoire)	ci
Eritrea	er	Jamaica	jm
Estonia	ee	Japan	jp
Ethiopia	et	Jersey	je
Falkland Islands	fk	Jordan	jo
Faro Islands	fo	Kazakhstan	kz
Fiji	fj	Kenya	ke
Finland	fi	Kiribati	ki
France	fr	Kuwait	kw
France, Metropolitan	fx	Kyrgyzstan	kg
French Guyana	gf	Laos	la
French Polynesia	pf	Latvia	lv
French Southern Territories	tf	Lebanon	lb

Lesotho	ls	Palau	pw
Liberia	lr	Panama	pa
Libya	ly	Papua New Guinea	pg
Liechtenstein	li	Paraguay	py
Lithuania	lt	Peru	pe
Luxembourg	lu	Philippines	ph
Macao	mo	Pitcairn	pn
Macedonia	mk	Poland	pl
Madagascar	mg	Portugal	pt
Malawi	mw	Puerto Rico	pr
Malaysia	my	Qatar	qa
Maldives	mv	Reunion	re
Mali	ml	Russia/Russian Federation	ru
Malta	mt	Rwanda	rw
Marshall Islands	mh	Saint Helena	sh
Martinique	mq	Saint Kitts and Nevis	kn
Mauritania	mr	Saint Lucia	lc
Mauritius	mu	Saint Pierre and Miquelon	pm
Mayotte	yt	Saint Vincent and Grenadines	vc
Mexico	mx	Samoa	ws
Micronesia	fm	San Marino	sm
Moldova	md	Sào Tomé and Principe	st
Monaco	mc	Saudi Arabia	sa
Mongolia	mn	Senegal	sn
Montserrat	ms	Seychelles	sc
Morocco	ma	Sierra Leone	sl
Mozambique	mz	Singapore	sg
Myanmar	mm	Slovakia/Slovak Republic	sk
Namibia	na	Slovenia	si
Nauru	nr	Solomon Islands	sb
Nepal	np	Somalia	so
Netherlands	nl	South Africa	za
New Caledonia	nc	South Georgia and South Sandwich Islands	gs
New Zealand	nz		
Nicaragua	ni	South Korea	kr
Niger	ne	Spain	es
Nigeria	ng	Sri Lanka	lk
Niue	nu	Sudan	sd
Norfolk Island	nf	Surinam	sr
North Korea	kp	Svalbard and Jan Mayen Islands	sj
Northern Mariana Islands	mp	Swaziland	sz
Norway	no	Sweden	se
Oman	om	Switzerland	ch
Pakistan	pk	Syria	sy

Taiwan	tw	United States	us
Tajikistan	tj	Uruguay	uy
Tanzania	tz	U.S. Minor Outlying Islands	um
Thailand	th	U.S. Virgin Islands	vi
Togo	tg	Uzbekistan	uz
Tonga	to	Vanuatu	vu
Trinidad and Tobago	tt	Vatican City State	va
Tunisia	tn	Venezuela	ve
Turkey	tr	Vietnam	vn
Turks and Caicos Islands	tc	Wallis and Futuna Islands	wf
Turmekistan	tm	Western Sahara	eh
Tuvalu	tv	Yemen	ye
Uganda	ug	Yugoslavia	yu
Ukraine	ua	Zambia	zm
United Arab Emirates	ae	Zimbabwe	zw
United Kingdom	uk		

Where Are the Subscribers?

The data about Internet users vary from one source to another, and they do not necessarily all agree. Most surveys conducted through the Internet are done on a voluntary basis, which is not necessarily representative of the whole Internet population but rather represents the Internet population that has a propensity toward volunteering information about themselves.

However, a study conducted by phone in early 1998 found that 70.5 million people were on-line in the United States, which represents about 35% of the total U.S. population and about half the total Internet users worldwide. Furthermore, almost 50% of the people between 16 and 34 years old were on-line, of which women accounted for about 43% and mature citizens (over 50) about 17%.

The end of 1998 surveys placed the total number of subscribers worldwide at over 150 million, of which about 57% are in the United States. It seems that the current trend is toward the U.S. percentage slowly losing ground as other countries gain subscribers in increasing proportions.

While the United States still has the most subscribers, other users are distributed as shown in Figure 4. This means that, for the time being, you are more likely to find the majority of your Internet

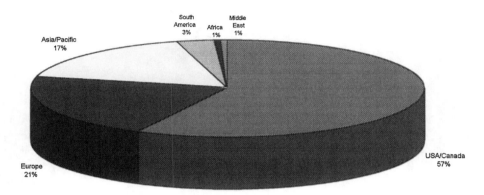

Figure 4 Worldwide Internet users.

customers in North America, but the trend is a higher growth in the rest of the world than in the United States from now on.

For up-to-date information about worldwide statistics, go to:

http://www.nua.ie/surveys

http://www-survey.cc.gatech.edu

http://www-personal.umich.edu/~sgupta/hermes

http://www.nw.com/zone/WWW

http://www.mit.edu/people/mkgray/net

http://www.cyberdialogue.com

2 Who Are the Users?

If you are going to do business on the Internet, you need to know who the Internet users are. Just as you need to know who your customers are in the real world, you need to know who your potential Internet customers are in what is called the "cyberworld." The Internet has its particularities, and its users have characteristics and a culture that are specific to that medium. One cannot assume, therefore, that the same marketing principles apply automatically. The Internet has its own rules.

Before attempting anything, it is wise to get to know the people, what they expect, what they want and what they will not accept. You gain nothing by offending your future customers. If your attempt is not appropriate to the Internet culture, you will at best be ignored and at worst be chastised. Furthermore, you need to determine what you can realistically expect, given the potential the Internet offers.

This chapter offers statistics and describes the users' profile in terms of age, gender, tastes, preferences, etc. Also discussed are the culture that is found on the Internet, as well as current ethical problems and pitfalls.

Who Are the Internet Subscribers?

Depending on the country, women represent between 40 to 45% of Internet users. The gap between male and female Internet users has been narrowing regularly since 1994, when women accounted for less than 5% and men over 95% of total Internet users. Note that in recent

15

months, the demographics seem to be changing. There are more younger users, and among that clientele, the female population is represented in equal or greater numbers. It seems that young women are getting involved with the Internet in greater numbers than before and young people are using the Internet in a higher proportion than before. The largest group of users is between 16 and 45 years old. However, a definite trend of an increasing segment among seniors is also seen.

The education curve of Internet users is gradually changing as well. Because the Internet was initially available through universities, Internet users with the most experience tend to have a higher level of education (advanced degrees such as master's and Ph.D.) than those with less experience. Today, Internet users still tend to have a higher level of education than that of the general population, but the difference is not as acute as before (i.e., most of them have at least some college experience and about half have a university degree). This means that the Internet is increasingly accessible to more people and that the general population is gradually becoming better represented among users. This also has an effect on the type of consumers one will encounter on the Internet.

That brings us to the average income of Internet users. Recent surveys show that about 50% of Internet users earn over $50,000 per year, with the largest percentage between $50,000 and $75,000. This has also varied slightly in recent years. The average income is now about $65,000, whereas it was over $70,000 per year previously.

What Do Subscribers Like to Use the Internet For?

About 60% of people use the Internet for more than ten hours a week. Most of those hours are spent surfing the Web. In fact, the Web is about as popular as e-mail, which comes in first but requires less time on-line. Reading and writing e-mail messages can be done off-line, and it takes only a few seconds to send or receive a message as compared to Web surfing, which requires longer periods of time.

The two most popular services, then, are e-mail and the World Wide Web (see Chapter 3). Next come Java and chat, with audio not very far behind (see Chapter 4). Video, at less than 10%, has yet to take its rightful place, along with Internet phone, fax (see Chapter 4) and push (see Chapter 6). This is probably due to the fact that video takes up more bandwidth and requires additional equipment, as discussed later.

Electronic Commerce

According to a Nielsen study, about 28 million American Internet users have purchased something on-line at one point or another. However, there still seems to be some reluctance to make purchases on a regular basis. One of the main reasons is the concern about security when paying with a credit card (i.e., disclosing one's credit-card number on-line). Other important deterrents to on-line buying are the fact that users are not able to evaluate and gauge products as they would in person, as well as fear of personal information being disclosed to other parties. In addition to these is the fact that customers do not know who the seller is and some prefer faster, in-person purchases where they get their merchandise right away. This gives you a global picture of the e-commerce world, where you have to be convincing and flexible in dealing with your Internet customers. Remember that there are still enough people willing to do transactions over the Internet to make a Web site successful and profitable. But why not offer your customers more options than less?

What Do Internet Users Buy?

Although people use the Internet primarily to seek information about products, on-line purchasing is growing rapidly. Computers and related products are, as might be expected, among the most popular purchases, and that includes both hardware and software. For instance, at press time, Dell Computer was selling over $6 million per day in computers through its World Wide Web site. Other products are popular as well: music and books, travel arrangements, used cars, apparel and accessories, flowers, appliances, gifts, food and beverages, furniture and housewares and investment services. There is also an increasing trend toward buying health products as well as other merchandise. Recently, a lot of Internet malls have been set up. Some are more successful than others, and some will survive while others will not. However, this only stresses the importance a businessperson must place on the setup and operation of a Web site as well as its relationship with the customer.

Finally, when Internet consumers buy, about one-third of buyers spend between $200 and $1,000 per year and another third spend over $1,000 per year.

The Internet Culture

The Internet has been around for a number of years. The Internet culture is thus inherited from the early users, and there are informal rules about doing things on the network. Although the medium is not regulated as such, there are some things that are well regarded and others that are not tolerated. The Internet community has its own tastes, likes and dislikes. The Internet is a tool for expression, and users are not shy about expressing themselves.

Internet users have certain expectations when they use the Internet. For instance, sending unsolicited advertising via electronic mail is not well regarded. This is called **spam**. Spam can provoke significant and massive adverse reactions on the part of Internet users. There is even anti-spam software on the market. This means that you cannot just decide to send unsolicited e-mail on a mass basis. Some people who have tried it have found that their servers became so overloaded with angry replies that they crashed.

Also, people expect the information to be free when they surf the Web. Part of this expectation stems from the fact that the Internet is probably one of the few places where there has been and still is an outburst of generosity from people all over the world who have given and are still graciously giving their time and creations in the form of free software and files such as images and text. In the past few years, the commercial side of the Internet has evolved tremendously, and more solicitation is now seen for commercial purposes as well as information and/or services for a fee. However, any advertisement must always be done in good taste and by invitation rather than pressure, while respecting established informal conventions.

The Challenges

In light of the promising potential for commerce as well as technology offered by the Internet, one of the main challenges is tapping into that most dynamic and gigantic market in an effective manner.

Offering customers what they want can be challenging when dealing with such a new outlet. Some principles are only now emerging, and there is still quite a bit of trial and error. Some new techniques also remain to be discovered in relation to the medium.

Internet commerce is probably the strongest competitor to regular mail order at the moment. Competing with traditional mail-order companies can be challenging. When targeting existing mail-order clientele, the Internet introduces three aspects:

1. It is easier to position a business among potential customers who are already familiar with the Internet. All you need to do is familiarize them with on-line purchasing and make it as easy for them to purchase as it is by mail order.
2. Competition will be a lot tougher to establish your business among non-Internet users. The challenge is double, and it is advisable to concentrate on the existing segment rather than try to "convert" nonusers to the Internet, which could prove to be very expensive.
3. Because Internet buyers place great importance on who the vendor is, you may have to work hard to establish your credibility. But remember that this is an important issue in real-life business as well as cyberbusiness.

Regulating the Internet

Governments have been considering regulating the Internet for some time now. The Internet is positioned high among the priorities of most industrialized world governments. Several governments have attempted, and in certain cases succeeded, to impose specific regulations on certain aspects of Internet operations. So far, however, the process has been similar to one step forward and one step backward. There is still much animated debate about whether or not to do it and how. Furthermore, the governments are attempting to regulate numerous aspects, covering taxes, copyrights, encryption and pornography, as well as more basic standards such as those for electronic data exchange and transactions. This is not an easy task. The debate is ongoing because the very nature of the Internet makes it extremely difficult, if not impossible, to control and therefore to regulate. Remember that states are heavily involved in subsidizing colleges and universities, which play an important role within the Internet and provide many network sites. However, that does not make the Internet totally vulnerable. Furthermore, because the Internet is considered a means of expression, it is even less vulnerable in court due to the importance, in America, of freedom of expression.

The fact is that no one has any real control over what is occurring on the Internet, and any restrictions are only temporary. When anyone does attempt to impose any kind of restriction, there is an immediate mobilization of forces over the Internet with an amazingly short response time from the on-line community. The speed at which the information circulates allows users to be informed instantly of what is going on and to react instantly — and they respond in a massive way. This changes the rules of the game and is bound to give politicians more than a mild headache.

However, politicians will continue to look at various ways of regulating the Internet as well as ways to gain financially from that potential gold mine. What would make the Internet community vulnerable would be apathy on its part — and Internet users are anything but apathetic. For instance, in a protest against the Online Indecency Law, thousands of World Wide Web pages went black during the 48 hours after President Clinton signed the Telecommunications Reform Bill. And over 20,000 Internet users protested against various Internet censorship bills. This is one strongly opinionated community!

Another problem that legislators encounter is boundaries and national jurisdictions. Given the nature of the Internet, if one Internet entity becomes outlawed somewhere, all it needs to do is relocate somewhere else outside of that jurisdiction; it does not even have to change its Internet trademark or identity. For instance, a World Wide Web site operator could simply move his or her Web site to another country while keeping the same domain name, and visitors would not know or notice it. This is one tough enterprise for legislators.

But that has not stopped them from trying to regulate the Internet. A number of issues are currently being examined. The following are a few examples of legislation and legislative attempts — some good, some not.

Pornography has been an issue in the United States for a long time, especially where children who use the Internet are concerned. The Communications Decency Act has caused a lot of controversy and has been overturned by the Supreme Court, which found it in violation of the First Amendment. There has also been some talk about imposing special taxes on the Internet. However, a two-year moratorium has been imposed to allow a special commission to study the issue and make recommendations to the president and the Senate. A recent copyright bill seeks to protect written material and sound recordings on the Internet.

These are but a few of the issues being debated in the United States and in several other countries. There is much activity on these issues because the Internet is evolving in several directions at an incredible pace. If you want to know more about these issues, do a search on "legislation" using one of the search engines.

3 Internet Services

You can use the Internet in two manners, which are really two different functions: as a user and as a World Wide Web publisher. The first is comparable to telephone communication (Figure 5). The computer (caller) uses a modem (telephone) to make a local call to a number (the Internet service provider [ISP]). A handshake (connection) and an exchange of data (conversation) ensue.

The second is comparable to having a giant billboard along with an information booth/store along a busy highway (Figure 6). People navigate the World Wide Web (travel the highway), see the home Web page (billboard), decide to stop and browse (park and go to the information booth) and might decide to make a purchase (go to the store and buy).

Basic Telephone Service

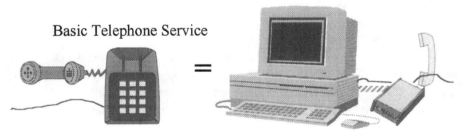

Internet Basic Service

Figure 5   Using the Internet to communicate with the rest of the world is similar, in principle, to using your telephone to speak to individuals and companies worldwide.

Figure 6　Having your own Web site on the World Wide Web is similar, in principle, to having a billboard along a busy highway.

These two distinct functions are independent of one another. The services that are related to the first function, the individual Internet user, are described first in this chapter.

When you connect to the Internet through a basic account with an ISP, there are several services that you can use. Each service has a specific role, and you must accordingly use the software that will allow you to access that particular service.

In the past few years, software has evolved tremendously, and software is now available that integrates several of the functions that are described below. Software is discussed further in Chapter 15. The various services are described in the following sections.

Internet Account/Connection

The very first service you must have is access to the Internet through an ISP. An ISP is a company that owns a server connected to the rest of the Internet network and allows you, for a fee, to connect to its server, through which you can access the rest of the network. There are numerous Internet providers, and they offer a range of connection possibilities. An ISP usually offers a set or unlimited number of connection hours per month for a set price.

In order to access the Internet, you need to open an account with an ISP, for the amount of time you desire and for the monthly budget you have. After you have contacted your provider, made arrangements to open your account and the connection process has been explained to you, the next step is to install the connection software on your computer. Most providers will give you that software, and there is also a lot of freeware available for that purpose on the Internet.

You may need your provider's help to adjust the various settings in the software. Those settings must be in agreement with the provider's own server settings in order to allow you to communicate with the server. There are several parameters that must be set up, such as Internet Protocol (IP) addresses, connection speeds and so on; once set up, they remain the same from then on. This is a relatively simple process and usually needs to be done only once.

In certain instances, the provider will give you preset software. Again, there is a whole range of possibilities. The best advice is to make sure that the provider you have chosen will assist you properly in your initial setup, as this is the most complex phase (although it is not really complicated with the help of a good ISP) of accessing the Internet. You must set the parameters for communication with the server, and those parameters are specific to each ISP. Next, you complete a similar setup for your e-mail and then for the World Wide Web navigation browser. Freeware or shareware is available for each of the services. **Freeware** is software that is available for free to the public. **Shareware** is software that the author makes available for a voluntary, usually modest, contribution. This allows you to try various versions of software. If you want additional features, you can then buy commercial versions, depending on your specific needs. A helpful ISP will most likely provide you with the basic software to complete your connection and access the basic services because this is the basis of its business.

Once the setup is done, which normally requires only a few minutes, it will be easy for you to access the Internet. You will not have to touch those setups again unless you make major changes in your programs or you encounter a major computer problem.

Electronic Mail

What It Is

Internet electronic mail, called **e-mail** (note that electronic mail systems exist outside the Internet), allows you to electronically send messages to and receive messages from any other computer that has Internet access. This service is similar to sending a letter through the regular mail, except it is a lot faster. Just as you can send small envelopes and packages through regular mail, you can also send small and large messages through e-mail, along with attachments such as various types of computer files.

The advantage of using e-mail is that you can send a message whenever you are ready, and the addressee reads it whenever she or he is ready. The message is sent, through the Internet, to the addressee ISP's server and is then stored on that server until the recipient is ready to retrieve and read it. The same thing happens when someone sends you a message: the message is sent to your ISP's server and stored there, in your special mailbox, until you are ready to retrieve and read it. This offers an important advantage in that the sender and receiver do not both have to be available at the same time, unlike a telephone call.

Messages can be saved for an indefinite period of time on your computer and can even be stored on your ISP's server. To take advantage of e-mail service, you need e-mail software that is compatible with the Internet. This software may be integrated with your browser. The software displays a window on your computer screen in which you type the desired message. You use the "Send" command when your message is ready to be sent. You do not need to be logged onto the Internet to prepare or read messages; you can use your e-mail software when you are off-line and use your connection time to send and receive only. This means that you open the software but do not immediately connect to your ISP's server. Some software will connect you automatically when you ask it to send a message.

The advantage is that you use very little of your available connection time for preparing or reading messages, allowing you more time for other services. Electronic mail actually requires very little time on-line. Sending or receiving a message takes only a few seconds, depending on the length of the message and the connection speed. Of course, if there are large attachments, you will spend minutes on-line rather than seconds.

Electronic mail messages are sent and received using e-mail software. Your World Wide Web browser most likely will have an e-mail function built into it. If you use an e-mail service without Web browsing capability, you can install specialized e-mail software. You can find on the Internet free e-mail services as well as free trial versions of commercial e-mail software that allow you to try the software before purchasing it. Commercial e-mail software usually contains many extra useful features that filter and organize your e-mail, as well as the documentation and technical support to use the software efficiently.

Basic e-mail services can be obtained for free from some providers that offer this kind of service. Yahoo (http://www.yahoo.com), HotMail (http://www.hotmail.com), Geocities (http://www.geocities.com), Juno (http://www.juno.com), Mirabilis (http://www.mirabilis.com) and Homestead (http://www.homestead.com) are among the major players. These services are based on what is sometimes called "viral marketing." This does not mean that they spread viruses, but rather that they use something similar to the virus reproduction method to do their marketing. Certain conditions apply; for example, each e-mail message might contain some kind of advertisement from the e-mail provider. Other services, which cost between $5 and $30 monthly, include a predetermined number of hours of use that can be spent on whatever service you choose: e-mail, World Wide Web surfing, chat, video-conferencing, Internet phone, etc.

A special feature of e-mail software allows you to attach other types of files to a message. For example, you can attach a Microsoft Word document to your message. This means that the addressee will receive your message plus the Word file; if the addressee owns the

Microsoft Word application, he or she will be able to work on the file as if it were his or her own. Files can be exchanged in this manner and used by both parties provided each has the proper software to access the file. Files can be text, images, spreadsheets or practically any type of file. Big files should be compressed, first to make downloading faster and second to preserve the integrity of the data during the transfer.

An emerging feature of e-mail is voice e-mail. It is now possible to attach to regular e-mail a voice that replaces the body of the message. The advantages are that it gives a message more "personality" and that recording requires less time than typing. You need the appropriate software to prepare voice e-mail, but the message can be read by a free voice e-mail player.

For more information, go to:

http://www.bonzi.com
http://www.phonesoft.com

What It Can Do for Your Business

Electronic mail allows you to exchange information and messages rapidly with customers, suppliers, colleagues and employees. It avoids playing telephone tag. It also saves time, as one often has to engage in some "social chat" during a phone call. Research shows that more than 85% of Internet e-mail reaches its destination in less than five minutes. The fact that a message is in writing, is dated and indicates the name of the sender allows you to keep it for future reference and for your records. Electronic mail can also be received from customers and answered rapidly, thus freeing up customer service phone lines; it makes you accessible to customers 24 hours a day, 7 days a week.

It is now possible to retrieve your e-mail by phone wherever you are or to receive messages on a pager or PC. There is also e-mail merge software on the market that allows you to customize e-mail messages for several recipients and to interact with databases. There is also what is called unified messaging software that allows integration of e-mail, voice e-mail and faxes. This is one service that will evolve tremendously in the near future.

For more information about e-mail, go to:

http://www.delphi.com/navnet/faq/mailq.html

World Wide Web

What It Is

The World Wide Web, as we know it, has existed since approximately 1992 and has seriously evolved since 1994. It is comparable to an electronic billboard. When you access the Web, from a user's point of view, it is presented to you in the form of information pages that contain text, illustrations, photos, animated pictures, sound files and video files. It can also contain automatic commands that will allow you to download files of various types or to fill out forms in order to obtain specific information.

To access the World Wide Web and "surf" it, you need software called a **browser**. This software allows you to navigate the World Wide Web and see the millions of pages that are available. Browsers are usually available for free, at least for now, because there is a competitive war between the two giants: Netscape and Microsoft. Note that there are also other free browsers available (listed in Chapter 15). Browsers have evolved substantially and now integrate several functions such as e-mail and FTP among others. The trend is for browsers to integrate as many Internet functions as possible, either into the software itself or through the use of plug-ins. A **plug-in** is a small software appendage that is added to the main software (the browser); it allows the browser to perform a specific additional function. Plug-ins are generally available for free on the Internet. For instance, they let you see video files, hear audio broadcasts, transfer files with FTP, read other file formats such as PDF files and decompress files. Plug-ins are discussed further later on.

The World Wide Web pages are grouped under Web sites, each of which has a specific address. A Web site is equivalent to an apartment building. A Web site has its own address, and each of the pages on a site has the Web site address plus its own address, just as an apartment building has a street address and each apartment has its own number. The address of a Web site is called a **URL** address, which stands for Uniform Resource Locator. Each Web site has its own URL address and can contain an unlimited number of pages. Within the Web site, each page also has its own address, which is composed of the URL address plus the address of the individual page.

You do not need to know the address of each page. All you need is the Web site address. Once you get to a Web site, you will be able to access each individual page of that site by clicking on links, which appear as underlined words within a Web page.

The text on a Web page is coded in **HTML**, which stands for HyperText Markup Language. Some of the words in HTML are underlined and appear in a different color. These are called **hyperlinks**. Hyperlinked words contain an address code that tells your browser to go elsewhere. You can click on these underlined words. When you do, they bring you to another section of the same page, another page of the same Web site or even to another Web site. The different addresses are discussed in more detail in Chapter 9. You can click on a picture as well; each has its own link that leads elsewhere in the same manner. You can link together anything that is on the Web. In addition, a hyperlink can create a message window that allows the user to automatically send an e-mail message to someone related to that Web site, with a predetermined e-mail address, while browsing the Web.

Whenever your pointer comes across a hyperlink, it turns into a little hand. That is how you know that you can click and access that link. The link can be just about anywhere on the Web. There is no limit to where you can go. You can find yourself on a totally foreign site miles away. Because there are so many interesting links, it is easy to lose your focus while searching the Web. That is why browsers contain one or more functions that allow you to retrace your steps back to the sites you have visited previously. They also contain several additional features that are discussed in Chapter 15.

What It Can Do for Your Business

You can use the Web in your business to do a lot of research on specific topics such as products, competition, target markets, suppliers and so on. You can use it to subscribe to news services and automatically receive audio/video broadcasts and newsletters. You can find out about potential markets and your competitors. You can instantly find zip codes, make travel arrangements and find out about flight schedules. The uses are almost unlimited. The main limit is the time you can spend using the Web!

Search Engines

With millions of pages available on the Web, it is a major challenge to find exactly what you are looking for. To help you, there are some tools that you can use to perform a search. These are called **search engines**. A search engine is a special program designed to help you perform a search by following specific instructions.

Currently, there are over 150 search engines on the Web, and most of them are free to users. Each has its own URL address and can be accessed easily by going to that particular Web site. Each has its own search method. Some are more like directories, where URLs have to be registered; others, called **crawlers**, perform an automatic search and census of World Wide Web sites on their own. Once you access a search engine, get familiar with the type of search it performs. The Web site for a search engine contains instructions for how to best use its specific search functions and how to perform your search for maximum performance and results. It is a good idea to take some time to read about the service offered because a lot of search engines are high-performance tools once you get to know how to use them. Several search engines are now called **portals** because they have evolved and assume new and more comprehensive roles. They are considered to be points of entry to the rest of the Internet.

When you give a search engine your criteria, it will get back to you with a selection of possible Web sites that contain information on what you are looking for. The quantity of information it will bring back is amazing. If you do not narrow your search, you can easily get several hundred thousand URL addresses that discuss the topic you are interested in, with more or less relevancy. Some search engines give you a summary of the content of the target Web site to facilitate your choice. This allows you to go through the millions of Web pages and other data banks in a fast and efficient manner, selecting those that contain your specific topic. Of course, most of the time, you get a lot more than you bargained for, but that's the richness of the Internet!

Mastering the use of search engines is very useful if you are going to do a lot of research. Because the amount of information available is overwhelming, learning how to narrow your search by using the specific features of each search engine will save you a lot of time. Time spent learning the features will be well worth it compared to the time you will save doing your search.

The following are a few of the main search engines, along with their URLs:

Yahoo	http://www.yahoo.com
Webcrawler	http://www.webcrawler.com
Alta Vista	http://altavista.digital.com
Infoseek	http://www.infoseek.com
Lycos	http://www.lycos.com
Excite	http://www.excite.com
HotBot	http://www.hotbot.com
DejaNews	http://www.dejanews.com
WWW Virtual Library	http://www.w3.org/vl
Northern Light	http://www.nlsearch.com
Google	http://google.stanford.edu
MetaCrawler	http://www.metacrawler.com
Argus Clearinghouse	http://www.clearinghouse.net
Ohio State Usent FAQ Archive	http://www.faqs.org/faqs
Inference Find	http://www.inference.com/ifind/

Also, you can check out the following sites for more information about search engines:

http://searchenginewatch.internet.com/webmasters/features.html
http://www.delphi.com/navnet/faq/search.html
http://www.delphi.com/navnet/faq/search1.html
http://www.delphi.com/navnet/faq/search2.html
http://www.delphi.com/navnet/faq/findit.html
http://cuiwww.unige.ch/meta-index.html

FTP

What It Is

FTP stands for **File Transfer Protocol**. It is a protocol that allows two computers to establish a direct connection with one another in order to exchange files. It is a file mover and differs from a browser. A browser allows you to read a page that is from a computer file. You cannot do anything to that page except copy it to your own computer. FTP allows you to access the computer hosting the file and move it; that is, you can transfer a new file to or remove a file from a remote server. FTP can be compared to the process involved in changing an advertisement on a billboard. When you read a Web page, the page itself is a file, and all pictures or graphic elements are separate files that are placed in the same directory on the server. A browser can read how to display the page on your screen, including the pictures that are to be shown on that page. With FTP, you can transfer, replace or remove any of those files individually on the computer without reading them; that is, you can retrieve them or put them in place so that people surfing the Web will be able to read them.

FTP transfers files in a reliable manner. It can also be used to download computer files, such as software that is available on the World Wide Web, while you are browsing. The file transfer protocol ensures the integrity of the transferred file. This is to avoid file corruption during the transfer, which might damage what you are transferring.

You sometimes see "Anonymous FTP Site" when navigating the Web; it is even advertised as one of the services offered by an ISP as part of Web hosting services. This means that the ISP is giving you (probably for a fee) some disk space to store software or files that will be downloaded at will by your customers with FTP. An anonymous site is one for which you do not need a special ID and password; therefore, you do not need to identify yourself to the server in order to get access. The user ID is simply the word "anonymous" in this case. The password is either defaulted or provided by the server itself. This is used mainly for software or files that are publicly available.

FTP requires the use of FTP software on the part of the user. The FTP software is used to transfer your Web page files to the server, integrating them into your Web site. It either stands on its own or can be integrated into the Web browser. Major Web browsers on the market have integrated the FTP function, allowing you to download software as you are browsing the World Wide Web. While browsing, you may come across sites that allow you to download software, software updates, video files and so on. A simple click of the mouse while browsing will set up the automatic FTP downloading function. Downloaded software is compressed with standard compression software. The decompression software can also be added to the browser as a plug-in. When properly installed, the decompression function will activate and automatically decompress your file as soon as it is finished downloading. All you have to do is let the computer work it through, and when it is finished, you either open or install the file, depending on the program and the computer.

What It Can Do for Your Business

FTP allows you to download useful software that is available on the World Wide Web. Such software includes free software that allows you to prepare Web pages, upgrades or updates of software you have purchased and new software that you purchase on-line.

If you have your own Web site, FTP software allows you to transfer your World Wide Web pages to the server for your Web site and also allows you to update them, replace them, destroy some of them or copy them back to your computer. If you include other types of files in your Web site (e.g., Microsoft Word or Excel documents), the FTP function of the browser lets you automatically download these files provided the file names have a hyperlink on a Web page. This can be done in lieu of sending the files as attachments through e-mail.

Newsgroups/Usenet

What They Are

Newsgroups, as they are commonly called, rely on Usenet. Usenet is not, as such, part of the Internet; it is a separate network that is carried by Internet connections, although that distinction may not be relevant to users because of the integration of that function into browsers. Newsgroups are sites where messages from different users discussing various topics are posted through Usenet. They offer a forum for public discussion on a variety of themes or topics. The newsgroup function is supported by several Web browsers.

There are numerous newsgroups, estimated at between 10,000 and 35,000, covering an incredible number of topics. Some of them are mainstream, while others are rather marginal. They can cover anything one can imagine. You can join a newsgroup and you can also start one of your own.

You can find a rare piece of information, but you can also spend a lot of time doing it because the content is less organized than on the World Wide Web. The advantage of newsgroups is that you can ask a question on one or several of them, and if anyone on earth has the answer or a suggestion, they will let you know in a short period of time. It is like a public forum. You might receive your answer from a specialist on the other side of the globe or from someone in your neighborhood. It can be a precious resource in certain instances.

The downside of newsgroups is that the information available is not verified and therefore not necessarily reliable. Anyone can say just about anything he or she wants. Unless the content is offensive or goes against the basic rules of the particular newsgroup, it will not be censored.

There are two kinds of discussions that can be implemented in newsgroups: linear discussion and threaded discussion. Linear discussion is one continuous string of messages that retains the flow in strict order of response. Threaded discussion allows a message to serve as a reply to a posted thread or to kick off as a new thread. This model makes it easier to navigate because it allows you to view thread headers and skip irrelevant tangential discussions.

Newsgroup names typically include the type of group as defined by the Usenet hierarchy, for instance, alt. for alternative, rec. for recreation, can. for Canadian, etc.

The incredible amount of information contained in newsgroups has prompted the emergence of special software to allow efficient and faster searches of newsgroups by topics and a variety of other specifications. If you are considering searching newsgroups extensively, this can be a good tool to use.

What Newsgroups Can Do for Your Business

As discussed above, you can use newsgroups in your business to find very specific information, either by searching them or by posing questions to them. Another application is to create your own newsgroup in relation to a topic that is of particular interest to your business. Some newsgroups have been created for business purposes and can be used efficiently as a promotional vehicle as long as you respect the context and purpose with which they have been created.

Netscape and Microsoft have integrated newsgroup capabilities into their browsers, but you can also use newsgroup reader software independently of the browser. For more information about newsgroups and their list of topics, perform a search for Usenet using a major search engine. You can also go to:

http://www.dejanews.com

Video and Videoconferencing

Video

What It Is

Videos clips and movies are now accessible on the Internet. Unfortunately, they are limited by the transmission speed of telecommunication lines, the size of video computer files and the modem speed of both user and server. Videos are large computer files that require a lot of memory to store and require more time to download than regular files. Some files (e.g., some music video clip excerpts and some movies prepared especially for the Internet) can be downloaded through FTP and then played on your computer. The speed limitation has also resulted in what is called video streaming, which is a gradual downloading of data of the video to be seen interspersed with viewing, which gives the viewer a chance to see a continuous flow of images while downloading the portion to be seen. This option, however, is not automatically available to the viewer for all videos because it still requires faster communication links as well as special software on the server.

What It Can Do for Your Business

You might consider publishing video files. This is used by the music industry in particular for video clips of songs, but it can also be used for business purposes such as broadcasting speeches, presentations, training sessions and so on. Because of speed constraints, a file should not be very long so as to keep its size reasonable for the user. Remember that while a file is downloading, the user has to wait, unless video streaming is used. In the same manner, you could use video capability to create special messages about your business that will be available on the Internet. However, due to the constraints mentioned above, these messages will need to be very interesting and present real value to users in order for users to download them.

Videoconferencing

What It Is

With videoconferencing, it is possible to see people live, in real time, through their own video camera, simply by downloading and installing a viewer on your computer. You do not need a camera yourself, except in cases where people require that they be able to see you in order for you to see them. It is possible to hook up a small camera to your computer and broadcast video live. Even if you do not have a camera, you can view a broadcast, provided you have the proper software. Depending on the setup, video transmission quality will vary according to the speed of telecommunication lines, modem speeds of both user and servers and bottlenecks on the Internet network.

Videoconferencing options range from very affordable setups, as described above, to expensive ones, depending on your requirements and budget. You can use a basic Internet setup with a minimum of equipment, such as a 56-Kbps modem and 150-MHz processor, to obtain reasonable output with a small camera hooked up to your computer. All you need to add is the appropriate software in order to see others and a camera in order for you to be seen. Small cameras sell for about $200 and usually come with their own software. However, do not expect this output to be perfect. If you want perfection, you will need to invest a lot more money in setting up a fancier arrangement, such as a television-based system with high bandwidth capabilities. **Bandwidth** is, in digital systems, the data speed (i.e., by extension, the physical capacity and space available to transmit data across telecommunication links). (For a more precise and detailed definition, see http://www.whatis.com/bandwidt.htm.)

If you do not need perfection, the simple setup allows for meetings with people in different places, even in different countries. When first-hand, person-to-person communication is useful to your business, even if you do not obtain a top television-quality image, your objectives might still be met while saving significant sums of money.

The camera is a special piece of equipment that is small enough to fit in the palm of a hand. It is usually hooked up on top of the computer, although some models now have their own table support. Special video software allows you to open a window on your screen and see the video picture in real time. The picture is available in color or in black and white, depending on the type of camera and version of software you use. Color uses more bandwidth and therefore requires a higher transmission speed to work well. Lack of sufficient speed will produce a jittery image.

There are a few companies that offer video software, and some software works better than others. To use the software, you either have to log onto a video channel to be able to view the desired video broadcast or you can open your own channel. You can try it by logging onto a site that is in permanent display. For example, there are permanent cameras on the corners of certain famous streets throughout the world. NASA also offers permanent viewing of its control room, and you can view some live broadcasts on The Media Channel. The URLs for NASA are

http://www.nasa.com
http://btree.lerc.nasa.gov/NASA_TV/NASA_TV.html

The software allows several people to see one another simultaneously, in which case a small picture of each one of them will be displayed on your screen, provided they also have cameras. You can limit access to only a few people and even allow only one person to see you at any one time.

What You Can Do with It

The videoconferencing capability allows people from the same company who are in remote locations to meet virtually on a more or less regular basis without traveling. This saves both time and money and allows more regular visual contact between members of the same company. Remember that in-person meetings will still be needed at some point because real people need to meet face to face once in a while. Therefore, you should not anticipate being able to replace all of your meetings with videoconferencing, but you can certainly use the Internet for a good portion of them.

Videoconferencing also permits a business to set up virtual teams that operate the business from a distance. For example, a team of independent specialists can come together for a project without being physically present at the same location. The teams would be composed of people who are in remote locations but who work together and meet through an electronic means. Some initial meetings may be necessary for the team members to meet one another, but videoconferencing allows a team to work across a wider geographical area and on projects of wider magnitude without losing contact with one another.

Videoconferencing also allows you to talk face to face with clients. It allows them to "see" you and/or specific items, thus improving and customizing contacts and customer service. If you cannot make it to the customer's premises, this is an interesting alternative that shows the customer that you care. Various meetings can also be organized with partners, suppliers, consultants and so on.

Videoconferencing is also an excellent tool for training employees and clients, as well as for providing distance learning opportunities.

What You Need to Use It

There are two options: the first is lower end and uses a regular phone line, and the second is through a higher speed or network link.

Option 1: The economical setup. This option allows from 2 frames per second up to 15 frames per second, whereas regular television gives about 30 frames per second. You will get occasional freezes, a grainy image and limited image resolution. Also, the audio may not be synchronized with the video (particularly at low speed), which may be an unpleasant effect if you are not used to it. Yet it can still be an effective tool for your business, especially if your financial resources are limited. Remember that the quality will definitely improve over time as technology evolves. This option definitely adds an extra dimension to an audio-only connection.

In this case, you need:

- A computer
- A video card for your computer
- An audio card for your computer
- A modem
- A small camera for your computer
- A microphone for your computer
- Video/audio software
- A telephone line
- An Internet connection

You also need to coordinate meetings by making formal appointments for meeting times as well as preparing agendas. Remember that each person who wants to communicate with the others will need a similar setup and will have to be on-line at the same time. To start the videoconference, the caller enters the IP address of the person being called. That person needs to be connected at that address and have compatible software running.

Note that some videoconferencing software includes audio capability, which will be handled by the audio card that the computer must have in order to get audio.

Option 2. If you are going to use video on a regular basis and for regular meetings, you may want to invest in an ISDN or faster link (64 to 128 Kbps), which will allow you to connect at a respectively faster rate to your ISP and, therefore, to the rest of the network. Telecommunication lines and specifications are discussed in Chapter 15.

You may also choose to use a local area network (LAN) connection or a wide area network (WAN) connection. If you are using either of those, you know that you can use them for faster connection. You can use a higher quality video camera as well as a microphone and speaker system with echo cancellation. The advantage of this option is the high bandwidth availability (which translates into transmission speed). Remember, however, that if at any point you have to go through the Internet, the speed will go down. This kind of setup is a lot more expensive than the first option described.

In this case, you need:

- A computer with the appropriate audio/video cards
- A network (LAN/WAN) with the appropriate equipment, or
- A high-speed telecommunication line (ISDN, ADSL, T1, T3, etc.)
- A high-quality video camera
- A microphone and speaker system
- Video/audio software

Remember that some products work better than others at slow speed, so you should take into account all the elements in preparing the final equation. Also remember that fancier equipment can be rented on an as-needed basis.

An interesting aspect of videoconferencing is that an event can be saved as a movie for further reference.

For more information about video and the possibilities it offers, go to:

http://www.connectix.com	Connectix
http://www.pine.com	CU-SeeMe
http://www.realplayer.com	RealNetworks
http://www.apple.com/quicktime	Quicktime
http://www.mpeg.org	Motion Picture Experts Group (MPEG)
http://www.microsoft.com/ windows/mediaplayer/	Video for Windows Runtime
http://home.netscape.com/ plugins/index.html	Netscape
http://www.apple.com	Apple VideoPhone Kit

http://www.diamondmm.com	Diamond Multimedia's Supar Video Kit
http://www.vtel.com	VTEL's Smart Station

You can also find out more at the following FTP sites:

BijouPlay	ftp.hawaii.edu
Sparkle	ftp.hawaii.edu
MPEGPLAY	quepasa.cs.tu-berlin.de
PMMPEG	ftp.cdrom.com

Audio

What It Is

It is possible to listen to a real-time audio broadcast through the Internet or to download audio files on your computer to listen to later. This is done with a plug-in that is added to the browser and that plays audio files as soon as you come across them on the Web. There are several Web sites that broadcast audio on the Internet. However, in order for you to broadcast, you need to get the audio software and install it on your server with the appropriate setup. Both software and plug-in are compatible and are available from the same company (RealAudio).

What It Can Do for Your Business

Audio opens new avenues to commerce. For example, it makes it possible for artists to distribute their music through the World Wide Web without the help of intermediaries. It is also possible to use audio broadcasts as a special information feature on your Web site. For instance, you can regularly provide your customers with information and interviews delivered in an audio format.

What You Need to Use It

To listen to audio files, you need to download the plug-in that corresponds to the type of files you are interested in. If you want to distribute audio files, you need the server software that allows you to put RealAudio libraries on the Internet.

For more information, go to:

http://www.realaudio.com

Internet Relay Chat (Chat)

What It Is

Internet Relay Chat is a real-time on-line exchange of typewritten information between two or more people. This means that you can have on your computer screen a written conversation in real time with one or more persons while you are on the Internet.

What It Can Do for Your Business

Chat allows several people to have a real-time exchange of written words, a written discussion. Such discussions can be performed in a very economical manner because the software is either freeware or shareware. Chats can be organized by a business around certain topics and held on a permanent basis or at scheduled times. This can draw groups of people to your Web site at specific times to hold discussions. Another use is for organizing virtual focus groups with live interaction. For instance, potential focus group participants can be invited by e-mail. Actual participants would then receive a URL address along with a password allowing them to participate in the focus group through the chat. A moderator would greet them and get the session started.

Note that you can open a public channel anytime, but you are not assured exclusivity of the channel name when you leave. For instance, if you open a channel called "#profits," someone else can reopen it after you close it and keep it running indefinitely, and there is nothing you can do about it. The alternative is to operate your own chat server with chat server software or to use one of the services that provide private chat options for a fee whereby you can keep ownership of your chat channel name.

Distance learning programs also benefit from chat sessions because they allow students to communicate on-line with the teacher. Chat can also be used between colleagues who want to hold a specific on-line discussion.

What You Need to Use It

To participate in a chat, you need:

- A computer
- A modem
- A telephone line
- An Internet connection
- Chat software and/or a World Wide Web browser
- A common time for the meeting
- A chat channel

Some advanced browsers have integrated the chat function, but it can also be used separately with chat software. When you first log on, you need to find a chat channel you are interested in or a server that offers chat channels. This is a central common point where the participants log on using the appropriate software in order to synchronize their conversations (i.e., a specific chat group). The software allows you to either participate in an existing chat or start your own chat. In the latter case, you have the option of accepting everyone who happens to arrive or only the participants you want. All you have to do is set up a meeting time and log on.

If you do participate in a chat, beware of Trojan horses (see Chapter 12). They are usually transmitted to your computer when you type certain Internet Relay Chat scripts.

When you are the first person to open a new channel, you automatically become the channel operator and have complete control over that channel as long as you are logged onto the channel or until you grant privileges to other participants.

To learn more about Internet Relay Chat and related possibilities, go to:

http://www.irchelp.org
http://www.mirabilis.com

Internet Telephone

What It Is

Telephone conversations are now possible on the Internet, as long as you have microphone and speaker capability with an audio card in your computer. Your modem must also have voice transmission capability. However, do not expect the same quality as you are used to on a regular telephone.

What It Can Do for Your Business

Internet telephone allows you to speak to someone far away without incurring long-distance charges and will soon allow you to hold conference calls without the hefty bills that usually accompany them. (To keep abreast of new developments in this field, see http://www.itca.org.)

What You Need to Use It

- A computer with an audio card
- A modem with voice transmission capability
- A telephone line
- An Internet connection
- Internet telephone software

To use Internet telephone, you need to set up a common time for a meeting with the people with whom you want to meet. You can obtain information about various telephone software at:

http://www.freetel.inter.net	FreeTel, one free version with very good performance
http://www.vocaltec.com	Internet phone is cross-platform compatible
http://www.intel.com/cpc	Intel Internet phone

Also see the Web site of a magazine devoted to computer telephony:

http://www.computertelephony.com

Intranet

What It Is

An intranet is like a private Internet that serves a specific group of persons inside an organization. An intranet uses Internet protocols and software but is invisible to the rest of the Internet in that it occupies a private section in a nook of the network. It is usually connected to the Internet through single or multiple access, at which point some protection from the "exterior" world (the rest of the Internet) is installed. That protection is called a **firewall**. Intranets and extranets are discussed further in Chapter 7.

What It Can Do for Your Business

An intranet can offer several services, such as resource references, document sharing, application sharing, time management, file exchange, news, etc., to people in your organization without being accessible to people outside the organization. The advantage of an intranet is that access to it is reserved to authorized people within a company, as opposed to the whole Internet community. You can, therefore, give users different levels of authorization for different types of documents or transactions.

With an intranet setup, people within an organization can send and receive e-mail that does not go through the Internet. They can share documents, appointment books, schedules, project management charts, etc. Documents such as Web pages and databases can be posted for consultation by employees only.

Of course, if you operate your business by yourself, you do not need an intranet any more than you need a network, unless you operate several computers all by yourself. (Don't laugh, it happens!)

What You Need to Use It

An intranet requires a more elaborate setup that involves a network of computers. Your network must be rendered compatible with the Internet Protocol. You may have to change some of your software. Security is also a very important aspect of an intranet, given the sensitive nature of some of the information that is carried within its network. If you link your intranet with the rest of the Internet, you will need a mechanism, usually a firewall, to limit access to authorized people only.

Extranet

What It Is

An extranet is like an intranet that gives access to specific outside users. It can also be a group of intranets in various locations that are linked together through the Internet, with protective firewalls at each boundary. Extranets link two or more businesses or organizations together. The information exchanged between those businesses generally uses private software to render it invisible and inaccessible to the rest of the Internet users. Confidential information can then be exchanged between companies.

What It Can Do for Your Business

An extranet allows a business to establish electronic links with suppliers, for instance, to rapidly order parts and supplies. It also allows links with corporate customers, in a closer manner than general Internet and World Wide Web access provides, with restricted access as well. For instance, if your company sells high volumes to another company, you can receive orders from that company through an extranet.

What You Need to Use It

An extranet requires a special network setup. You will need to consult a specialist, as there are several possibilities. Refer to Chapter 7 for more details.

Telnet

Telnet is similar in type of activity to FTP because it establishes a direct connection between your computer and a remote computer with which you want to work. It allows you to log onto that remote computer and use its applications as if you were using the computer locally. For instance, a remote computer might contain certain types of specific documents or libraries. The Internet allows you to access the remote computer from a distance.

For instance, if your Web site is on your ISP's server and you want to protect some of its sections with passwords, you would have to connect to the ISP's server with Telnet to make specific entries in the system, such as new user logins along with passwords to allow them to access your Web site — that is, if your provider gives you access to its server in that manner. This requires a knowledge of commands in relation to the server operating system.

Another possible application is to access a distant library's catalog as if you were on-site. Telnet is not as popular as the World Wide Web, but it can be useful with some sites that are accessible by Telnet only and for some specific uses.

4 Additional Features

Electronic Commerce

Electronic commerce is actually one of the most promising features of the Internet at the moment. It will have the highest growth and will benefit companies the most. It is done with various tools and in various ways. It entails working with several aspects, among which are Internet market study, World Wide Web marketing, Web site design, security for transactions, supply and delivery and so on.

What It Is

Electronic commerce is not a service as such but rather something that can be achieved in various ways through the Internet. It allows you to sell and to perform commercial transactions. It provides a virtual storefront, allowing merchandise and services to be sold and payments to be collected. It entails the display of products, both merchandise and services, on-line. It also requires good marketing, just as a real-world store does. As transactions are made, they must be organized and processed in a secure manner. Customer service must be assured.

What It Can Do for Your Business

There are several immediate advantages for a business. First, Web space is less expensive than floor space. A virtual store can be set up

49

for a lot less money than a physical store. Second, you are not limited to a geographical area in which to sell your services or merchandise. You can sell your products throughout the world if you want to. Third, you can handle order processing with computerized tools, such as databases and automated operations, thus avoiding expensive labor costs. All transactions can be performed electronically, provided you have the proper setup and security.

Customer service can be handled through the Web as well, and you can save considerable time and money and give better service by doing it this way. For instance, you can post specifications, information and descriptions that can be consulted by customers 24 hours a day, 7 days a week. Common questions, called **FAQs** or frequently asked questions, can be answered before clients even think of them.

All this gives you a lot of new possibilities. You are limited only by your own imagination.

What You Need to Use It

Setting up an e-commerce operation requires good planning and can be done in several ways. The subject is so vast that the next chapter is devoted to it. For now, suffice it to say that the possibilities are very real and show true potential for businesses of all sizes. Examining the electronic commerce issue carefully is worth your time.

For more information, go to:

http://www.electronicmarkets.org
http://www.oecd.org/dsti

Perl and CGI

Perl

Perl, which stands for Practical Extraction and Report Language, is a programming language used mainly by system administrators to automate tasks on UNIX systems. In relation to the Internet, many Web servers use the UNIX operating system. One of the great strengths of Perl in that regard is in writing Common Gateway Interface (CGI) programs and scripts. Perl is also great for Web maintenance in that it allows webmasters to write programs that can update HTML pages automatically, rather than having to update them one at a time. This may not seem like an obvious advantage at first glance, especially if your Web site only has a few pages, but when it has a couple of thousand pages, that's another story altogether. However, there are also other tools that perform automatic updates, such as cascading style sheets and commercial software.

For more information about Perl, go to:

http://www.perl.com/perl

http://www.ora.com

http://www.oac.uci.edu/indiv/ehood/perlWWW

http://www.geocities.com/SiliconValley/7331/ten_perl.html

CGI

CGI scripts are groups of text commands that can be compared to macros in word-processing software. These scripts can perform on their own or interact with a CGI program on a server.

CGI allows you to produce forms, within a Web site, that visitors can fill out to either provide you with data or place orders. It is a standard that allows external programs to interface with information servers, such as a Web server. CGI scripts are integrated into the HTML page. When a user fills out a form, the CGI scripts call on the CGI program on the server to perform specific tasks. It can also bring back information to the customer if, for instance, it is linked to a database.

CGI can be used to send data either to you through regular e-mail or to a database on a server. If you send information through your e-mail with CGI, you will get a series of comments without any identification as to which boxes have been filled in. This format can rapidly become confusing if your form has several fields, especially if there are boxes to check on the form, because you will only get an "on" or "off" message for each box. You may need software to interpret the data received this way in an e-mail.

If you send information to a database, the server must have the CGI program in a directory so that the Web server can execute the

CGI program and interface with the database that will accept, interpret and store the data. The Web page into which the CGI scripts are integrated sends queries to the CGI program on the server, which interfaces with the server and the database and returns information to customers. For instance, the information can be a special configuration of a set of products, confirmation of an order or a thank-you note for patronage.

Note that this kind of setup requires involvement from your Internet service provider (ISP) because the ISP needs to give you access to the CGI library and program on the server. Also note that you can achieve similar results, to a certain extent, by using JavaScript in your HTML page.

For more information about CGI, visit the following:

http://hoohoo.ncsa.uiuc.edu/cgi

Other Scripts: VBScript, Tcl, REXX

There are also other scripts available for Web sites. Script languages are easier to code than more structured languages. They also are more limited in their capabilities.

The list of script languages includes:

- Netscape's JavaScript (discussed later in this chapter)
- Microsoft VBScript
- UNIX-based Perl (which is more sophisticated than the other script languages)
- Sun Laboratories' Tcl
- IBM's REXX

Using scripts requires some technical expertise. If you are serious about using them, either do some research or talk to a specialist.

Imagemap

An imagemap is a large image on a Web page on which visitors can click in various places to lead them to various corresponding places on the Web site. For instance, clicking on one part of an image will bring the visitor to a certain page, while clicking on another area of the image will bring the visitor to another page. This means that the image has to be "programmed," with various areas delimited within the image and individually linked to Uniform Resource Locators (URLs). Those URLs will point to other Web pages or other areas of the current page.

Imagemaps are just another way of presenting links in a more graphical way on a Web page. They require more advanced skills than HTML but are not that complicated. Software is available to help you prepare imagemaps more easily.

For more information about imagemaps, visit:

http://hoohoo.ncsa.uiuc.edu/docs/tutorials/imagemapping.html

Java and Java Applets

What They Are

Java is a programming language that is platform neutral, which means that it can run in any environment and on any platform and network (e.g., Windows, Macintosh, Sun Solaris and others). It can also be used as an operating system. It is easy to transport over the Internet. The language allows a developer to embed small applications within World Wide Web pages.

Java is used on the Internet with Java-enabled browsers (i.e., those containing a Java Virtual Machine, as most of the recent versions of browsers do). When the browser comes upon a World Wide Web site that contains the embedded application in Java code, called a Java applet, only the bits of code needed to perform the task are downloaded onto the visitor's computer. The applet then runs on that computer. This applet's actions are restricted to its "sandbox" (i.e., the area of the browser dedicated to that applet). The applet cannot read or alter data outside of its sandbox.

Java can also be used to work with databases, to design, run and publish queries, reports and interactive computing charts through Web browsers.

The browser can interpret and run any applet written in Java. It seems that in order to achieve 100% platform compatibility, the applets must be 100% pure Java and not intermixed with something else such as JavaScript. Mixing will produce error messages with some of the browsers and seriously decrease stability. Java is not quite mature yet, but it is promising and will have a lot to offer in the coming months and years.

What They Can Do for Your Business

Java can do interesting things for your Web site if you can live with its downsides. With it, you can integrate animation into your site. You can use it to make your Web site interactive with a customer or to allow a group of people to interact on the Web. It can be used to work with your database, to produce forms and charts. You can use it to build business solutions that take full advantage of the Internet. With it, you can create toolbars and buttons and prepare dynamic visual presentations and even interactive multimedia presentations. You can offer your clients searchable product catalogs, and you can use it to process electronic transactions. It can be used on an intranet as well as an extranet. It allows you to access existing databases as well as new applications.

As an indication of how popular it is, about half of companies with over 1,000 employees are actually using Java, and another 22% are considering using it. Note, however, that some companies will not allow Java applets to come through their intranets. This means that employees from those companies who are connected to the Internet through an intranet cannot receive the applets and will therefore see an error message each time they access a Web page that contains one. The reason behind this is that there is the risk of virus infiltration because an applet is executable. Therefore, certain companies and government organizations block any Java applet from entering their networks.

If you decide to use Java, really test it on several platforms before implementing it on your site. There are still innumerable problems on sites where Java is used. Either pages take forever to download or the browser crashes.

What You Need to Use Them

To view Java applets, all you need is a recent version of a World Wide Web browser that contains the Java Virtual Machine. Because the Java Virtual Machine is already integrated into the browser, you do not need to download it, as you would a plug-in.

To use Java to develop applets, you need the Java development software and you need someone who knows how to program Java. It is also possible to use prepared applets that are freely available on the Internet. In this case, it is of the utmost importance that you ensure that those applets are what they are advertised to be and not viruses in disguise.

To find out more about Java, go to:

http://java.sun.com

http://www.internetuser.com

http://www.developer.com/directories/pages/dir.java.html

JavaScript

What It Is

JavaScript differs from Java in that it is a scripting language. Its command set is a subset of Java's. JavaScript capabilities have been built into the Netscape browser since the release of Navigator 2.0. Microsoft Explorer Version 4.0 and higher can also read JavaScript.

As a programming language, Java's source code needs to be compiled to transform it into executable programs. JavaScript's source code is embedded into the HTML page and read by the browser (actually, one of the engines running in the browser interprets JavaScript).

What It Can Do for Your Business

JavaScript can:

- Manipulate a Web page (i.e., change the background, text and link colors according to user preferences). In addition, some special effects can be created, based on the PC's internal clock. For instance, a banner or message that changes according to various periods during the day or night can be displayed.

■ Store and retrieve information in order to personalize interactions with customers/visitors. This can include registration forms that are stored in cookies which can be retrieved later by other scripts to personalize messages for visitors. It is this function that can be used for shopping cart applications, in relation with the following point.

■ Display dynamic data, if used with tools that connect with databases. Of course, you need a database that is compatible with those intermediary connecting tools, in which case this setup can allow you to display the content of your database to your customers. For instance, you could show products tailored to customers' specifications or sets of services tailored to customers' requirements.

■ Communicate with applets and plug-ins in order to interact with your visitor. You could, for instance, retrieve your visitor's name from a cookie and post a personalized welcoming message on the screen, or you could use JavaScript to interact with plug-ins to perform certain other tasks.

JavaScript represents an interesting option as it is free and easy to learn. It allows a great amount of flexibility at a very low cost. Another advantage is that, because it is not executable, it is less prone to viruses than Java applets are. JavaScript is not usually blocked by networks, as Java applets are, and it takes full advantage of some browsers' power without burdening the user with extended download time. Some JavaScripts are available on the World Wide Web and perform specific tasks on your World Wide Web site, such as color changes, pop-up windows and so on.

For more information about JavaScript and connecting tools, visit:

http://home.netscape.com/
http://home.netscape.com/eng/mozilla/3.0/handbook/javascript/
http://developer.netscape.com/docs/manuals/communicator/jsguide4/
http://developer.netscape.com/docs/manuals/enterprise/wrijsap/
http://rhoque.com/book/

http://www.jsworld.com
http://www.tradepub.com/javascript/

Cookies

What They Are

A cookie is a small piece of information that a Web site you visit sends to your browser. That information is then stored in your browser's files and can be read by the same Web site or other Web sites when you visit again later.

This can be a bit touchy, depending on the kind of information that is gathered and who has access to it. Cookies are, in general, largely misunderstood by Web surfers. Cookies are somewhat controversial on the Internet because they are perceived by some Web surfers as an invasion of their privacy. This may be true in certain instances, but if used with some good ethics, cookies can also prove useful for business purposes for both the visitor and the business to which the Web site belongs. For instance, if an insurance company were able to retrieve information from a cookie about medical Web sites you have visited while researching cancer topics and later base its acceptance of your life insurance application on that information, this could be very prejudicial against you. The insurance company would not know, for instance, that you were doing research on your parents' behalf. This is an example of negative use of cookies. A more positive use would be a one-time registration, after which the user does not need to register or give a password again every time he or she wants to access the same information.

Some people argue that the information contained in a cookie and downloaded to a surfer's browser takes up space, which is true but only up to a maximum size of 4 Kb per cookie. They are afraid that cookies will take up too much space on their hard disk, but that depends on how many cookies a visitor accepts.

What They Can Do for Your Business

You can use cookies on your Web site for various purposes, such as:

- Customizing the information presented to a visitor
- Tracking visits to pages throughout your Web site and measuring the visitors' interest in each page in a consistent manner (which can be achieved by other means as well)
- Displaying selective advertising (e.g., not showing an ad again if a person has already seen it)
- On-line ordering (cookies store item selections until the visitor is ready to complete the transaction)
- Identifying a visitor

What They Will Not Do

An HTTP cookie cannot be used to get an e-mail address, obtain data from a customer's hard drive or steal personal information. It also cannot infect a visitor's computer with a virus, unless it is executable, which is very unlikely.

But what cookies cannot do, as described above, is not necessarily obvious to a customer. Cookies are mysterious to a lot of people, in which case they might not allow them. Remember that browsers allow you to completely disable cookies by setting up preferences to that effect in the browser menu.

Therefore, if you intend to use cookies, it may be advisable to inform visitors, through your Web site, about the purpose of your cookies (i.e., what they do, the information they will gather and, most of all, the benefits they offer). Of course, cookies should benefit your customers, and that is what you should emphasize so that you will get more cooperation and your data will of better quality and more reliable.

What You Need to Do to Use Them

A simple set of commands used in the HTML code of a document tells the browser to set up a cookie. A name or a value is specified for the cookie, along with an expiration date, a path and a domain name. The command can be prepared using either CGI scripts or JavaScript.

For more information about cookies, go to:

http://www.cookiecentral.com
http://home.netscape.com

E-Mail Feedback

You can set up your Web site in such a way that a visitor will receive an automatic reply to an action. The reply can be an order confirmation, acknowledgment of an e-mail query and so on. When you receive a query, you can either reply manually or program the server in accordance with the rest of your setup to send an automatic reply or confirmation.

This option is very positive in terms of marketing because it lets the visitor know immediately that the query/order has been received and that someone is taking care of it. However, if you use it, be sure to follow up with a more tangible action such as confirmation of the cost of the order, the delivery date of the merchandise and so on.

VRML

VRML stands for Virtual Reality Modeling Language. It is used to describe three-dimensional images and user interactions with those images.

For more information, see:

http://www.whatis.com/vrml.htm

SGML and XML

SGML is the acronym for Standard Graphic Markup Language. It is the forerunner of HTML and XML (i.e., HTML is derived from it). XML stands for Extensible Markup Language and is also a subset of SGML. These are both technical languages.

For more information, go to:

http://www.whatis.com/sgml.htm

http://www.whatis.com/xml.htm
http://www.delphi.com/navnet/glossary

Specialized Advanced Research Services

In addition to regular search engines, there are more specialized search engines that are topic specific. There are also commercial research services that can perform a specific search for a fee. Some forums are dedicated to special interests. Professional databases include popular legal databases. You can search chat groups and newsgroups, but note that the information contained therein is a mix of expertise and more or less informed opinion. Some encyclopedias are available in the form of Internet-accessible CDs. Libraries and bookstores have tremendous collections of files. The following resources can help you with a search:

http://www.dejanews (newsgroups)
http://www.aol.com (America Online)

- Encyclopedias
  http://www.eb.com (Encyclopedia Britannica)
  http://www.encarta.com

- Search tools
  http://www.delphi.com/navnet/faq/findit.html
  http://www.lincon.com/srclist.htm
  http://www.whatis.com/search/default.html
  http://www.whatis.com/search/searchen.htm

- Legal databases
  http://www.westlaw.com
  http://www.lexis-nexis.com

- Bookstores
  http://www.amazon.com
  http://www.barnesandnoble.com

- Libraries
  http://lcweb.loc.gov (Library of Congress)

UNIX

UNIX is an operating system that is still widely used among Internet service providers and on various servers because it is robust and reliable. UNIX commands are short cryptic commands that perform various tasks on a server.

If your Web site is located on an ISP's server, chances are you will not need to get involved with UNIX, unless you have special needs for specific tasks. For instance, suppose you want to arrange a setup whereby access to a portion of your Web site is restricted to users who can access it only if they have the proper password. In that case, you might want to arrange to register new logins and passwords yourself, thus giving your customers access without involving your ISP's technician every time. Remember that every time you need your provider's intervention, it will probably cost something and you will have to wait until a technician is available. However, that kind of setup can be achieved in other ways as well.

Mirror Site

What It Is

A mirror site is an exact replica that reflects the content of the original Web site on another server. This achieves two purposes: it reduces traffic on the original Web site, thus ensuring availability, and it ensures that, should one of the servers fail, the Web site remains available through the alternate server. In some instances, when huge distances are involved and a site is very popular, a mirror site may be installed in different countries to distribute traffic and free the network. This might happen between Web sites located in the United States and Asia. In other instances, some Web sites with low-speed telecommunication links may benefit from a mirror site with a higher speed link somewhere else.

What It Can Do for Your Business

A mirror site is a good precaution to ensure that your Web site remains available at all times. Also, if you want to organize a promotional event around your Web site, setting up even a temporary mirror site can ensure that a sudden increase in traffic will not overwhelm your original site.

Fax Service

It is possible to use the Internet to send and receive faxes. One option is to send a fax from a fax machine to a local number, whether an ISP, a specialized company or a corporate network that has the appropriate software for sending and receiving faxes. Then, the faxed document is sent through the Internet to a server that is close to the fax destination. From there, it can be sent to the local destination fax machine or accessed through a local corporate network. This means that long-distance calls for faxes thus become local calls. Other options will develop in the future, so this is one sector to watch.

In 1997, it was estimated that it cost $60 for a company to send a fax around the world. Some companies have been created specifically to provide fax services over the Internet for a fee, which is lower than regular telecommunication fees.

This is still an emerging technology. Among various products on the market, some are free and some cost up to $6,000 (including a server). The free service does not cover all geographical locations.

For more information, go to:

http://www.savetz.com/fax
http://www.tpc.int

The following companies offer various fax solutions:

http://www.faxsav.com	FaxSav
http://www.atfax.com	@fax
http://www.castelle.com	Castelle
http://www.omtool.com	Omtool
http://www.brooktrout.com	Brooktrout Technology

http://www.faxserver.com	Interstas Technologies
http://www.panasonic.com/internetfax	Panasonic Office Products
http://www.rightfax.com	RightFAX

II Commercial Possibilities Offered by the Internet

5 Commercial Opportunities

A New Way of Doing Business, A New Form of Marketing

The Internet is not called the "cyberworld" for nothing. Entering the Internet is indeed like entering a different world. Doing business electronically is a new experience, whether you are the buyer or the seller. As a matter of fact, the phenomenon is so important that it has been forecasted to displace the existing economy and force it to be reshaped in the near future.

Electronic commerce has its own opportunities and also its own challenges. Its development is still very young and its growth has been phenomenal. For instance, in 1997, purchases totaled $8.5 billion in the United States and over $2 billion outside the United States, for a total of over $10.5 billion. The forecast for 2001 is $155 billion in the United States and $68 billion elsewhere. For 2002, the estimate is over $300 billion in purchases worldwide. These figures may vary somewhat in the future, depending on whether or not certain obstacles are overcome, but one thing is certain: e-commerce will occupy a very important place in the economy.

Despite all the potential it has to offer, there are at the moment still several deterrents to e-commerce. It is interesting that they are not perceived in the same manner by customers as by merchants.

For instance, one of the main debates is over relaxation of regulations for encryption. Encryption is one of the most important components of secure commercial transactions because it allows transactions to be processed in a secure manner. Compatibility for electronic data interchange (EDI) is another major preoccupation, as incompatibility between EDI protocols has adverse effects for obvious reasons. EDI is among the current priorities of several governments. Allowing various entities to exchange data securely with one another is important to successful e-commerce.

However, for customers, the main concern is not necessarily the security of transactions, although it remains high on their list. It is, rather, the fact that they do not know who they are dealing with in many cases. Not being able to meet the merchant face to face, not being able to visit physical premises and not being able to assess product quality can be disturbing to customers and has to be overcome or compensated for in order for e-commerce to be effective.

The key to successful e-commerce is, first and foremost, a thorough understanding of the clientele — how people think, how they react, how they behave on the Internet, what they expect, what attracts them, what they use as their Internet tools, what their needs are, what they dislike, how to best approach them, how to contact them.

As an additional element, it should be noted that the trend over the past few months has generally put more of a burden on merchants in cyberlife than in real life. A World Wide Web electronic business operates in a different context than a real-world business. It is comparable to having millions of stores on the same street for people to visit. That would not be possible in the real world. The potential is also grand in scale. Using the same example, imagine a store that most of the people throughout the world could visit on a continuous basis, 24 hours a day, 7 days a week.

There are other phenomena that are specific to the Internet. One example is disintermediation, which is the process of cutting out the middleman. This means that it is possible for companies to deal directly with customers. Another phenomenon is the appearance of "cybermediaries" and "infomediaries." Cybermediaries are a new breed of middlemen, whose role is quite different from traditional intermediaries in that they offer advice and price comparisons. They are more like matchmakers or order desks. Infomediaries are specialized agents who search the tremendous amount of information that is available on the World Wide Web and organize it in a way that is accessible and useful to customers. Indeed, when one considers the vast amount of resources the Web offers, consumers cannot individually spend the incredible amount of time it would take to sort it all out. That would defeat the purpose of the Web, which is to make things easily and rapidly available.

Having said that, it is important to note that most of the same operations that must be accomplished in real-world commerce must also be accomplished in cybercommerce, but in an electronic form. An electronic operation is not simply a replica of a real-world operation. This alone can represent an additional challenge, depending on a merchant's level of technical competence.

One must therefore "immerse" oneself in what it means to do business electronically. As a reference, let's discuss each of the steps that are involved.

The main elements involved in organizing e-commerce are as follows:

For Selling Merchandise	*For Selling Services*
■ Define products (merchandise)	■ Define products (services)
■ Choose server	■ Choose server

■ Display merchandise
  □ On-line store
  □ On-line catalog
	■ Display service description

■ Provide customers with ordering facilities
  □ Shopping carts
  □ Ease of use
	■ Provide customers with inquiry facilities
	  □ Questionnaire to help customers define needs (in order to receive quotes on jobs)

■ Provide customers with methods of payment
  □ Checks
  □ Credit cards
    ◊ On-line
    ◊ 800 number
  □ Electronic cash
  □ COD
  □ Purchase order	

For Selling Merchandise	For Selling Services
■ Provide customers with delivery options	■ Provide customers with conditions and specs for delivery of services

■ Order processing
  ☐ Confirmation of orders
  ☐ Confirmation of costs
  ☐ Confirmation of delivery
    ◊ Specifications
    ◊ Delivery tracking
  ☐ Possible fax confirmation
	■ Provide quotes to customers
	■ Obtain signed agreement and deposit
	  ☐ Deliver work
	  ☐ Obtain final payment

■ Track Web site and Web store activity
  ☐ Divulge what you do with customer information
	■ Track Web site visits
	  ☐ Divulge what you do with customer information

■ Marketing and seek out traffic	■ Marketing and seek out traffic

Internet commerce operations are very similar to real-world operations. However, the way they are run and the tools used are quite different. Let's examine what they are by analyzing Figure 7 and how it applies to the Internet.

If you would put your merchandise on shelves in a real-world store, you need to adapt this action to the virtual store. This means presenting your products on an electronic page. Products must be photographed, described and presented in an attractive manner. You must determine the following:

- ■ How many products are going to be presented on your Web site.
- ■ How many products there will be per page.
- ■ What material you will present. Will you give a summary or brief description as an introduction to customers, with a more detailed description available on request? If you are going to give customers a lot of information resources, how will that be organized? Will you offer an on-line library? Will there be an FAQ (frequently asked questions) section? Will there be chats?
- ■ How you will organize the overall information to make it easy for customers to find:

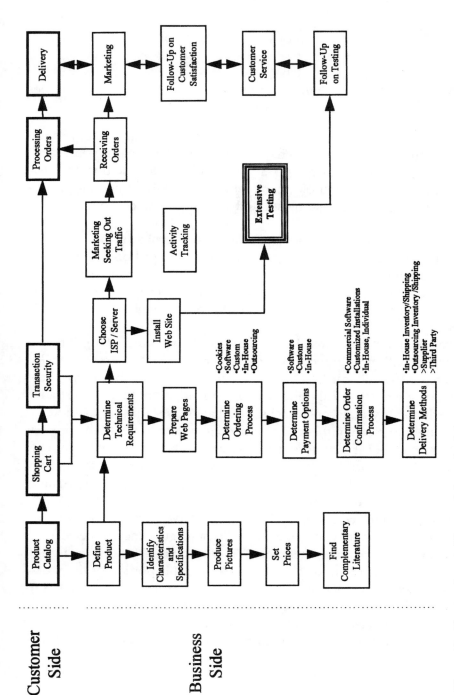

Figure 7 Electronic retailing activity schedule.

- ☐ Will there be various categories of products?
- ☐ If so, how many categories?
- ■ What the prices will be.
- ■ What the shipping fees will be as well as any other fees customers will have to pay.

The next step is to determine the technical requirements in relation to the previous elements. What will you need to make your sales? Evidently, you need to set up a Web site, but in addition to basic HTML pages, what kind of e-commerce setup do you need to implement? Do you need a sophisticated setup with a completely automated process?

On the administrative side, you need to organize in parallel your inventory of products (ordering and stocking), your bookkeeping and your marketing. The ordering process (i.e., what is called the shopping cart) must be set up. Will you use available software, will you do it in-house or will you outsource the processing? How much will it cost?

Payment options must be determined. What kind of options for payment will you offer your customers? Money orders? Checks? CyberCash? Credit cards? COD? For each method of payment, there will be some technical requirements, in addition to administrative procedures. If you accept checks, you have to establish a method for verifying and clearing them. If you need a system to verify them, what will the cost be? If you accept credit cards, which bank will you use, what will the procedure be, how much will it cost and how will they be processed? In this case, you will need some technical assistance.

How will you confirm orders with customers? What kind of delivery methods will you use? Will customers have a choice? What kind of arrangements do you need to make sure customers receive their merchandise in a timely manner? Will you maintain stock and fulfill orders as they come in or will you outsource this portion of the work?

How will you track your Web site? Will you install special software? Will you ask your Internet service provider to do it? Will you outsource that task to an outside company?

It is clear that each step has to be planned and organized properly.

Selling Services

If you are selling services, your Web site will be slightly different in that it needs to be organized in a way that will attract customers to using your services. This means that you will need to establish a more personal and one-on-one relationship with your customers early on. It also means that your customer base will not be as broad as if you were selling merchandise. The quality of the relationship is different. When you are dealing with a mass of customers, the bigger the mass, the more automated your operations need to be. When you are offering services to customers, the emphasis is on the individual relationship and the quality of your services. The approach of the Web site will thus be different in that it will seek to establish that individual relationship with customers. The setup is usually simpler for this type of Web site, but it must also be well prepared and planned.

Selecting Software

If you are going to implement software on your Web site to automate your operations (e.g., for feedback, transactions and so on), you will need to evaluate the software that is available on the market and determine which is the most appropriate to meet your needs and requirements. You will need to test the software thoroughly before launching it on your Web site. You need to make sure it does what you want, what you need it to do and that there are no glitches or bugs. Find the bugs before your customers do. Determine how you will evaluate various software and how much time you will need.

Advantages

The Internet allows the creation of completely new businesses as well as the conversion of existing businesses into virtual businesses. It also offers new opportunities to existing businesses.

There is the potential for instant sales at very little cost, if the proper conditions are met. To some extent, small and medium businesses have an advantage over large businesses. They have the flexibility required for setting up and operating a Web site, which large businesses do not have because of their complex structure. Other than a few notable exceptions, the Web sites of most large businesses merely offer general information and job ads, with little else. This is far from the "cyberexperience" sought by Internet users. In that respect, smaller businesses can take advantage of their short response time, high adaptability and operation flexibility to establish a strong Web presence in a relatively short time, with the appropriate resources to maintain the Web site in a more dynamic manner. Heavy bureaucracy is a terrible thing for Web sites and can easily be an immobilizing factor.

Another use for e-commerce is business-to-business transactions. Businesses can reach a wider base of suppliers through the Internet, thus making it easier to compare service or product offers, obtain better deals and decrease the time needed to do so. Transactions can also be conducted over the Internet; orders can be sent out and billing can be done electronically.

Challenges

There are differences between doing business in the traditional way and on the Internet. On the Internet, there is a power shift from the business to the consumers, because they can obtain information more easily and more rapidly. For instance, consumers can compare prices faster and shop around in a lot less time than when they have to walk from store to store. There are even specialized services that can offer consumers price comparisons in one visit to a Web site.

There is always the risk of your Web site not being found by the search engines or being lost among the hundreds of thousands of Web sites, especially if META tags are not written properly. In addition, marketing your Web site requires special finesse if it is to be done in an effective manner.

Important Considerations

The content of your Web site must be compelling in order to attract visitors. It must also be renewed and/or updated on a regular basis. The relationship between the various e-commerce components is critical. If those components are not well adjusted, you will not be able to make sales through your Web site.

As for consumer acceptance, products to be sold on the Internet can be divided into two main categories:

1. *Products that customers do not need to see in person.* These products are easy to sell on the Internet because they are naturally adapted to that kind of selling. Most of the products that are sold through mail order fit into this category. There are also virtual services (i.e., services related to the Internet, such as Web page preparation, electronic commerce services, price comparison services and so on).

2. *Products that need to be seen or assessed (e.g., fruits and vegetables for freshness; clothes for fit, color and feel).* This kind of product is adapted less naturally to the Internet and requires special treatment to be sold effectively. For instance, in the case of clothes, you can scan a piece of fabric to allow the customer a closer look and a "virtual feel." Some stores have set up services where a person enters his or her measurements and the Web site suggests clothes that complement his or her shape.

Customers need to be reassured on several issues to be confident enough to make on-line purchases. These customer requirements and concerns are more than are usually encountered in traditional commerce and require handling in a way that has not been addressed before.

On another level, cryptography is an important element in electronic commerce and presents its own challenge as there are at the moment several standards that do not work with one another. Choices must be made and efficiency must be kept in mind.

Furthermore, the Web allows for contextual selling. This means placing on the Web site informative content that generates interest for products that are sold and enhances the user's experience. So far, this has been one of the most effective ways of selling on the Internet.

To be successful, you have to really explore the opportunities in a new light, especially if you are already in business.

Steps for Electronic Commerce Implementation

Implementing a Web site requires very clear thinking as to the desired outcome as well as the way information is going to be presented to customers. There must be an added value and customers must be able to understand your proposition before thinking about getting involved with it. And you have only a few seconds to do so. This is quite a challenge!

Good planning is essential. If you have surfed the Internet, you have surely seen Web sites that are confusing. Some do not even clearly explain what the company is all about and what it does. Set objectives as to the message you want to send, and take into consideration that not everyone knows your company. In fact, unless your business is among the stars of its industry, chances are there will be more people who know nothing about it than there are people who are familiar with it.

In designing your strategies, establish the following:

- Is your Web site for informational purposes only?
- Is your Web site designed to make initial sales (i.e., the first sale to a customer) or is its main purpose to handle repeat orders at a low cost, following the initial order?
- Is your Web site for specific tasks such as distance learning?

Each of the tasks requires careful setup. As for any other business projects, the preparation steps are always the same. Based on your objectives, determine your Web needs pursuant to presenting your content: images, frames, plug-ins, databases, security. Prepare a plan according to what you want to accomplish.

Opportunities

The Internet allows you to reach existing customers as well as new ones. However, the approach to reach each of those types of clientele is not exactly the same. You can also establish a new kind of relationship with those two kinds of clientele.

Reaching Existing Customers

The Internet allows you to reach some of your existing customers and offer them better and additional services. When reaching existing customers, you need to know:

- Who they are
- What their relationship is with the Internet (Are they familiar with it? Are they using it?)
- What your present business is
- How your business operation can be extended to the Internet (existing products, additional products, improved customer service, faster order taking, permanent access for your customers)
- How you can help your existing customers make the transition

Reaching New Customers

When reaching new customers, determine:

- What kind of new Internet customers would be interested in your products
- How much you would like to widen your territory for new markets
- What kind of strategies you can prepare for new market penetration

Feedback

It is possible to obtain instant feedback from visitors and from existing and potential customers, provided you have the proper setup on your

Web site. Feedback can be obtained by asking the customer to type a short message in an e-mail window that is linked to a clickable e-mail address in a Web page. This method is very easy to implement, does not cost anything and is simple for customers, although they have to do some typing. The other option is to have a form that customers fill out. This requires a setup on the server with one or more tools such as scripts and databases. Allowing customers to send you feedback one way or the other can be considered to be a certain level of interactivity.

Interactivity

Real interactivity is easy to achieve on the Internet. Data collection is rendered simple and can be done in a massive way. For instance, if you offer a free service, you can require people to fill out a brief questionnaire in order to be given access to the service. You can program your site so that the customer receives automatic feedback and replies as well as personalized information, which allows customers a more interesting experience than just reading a standard Web page among millions of others.

Preferences can be recorded using cookies. Databases allow you to present customers with customized products according to their specifications.

Interactivity can also be achieved in a simple manner (e.g., using basic JavaScripts). This is done rather simply by copying the desired script into your Web page, and it does not cost anything. The Internet offers several possibilities for interactivity with customers.

Cybermalls and Internet Shopping Centers

There are on the Internet several Web sites that offer space in a virtual shopping mall. They offer different formulas. Some offer a simple space on their Web site with prepared pages that all look alike, where you enter a minimum of information for the Web page to appear in your business name. Some offer a "miracle formula" and promise high traffic. Among those, some live up to their marketing promises and others do not. Some ask for significant sums of money, while others offer to simply provide your Web site with the electronic commerce part, which is the most technical part, including order forms, shopping carts, electronic transactions and security. There are even companies that are organized around a formula where they assemble a group of people (up to 20) and sell them some sort of franchise in a specific theme store. People in those ventures each invest a sum of money, generally several thousand dollars, and are given some responsibilities and management tasks.

Before entering any of these ventures, it is recommended that you read further on the subject in general in, for instance, Internet magazines and specialized books and on the specific company in particular. Don't be afraid to ask questions; if someone cannot answer your questions, talk to someone who can. As Internet commerce grows, there will be an increasing number of both scams and good proposals. Remember that the ultimate goal of all this is to serve your business purposes and meet your objectives.

The following is a brief list of magazines that regularly discuss electronic commerce. Some are printed, and others are electronic only. It is difficult to indicate which are print versus electronic because recently at least a couple of them stopped being printed and are now available only on-line.

Internet World	*PC World*
Web Guide Monthly	*Small Business Computing*
Wired	*Entrepreneur*
Business 2.0	*Sys Admin*
ZDNet	*Upside*
Yahoo! Internet Life	*Windows Magazine*
Business Week	*MacWorld*
The Industry Standard	*MacUser*
Computer World	*Home Office Computing*
PC Magazine	*PC Week*
PC Computing	*Inter@ctive Week*

You can also perform a search using one or more of the search engines to find more about them.

Affiliate Programs

Affiliate programs are a new phenomenon brought on by the World Wide Web. They work in the following way: You agree to set up a hyperlink on your Web site that leads to another popular Web site, which is an Internet store, such as amazon.com or barnesandnoble.com, which are among the most familiar ones. When a customer leaves your site to go to the affiliate site and makes a purchase on that site, you are awarded a commission on the sale.

For instance, if you put a hyperlink on your Web site leading to barnesandnoble.com or amazon.com and your visitors go to those sites and make book purchases, you will get, from those suppliers, a percentage of the sale price. In order to place that setup on your Web site, you have to follow the procedures described on those suppliers' sites. The suppliers are responsible for tracking the sites from which customers come, and they take care of all aspects of the transactions as well as payment to you.

If you are really serious about doing business on the Internet, think about what an affiliate program could do for you. Would the benefits outweigh the downsides? Would a few cents or dollars be worth sending your valued customers to another Web site, possibly depriving you of your own sales? There is no clear-cut answer. It depends on how you are organized and what you want to achieve.

Things to Avoid

Watch the angle that is presented to people when they visit your Web site. They are not coming to your Web site simply to see another plain advertisement. In the real world, people are constantly bombarded by such ads when they walk on the street, go shopping, drive on the highway, listen to radio, watch television, read their newspapers and magazines and open their mail. They need a lot more — something that will transform their visit into an enjoyable or enriching experience. They need to be informed, to be entertained, to learn something.

When you receive queries from customers, avoid simply sending them a phone number to call because this totally defeats the purpose of using the Internet. People using the Internet expect to be able to conduct business and communicate through the Internet. Otherwise, they could very well have picked up the phone and called you in the first place. If they are inquiring through the Web, they expect a prompt answer by e-mail, and one that is satisfying. Otherwise, it might very well be their first and last inquiry. And your reply should not be to come and visit you. You never know where they are located.

Useful Sites

In conclusion, stick to the KISS principle and you will not go wrong: "Keep It Simple, Stupid." The simpler and more logical your Web site is, the better it will work and the better your results will be.

The following sites can be useful for electronic commerce:

- Software and software providers

http://www.icat.com	Electronic Suite (iCat)
http://www.shoppingcart.com	Smart Cart
http://www.shopsite.com	Shop Site
http://home.rocketfuel.com	Rocket Fuel Buildashop
http://www.microsoft.com	Site Server Commerce Edition (Microsoft)
http://www.softcart.com	Mercantec Softcart
http://www.virtualspin.com	Virtual Spin Internet Store
http://www.ups.com/tools	UPS integrated Quick Cost Calculator Tool

- Electronic malls

http://www.yahoo.com	Yahoo Store
http://www.icat.com	iCat Commerce Online (iCO)

- Electronic solution providers

http://www.netavenue.com	An affordable electronic shopping solution
http://www.internetmall.com	The Internet Mall

http://www.oracle.com	Oracle
http://www.ibm.com	IBM

■ Other useful sites about electronic commerce

http://www.ecommerce.gov	U.S. Government site on e-commerce
http://www.WebChamber.com	The World Wide Web Chamber of Commerce
http://www.iwlabs	Internet World Online
http://www.wilsonweb.com	A site about Web marketing

Do not hesitate to do more research on each topic to obtain up-to-date information.

6 Electronic Publishing and Broadcasting

The Internet has added new dimensions to publishing. Various documents (books, letters, newsletters, magazines, administrative documents, etc.) can now be published electronically in a variety of formats.

The fact that you do not have to print on paper and pay for postage reduces publishing costs substantially. It also saves a lot of time in sending documents, as you can send your documents to a lot of people simultaneously. The Internet provides instant delivery and/or access.

There are two basic methods of publishing on the Internet:

1. Sending documents to subscribers through the Internet
2. Posting documents on a World Wide Web site and making them available to Internet users

Let's take a closer look at these methods.

Sending Document to Subscribers

Sending an "Information E-Mail" on a Regular Basis

This is basically an electronic message that is sent to a list of users. After preparing your message content, you simply e-mail it to a predetermined list of people. Software for e-mail allows you to store a list of e-mail addresses to which you can send the same message simultaneously. All you need is the appropriate e-mail software. When using this method, be careful to avoid inadvertently publishing the e-mail addresses to which the material is sent (i.e., do not allow the e-mail addresses to be visible to all recipients). Failure to keep the addresses confidential could cause problems if some of the recipients use the addresses for their profits and/or for spam.

This function can be used for up to a certain number of e-mail addresses, depending on the software you use. Above that, you will need to use an automatic mailing list. Software is available for that purpose.

Sending an Electronic Newsletter

A newsletter can be prepared with regular e-mail software. It is similar to the e-mail described above, only with a more defined layout (i.e., you can add a special header and/or footer, borders, a signature, etc.) that is specific to the newsletter and remains the same for each issue. Such an identification mark will give your newsletter character and help people identify it. The newsletter will also have an issue number, the same as any periodical. Giving your newsletter a clear identity will distinguish it from spam and will position it as a useful piece of information. Some e-mail plug-ins allow you to give a newsletter a fancier look.

You can publish your newsletter in the form of an HTML page if you use an e-mail builder integrated into an HTML browser. The newer browsers have an integrated e-mail function that allows you to compose a message that has the same appearance as a Web page. This gives you more latitude in terms of what you can include in your message and allows you to incorporate images and attach documents. It is produced in HTML format. You can still send it to people who have basic e-mail software. What they will receive in that case is your plain message followed by a lot of HTML code (the browser's message composer can be set up to send a basic e-mail as well as the HTML page, in case the receiving e-mail software cannot read HTML).

There are numerous newsletters available on the Internet on a variety of topics. All you need to do to receive the ones you are interested in is subscribe to them whenever you find one of particular interest on a Web site you are visiting. Just follow the instructions, which consist mainly of giving your e-mail address, which will be followed by an e-mail message that you will have to confirm, also by e-mail, within a certain period of time.

In the same manner, you can offer to your existing and potential customers a newsletter on a topic of interest to them in a field directly related to your business. This has the advantage of maintaining a continuous presence among your clientele. The offer can be made on your Web site. Asking for registration from potential customers allows you to add their names to your distribution list.

The newsletter layout need not be very elaborate. It can be a simple, well-organized, one-page e-mail message that gives your customers information about specific topics of interest. Be careful not to produce just plain advertising because Internet users will not appreciate it. The key word is *information*.

This is a rather inexpensive and quite effective means of communicating with your customers, provided you offer products and services that can be marketed efficiently with that medium.

Mailing Lists

When your electronic newsletter grows to several hundred subscribers, mailing lists such as LISTSERV allow you to automate sending it to all subscribers simultaneously. Such mailing lists are automated and use e-mail rather than Usenet, as newsgroups do. The registration process is automated. Customers can subscribe voluntarily and can also cancel subscriptions at will to mailing lists of their choice.

These mailing lists can be centralized and contributed to by one person only or can accept contributions from several or all participants. There are also other types of mailing lists: mailserv, majordomo, listproc, mailbase.

For more information about mailing lists, go to:

http://www.liszt.com
http://www.delphi.com/navnet/faq/mlists.html

If you plan to publish a document of this type:

- Plan the frequency of issues and maintain a regular publishing schedule.
- Plan the program, content and features of each issue.
- Make past issues available to subscribers for future reference, for instance by building an archives section into your Web site.
- Send out each issue diligently and on time according to your publishing schedule.

A Word About Spam

Spam is an unsolicited and unauthorized message sent indiscriminately to users, whether through regular e-mail, electronic mailing lists or newsgroups. The phenomenon is often compared to junk mail. Advertisements can be considered as spam, but spam can also be other types of messages. Spam is a serious problem because it is a massive waste of precious Internet resources. It is argued that, in the real world, junk mail is paid for by those who send it. In the cyberworld, spam is paid for by the entire network, from the people who own and maintain the network infrastructure to your Internet service provider and you. No cost is assumed by spammers other than the proportional share that everyone else pays indirectly.

There is on the market software that filters, intercepts and prevents spamming. For instance, some software can detect and block messages as well as copies of messages sent to mailing lists.

This poses a dilemma when publishing content for multiple distribution. Be careful how you do it. Asking people to register in order to receive your newsletter cannot be considered as spam because they have asked to receive it. But if you were to send that newsletter in an unsolicited manner, it could be considered as spam, regardless of the quality of your content. So be careful how you proceed, especially in view of the fact that the line between information and spam is very thin these days and some people tend to confuse the two.

To learn more about spam and the issues that are involved, including the names of blacklisted advertisers and the reason for their being on the list(s), as well as how to advertise without getting blacklisted, go to:

http://www.tardis.ed.ac.uk/~charlie/nonfiction/journalism/spam.html

Posting a Document on Your World Wide Web Site

You can do your publishing in another way, in the form of Web pages (i.e., in HTML format) in a special section of your Web site. Whether you publish an electronic magazine or another type of document, you can format the Web pages to serve your purpose by giving them an appropriate layout of your choice.

World Wide Web browsers have evolved to the point where you can build a page almost as sophisticated as a magazine page. However, remember that not all browsers will necessarily be able to read pages in the same manner and produce identical results on users' computer screens. It is a matter of software and versions, as discussed in Chapter 4. For instance, if you use features that can be read only by the latest versions of software or by one browser, some people will not be able to see your page displayed properly and might even get an error message and not see it at all. Additional specifications about this topic are provided in Chapter 11.

PDF

Another method for posting documents on the Web is the Portable Document Format (PDF). This allows you to reproduce a page exactly as it was printed on paper or published using desktop publishing software. Of course, this requires one extra step: first preparing the page in a layout appropriate for printing (but not having it printed) using other software. The widest use of this method is for rapidly putting on the Web material that has already been published or otherwise prepared on paper. This can save a lot of time compared to redoing the whole document in HTML format.

PDF allows exact reproduction of a magazine and thus a more precise rendering in that it can copy the exact layout of a page produced by other software (such as Microsoft Word, Excel, Adobe Illustrator, Adobe PageMaker) or of printed pages that have been scanned. PDF also allows you to include HTML links within Web pages, linking them with other PDF pages or HTML documents anywhere on the Web.

With this format, the page looks like a photocopy or a high-quality fax. The whole page is processed like a picture instead of being prepared with HTML. However, the final product is not as large as other types of pictures in terms of file size (i.e., it takes less space than the GIF or JPEG equivalent).

In order to produce a PDF page, you need software that allows you to translate the page into PDF format, such as Adobe Acrobat. The authoring software must be bought and mastered in order to produce a page. However, all customers have to do is download the Acrobat Reader once and install it as a plug-in in their browsers. Then, each time they come upon a PDF document, the plug-in will automatically activate and read the PDF files from your site. A lot of Internet users have already installed the Acrobat Reader. The Acrobat Reader can also be used as a stand-alone (i.e., PDF files can be viewed independently without the use of the browser).

Possible uses of PDF files include:

- Paperless proposals
- Operation manuals
- Newspapers
- Magazines
- White papers

For more information about PDF, go to:

http://www.adobe.com

Push

What It Is

As opposed to Web surfing, where users access data by retrieving it from the Web, push is a process by which preselected content appears directly within the customer's browser as an HTML page, right on the computer screen. From a business point of view, it could almost be said that it is a hybrid between an electronic newsletter and a customized Web site. This technology applies to fourth-generation browsers only. With this technology, users select a "channel," on Web sites that offer that option, as well as specific content they want to automatically receive, such as news, weather, stock reports and so on. The word channel in this context refers to a specific Web site that is selected and that automatically sends the user information according to preselected categories, for either immediate display or viewing on request.

There are sometimes fees associated with receiving the information, although most of the services are now free because they are financially supported by advertisers. There are costs associated with producing that kind of push content and for broadcasting it, or rather webcasting it, on the Web. Those costs are related to installing special software on the server and on the channels used by content publishers (there is a fee per channel).

Users can determine what they want to receive and at what interval they want to receive that information, and they remain in full control of the viewing. The information can be presented on a small window while users are browsing the Web, or users can immediately view a predetermined screen as soon as they log onto the Internet.

This technology was pioneered by PointCast, which has brought it one step further. Now it does not merely copy Web pages to the desktop but delivers a consistent and versatile product.

The PointCast technology is available to businesses, and push technology is also available from other suppliers, including

http://www.poincast.com

http://www.marimba.com

http://sitesearch.netscape.com/communicator/v4.0/faq/netcaster.html

http://www.backweb.com

http://www.intermind.com

http://www.microsoft.com

http://www.netscape.com

What It Can Do for Your Business

Push technology offers new avenues for delivering custom content in a timely and automatic manner. It brings the sophistication for delivering information to users one level further. Whereas a newsletter brings subscribers the same information in the same format, push lets users customize the information they receive exactly according to their needs and schedules.

Webcasting, Multicasting, Unicasting, Intercasting

Webcasting is the ability to use the Web to deliver video and audio broadcasts. When applied to push technology, it is the transmission over the Web of preselected material at predetermined intervals, on demand or on a continuous basis.

Multicasting is sending a *single* copy of data to multiple receivers. This has the distinct advantage of conserving bandwidth.

Unicasting is sending *multiple* copies of the same data, through the Internet, to a fixed number of receivers.

Intercasting is the creation on the Web, by a television station and network, of interactive content built around a television program. This allows people to discuss and interact with program content and allows producers to add material that does not fit into regular episodes or to ask for feedback about previous episodes to guide them in developing future episodes.

Archiving Documents

If you publish information on your Web site, you will need to plan a hierarchy for your previously published documents as well as for current information. The archives should be organized in a way that will make it easy for users to access and find what they need, should they want to refer to previously published material.

If many of your documents are archived, it may mean integrating a search feature into your Web site in order to make finding the information easier. You could also use an HTML catalog in the form of a table of contents, depending on how you structure your information and the quantity you have. In any case, you will definitely need a good classification system if you want it to be useful at all, and that means planning.

Remember that a search feature is a useful tool, but it does not necessarily help find something when users do not know the keywords to work with (i.e., when they can't think of what keywords they should use). Pages that offer only a search window and not much more are sometimes a turn-off, especially when users try a couple of keywords and none of them work. Keep in mind that there are always several ways to present the information and several ways to name things. Unless you have thought of including them all in your database, users may obtain a lot of empty replies to their keyword queries.

Capturing the Customer's Interest

Capturing the customer's interest is one of your main objectives if you want to get your message across, especially when publishing. This requires giving users what they need, want, expect and are looking for. You can achieve this in several ways and with several tools. First and foremost, find out who your target users are and what they want and need, just as you would do in the physical world.

Second, make your publications interesting and coherent. They must be easy to read, reliable and attractive. The content should be well planned and useful to your readers. Advertising should be done in an informative way. Pay attention to presentation and graphics, just as you would in a paper publication.

Offer something of value to readers, that is, information they can use immediately to improve their operations, their lifestyles — anything that can help them. Internet users are accustomed to receiving lots of information for free. They expect something of value from any Web site and get turned off fast if they don't get it, especially when viewing pure advertising only.

Prepare a schedule of what you want to publish, when you want to start publishing it and what the themes will be. You can add teasers in each issue to advertise upcoming issues.

Practical Publishing Applications for Your Business

Electronic publishing can be used within your business, on an intranet, to allow circulation of internal documents among employees and sales representatives. New features, new specifications and new policies can be published and communicated expediently to the right people. Compared to printed document circulation, this represents an important advantage, especially for companies that are at the leading edge of technology and want to keep up with rapid change.

For instance, if your company uses a catalog, putting that catalog on-line means that representatives have immediate access to up-to-date information, specifications, prices and availability for anything they are selling. They can also receive bulletins, updates, special notices, performance reports, customer leads and so on.

Documents can be sent as attachments for comment, revision and correction without limitations in relation to location. Communication between separate locations or offices is therefore facilitated and accelerated. Procedures can be immediately posted and updated, thus making changes and updates instantly available companywide.

Electronic magazines can be published for customers and employees, for sales support and to make information widely available to existing as well as new customers. For certain businesses, publishing is a core activity in their operations as well as an important tool in business development.

III Applying Internet Technology to Your Business

7 The Internet for Corporate Use

Whether your business is very small or large, you surely have identified some benefits you could realize by integrating the Internet into your daily operations. Basic Internet services and features were discussed in Chapters 3 and 4. If your business is very small, basic services may be all you need for the time being and may fulfill most of your immediate business needs. However, if you plan on growing your business or you want to expand it, or if your business is already medium size, the Internet can offer additional benefits and services.

The Internet offers tangible advantages when used within a corporate environment. The first is the amount of money that can be saved when using it for activities that reach both inside as well as outside of the business. The second advantage is its ease of use; it cuts down on learning time and expenses.

Internet corporate use goes from a basic Internet account to a Web presence to a more sophisticated setup involving intranets, extranets and virtual private networks.

Provided it is done in an organized and well-planned manner, implementing the Internet in your corporate environment will have a positive impact on:

1. The efficiency of your operations
2. Your level of expenses
3. Your employees' performance
4. Your bottom line

The efficiency of your operations can be improved because you can simplify them and reduce the time it takes to accomplish certain tasks, especially those that relate to the exchange of information and research of information. Among these tasks are exchanges of documents for information purposes, for comment, for reference and so on. It is possible to set up a document management system as well as a knowledge management system using the Internet Protocol (IP), within an intranet. Research takes less time when the information is centralized and easily accessible.

Your expenses will decrease because, although implementing the Internet entails some costs, if done well the costs are far less than other systems that accomplish the same thing. The reason is that the main core of the Internet is subsidized and freely accessible; you only pay for a portion of the operations at your end, compared to paying for the total cost of a project (e.g., a communication system). It should be noted, however, that a fair amount of money can be spent when putting a very sophisticated Internet setup in place. This happens mainly when people have not assessed their situation carefully and choose solutions that are much too powerful and expensive for their needs. It is up to you to decide on the kind of setup you want to start with and the specific amount of money you want to invest.

Your employees' performance will be improved because using the Internet will save time and effort in many cases. It also gives employees new opportunities as well as new responsibilities. The Internet opens up a whole new playground. When employees use it for their work, they need to use it in a responsible manner. Another consideration is the kind of training your employees will need. While using Internet services generally requires little training, this may not be the case if people are not already familiar with computers or if specific employees need to get involved with more advanced tasks, such as HTML authoring, CGI and Java/JavaScript programming, database administration and Web site management.

Your bottom line will improve because some of your expenses are bound to come down when the Internet is used efficiently, and your revenues might increase if you develop your niche successfully in the new economy. For instance, courier fees can be reduced substantially when documents are transmitted electronically. Long-distance costs can be reduced. Time saved also has a financial value. After analyzing your existing operations, as well as the impact your Internet setup will have on your operations, you will have a better idea of how much you can save.

Business Use

Among the basic services that are immediately available to your business at a very low cost are e-mail and Web surfing. But there are many more options that you can use in your business operations:

- Electronic communications
- Networks and intranets
- Shared software (scheduling, appointment books) and groupware
- Document management systems
- Virtual private networks
- Extranet, electronic data interchange
- Internal and external job posting
- Report filing
- Internal publishing (bulletins, newsletters, procedures, modifications, spec sheets)
- Transaction processing
- Videoconferencing and Internet phone
- Training

Electronic Communications

Electronic communications can be used extensively in the business environment, and their features bring additional useful elements to business operations. Electronic mail allows you and your employees to communicate with one another without delay and without playing phone tag. You send a message when you are ready, the recipient reads it and replies when ready and you read the reply when it is convenient for you. Electronic mail systems are available on business networks without necessarily being connected to the Internet. An example is Lotus Notes or Group Wise. In turn, they can also be connected to an intranet and used to send and receive e-mail inside the business as well as on the Internet.

For instance, e-mail allows collaboration by sharing information and exchanging documents. The sending or receiving date is automatically recorded on each message, and an automatic confirmation, in the form of a notification to the sender, can be obtained when the recipient opens the message. Messages can be organized by date, topic, sender, etc. Messages can be archived for later reference. Over 85% of Internet mail arrives at its destination within five minutes — a definite advantage. Another interesting use of e-mail is voice e-mail. You can now send a voice message attached to regular e-mail. This is faster than typing, and the message still bears the date and originator and can be kept for future reference.

Of course, if you have a network, an appropriate setup is required in order to link your network with the Internet. Most of all, appropriate protection of your network from unauthorized access from the outside is necessary. Electronic mail has become an indispensable tool for businesses. When implementing such a system, make sure it is compatible with the Internet to avoid having to purchase additional software and redo expensive installations.

Networks and Intranets

If your business uses more than one computer, chances are you already have a network. This means that your computers are linked with one another. The setup can be as simple as sharing a printer, but it can also be more extensive, such as sharing multi-user software through a server. A network can be established very simply or done on a wider scale, including several computers connected to a server which is connected to the Internet as well as to several printers and peripherals.

An intranet is like a private Internet. It is a business network which is built on the same principles and with the same protocol as the Internet but is for private use only within a business. It links people who are located at the same premises, with an outside link to the Internet. It is an alternative to a traditional network that operates with proprietary standards. An intranet uses the IP and is connected to the rest of the Internet, and is therefore completely compatible with it, through a firewall that prevents access to the intranet by unauthorized outsiders. It is a network that lets a business use Internet technology to host its private local area network or wide area network. It is based on the same principles as the Internet, but it is protected from the rest of the Internet by special measures that prevent unauthorized users from accessing everything on the network.

For instance, you can set up a Web site that is accessible to the general public or to all your customers, while reserving another Web site on your intranet for use by your employees only. You can even grant various levels of access to various employees. For example, you can grant minimum access to regular employees and another type of access to executives.

In any case, every time you make a decision to implement something new, always keep in mind the next steps (i.e., what your future needs will be) as well as what you already have, and make your investment in a way that is and will remain profitable. This means a little planning to make sure that whatever products or services you purchase and install now will be usable and compatible with future steps in building your network.

For more information about intranets, go to:

http://www.intraware.com/library

Shared Software and Groupware

If you have a network that includes a server, it is possible to install multi-user versions of software on the server. This means that every time someone wants to access an application, the request is sent to the server and use of the software is shared by the users. Thus, software resources can be used more efficiently because not all people are using all software 100% of the time. There can be other advantages to this type of sharing. For instance, when trying to organize a meeting, it is possible to ask the time-management software to find a common time slot that is available in everyone's appointment book. It is possible to implement the Internet in a business while maintaining that kind of setup.

Document Management Systems

There are some document management systems (DMSs) that are compatible with the IP. A DMS is like an electronic filing cabinet that allows you to manage documents efficiently throughout your business. When there is a large number of documents, and when those documents need to be accessed by several people in the business, it is essential to put in place a good and reliable system to facilitate sharing and to ensure that documents are properly managed. That means making sure that current documents are available when people need them, that updates are done correctly and in a timely manner, that copies exist and are archived and that access is given only to authorized people.

Some DMSs use the IP, which makes it easy for people to learn how to use them. In addition to managing documents, the information those documents contain must also be managed. Documents can have many forms and formats: they can be text, images, spreadsheets, sound, video, etc. They can be in electronic or paper format. They can be used by one or several different departments in a business: customer service (correspondence with customers, suppliers, etc.), accounting, legal, project management, etc. Speed and efficiency of processing, retrieval, consultation, transformation, archiving and indexing are important to a business because an incredible amount of time can be spent trying to locate documents, which decreases productivity significantly.

Document management is very important to a business, and the more a business grows, the more critical good document management becomes. It is easy to lose control of document management, regardless of the size of a business. Being organized saves a lot of time and avoids headaches. Imagine what would happen if you could not find a legal or financial document.

A good DMS can also allow publishing of document databases on the Web, thus allowing use through an intranet or extranet. This means that the document database is rendered accessible to a select group of users through a Web page. This may also mean integrating Web hyperlinks into documents as they are processed. The main advantages are ease of use and efficiency.

For a sample of what can be achieved with a DMS, go to:

http://www.blueridge.com (This company offers its software for free if you are a single user. It is available for both Macs and IBM compatibles.)

http://www.lotus.com

http://www.infologics.com

http://www.aviatorsoftware.com

http://www.bscw.gmd.de

http://www.imt.net/~jrmints/denhome.htm

http://www.compinfo.co.uk/index.htm

http://www.archivebuilders.com

Virtual Private Networks

A virtual private network (VPN) is like an intranet that extends farther geographically. It can link together offices that are in remote locations. It allows sharing of information efficiently and rapidly by using the Internet infrastructure, without allowing regular Internet users to see what you are doing. The Internet structure is used by a business to create a kind of "private corridor" for its data to travel through, therefore rendering the data invisible to the rest of the Internet.

A VPN is not quite an intranet in that additional security is required, such as user authentication, encryption and so on, which are not necessarily used inside an intranet. Interception and infiltration are prevented by using dedicated IP addresses which are authorized by the system. The transaction is the same as if users were surfing the Web with a browser, but the connection is faster and stronger and the site is secured. This kind of network can save around 30% on telecommunication costs if a company has offices around the world.

You can either build your own VPN or subcontract that task to specialists. Of course, building your own VPN requires specific technical knowledge that you will need to acquire or hire. If you want to concentrate on the services or products you offer rather than the technical aspects of the Internet and VPNs, using a third party's VPN facilities can represent an interesting alternative, especially for small and medium-size businesses. In addition, the third party is responsible for the security of the VPN and can be held liable for all data transferred. The hardware setup for that kind of service is a link between your office server and the VPN provider through a little black box.

The service is usually billed at an hourly fee. Sprint, AT&T, MCI and UUNeT offer such service. The VPN provider segregates a designated slice of network for your business needs and makes sure that only your data is carried on that bandwidth. Rates for VPN services can include installation fees, monthly fees and hourly user fees. Some companies charge one or two of the three types of fees. Inquire carefully and keep an eye on the fees, as VPN is bound to increase in use over the next couple of years, thus bringing the fees down.

For more information, go to:

MCI	http://www.mci.com/
AT&T	http://www.att.com/
Sprint	http://www.sprint.com/
UUNeT	http://www.us.uu.net

Extranets and Electronic Data Interchange

An extranet links several organizations that are not on the same premises, using the Internet infrastructure and protocol as well as part of the public telecommunication system. For instance, it can link several intranets in different geographical locations that belong to different companies, thus allowing business-to-business transactions with suppliers, customers, dealers, etc.

It allows safe exchanges of confidential information and transactions while going through the Internet. Of course, this means that proper security must be installed, in order to preserve confidentiality and secure transactions. The main difference between an extranet and a VPN is that an extranet uses the Internet in the standard way whereas a VPN uses specifically reserved corridors on the Internet network.

For instance, an extranet allows a company to grant access to a part of its intranet to wholesalers for up-to-date information about product specifications and prices. A large customer can place direct orders with a supplier. Joint projects can be developed between different companies, using collaboration tools.

For more information on extranets, see:

http://www.sitesearch.netscape.com/products/whitepaper/extranetstds.html
http://www.netg.se/se/~kerfor/extranet.htm

Internal and External Job Posting

Finding qualified candidates for specific tasks can sometimes be a challenge for businesses of all sizes. To that extent, the Internet is an excellent way of finding resources fast and communicating with them instantly, whether for hiring or outsourcing purposes. Many consultants have their own Web sites, and a search will identify them. Looking at their Web sites will give you a good idea of what they do and how they work. You can send them an e-mail instantly and inquire about more specific topics or concerns.

For large businesses, job posting (internal and external) and candidate searches can be performed efficiently on the Internet. A lot of good candidates post their resumes in job banks. Employers visit those job banks to shop for candidates. Employers can also post their job openings on World Wide Web job banks.

If your have an intranet, you can use it to post jobs that are available to employees internally, without the rest of the world seeing it.

Either of the above solutions allows a business to rapidly obtain resumes for review and to build its resume bank. The search is shortened and communication between candidates and potential employers is accelerated.

Report Filing

The Internet, intranets and extranets can be used for electronically filing various reports, such as sales reports, meeting reports, attendance reports, sales leads and so on. Other documents can also be made available through the same means. Those documents are immediately available and can either be sent as attachments or posted as private or public Web pages. This means that employees working in remote locations can stay in touch and file their reports without delay.

They can also have instant access to the latest version of updated data.

Making documents available instantaneously represents a definite advantage to a business. Saving time often translates directly into saving money.

Internal Publishing

Imagine having notices, technical documents and specification sheets widely available as soon as they are ready. Compare the time it takes to print them on paper and distribute versus instant shipping through electronic means. This is particularly advantageous when, on top of everything else, you have to redo an entire document in order to correct a mistake!

Electronic publishing can be used for internal newsletters, bulletins, procedures, modifications, announcements and specification sheets. It can be used to communicate with customers or independent agents in the same manner. It can also be used to submit paperless proposals in a fast and efficient manner.

Transaction Processing

Electronic transactions can be integrated into your operations as an extension of your intranet, within either a VPN or an extranet. For instance, if a customer company has its own intranet, it can be linked to yours as part of an extranet. This gives the customer company limited access to your intranet, allowing it to prepare and send its orders.

Videoconferencing and Internet Phone

As discussed previously, videoconferencing and Internet telephone can be used effectively for internal communications. In addition, they can be used with customers, to give the participants in an electronic conversation or virtual meeting more of a feeling of speaking "in person." Visual contact is often necessary when conducting business operations. Videoconferencing can therefore play an important and useful role in a company.

From a business's point of view, it is important to keep on top of technical requirements for virtual meetings and Internet communication, in order to be able to use the technology efficiently. Yet virtual meetings and conversations also need to be planned and coordinated. In the case of videoconferencing, you need to find a common time when everyone will be available because the conference takes place in real time. Once the time is agreed upon, the setup needs to be completed at both ends, which means that each remote party must connect at the predetermined moment. This also applies to Internet telephone. Of course, appropriate software and/or a camera must be installed beforehand. Once you get the hang of it, the setup for each meeting can be done very fast and will become routine.

Training

The Internet can be used efficiently for training by taking advantage of its capacity to implement distance learning. If you have a one-person business, you can take advantage of the Internet to obtain training through distance learning programs, right from your home or office, without the need to spend time traveling. In addition, the learning is done on your own schedule, when it is convenient for you and at your own pace. If your trade is training, you can set up your own distance learning program and offer it to the Internet community or to specific customers. You can use it to create a new stream of revenue for your business.

If you have a larger business, in addition to the above, you can use the Internet to train your employees, either at your premises or in remote locations. If you already have a training program, it will have to be adapted for the Internet. If you do not have a training program, you can either find one that suits your needs from those available on the Internet or build one that will be suited to both your business and the Internet, for delivery to your employees.

Distance learning programs can be built in several manners. Some are quite expensive, and others are very affordable and cost effective. It depends on your specific needs and how the program is prepared. For instance, if you need to use a lot of video material or want to have a lot of "bells and whistles," you may end up with a steep invoice, but if you design a program to take full advantage of what the Internet has to offer (i.e., all the free services, material, plug-ins and so on), you will be able to accomplish a lot with relatively very little investment.

There are not a lot of resources on the Internet on how to prepare a distance learning program. There are, however, several organizations that offer distance learning programs, including virtual universities. If you perform a search on "distance learning" using one of the search engines, you will find several outlets that offer some kind of distance learning.

Issues Raised by Corporate Use of the Internet

The above options raise several issues:

- Security
- Training employees
- Monitoring employees' use of the Internet
- Legal issues

Security

Security is an important consideration and is tied to several aspects of your business in addition to Internet use. It has major implications for your profitability. It also brings up several technical considerations, which are discussed in Chapter 12. However, security is not contingent only on technical aspects. Company personnel are directly involved in preserving the integrity of the information and how it is used.

In a corporate environment, security can be breached as easily from the inside as from the outside. According to statistics, it happens regularly. If you have a one-person business, you will have more to fear from the outside than the inside, although you may suffer damage from the inside because of negligence on your part in following some basic rules and taking precautions to preserve your data. Your data can be destroyed by a computer crash or a natural disaster such as flood, fire, etc. On the outside, you have to protect your business from hackers and crackers.

If you have a larger business, employee use of the Internet may have an impact on your company's security on several levels:

1. Importing contaminated data (i.e., documents that contain viruses and other similar contaminants)
2. Revealing, knowingly or unknowingly, trade secrets or confidential information to external parties, such as competitors
3. Actions that breach your security system (e.g., by installing a modem directly connected to the outside world, thereby bypassing your firewall)
4. Ignorance of basic procedures or their purpose (e.g., sharing passwords or failing to back up important data)

This means that if you have employees, you need to establish clear policies for how you expect them to use and behave on the Internet, as well as some specific guidelines for the general use of computers. Employees must be well informed about the rules and guidelines. That includes new employees as soon as they come on board. You also need to establish the kind of Internet access you want to allow employees and the operations you will allow to take place. How will employees spend their time while surfing the Internet? Will they be able or likely to use it for fraudulent purposes? How could that impact your operations and your bottom line?

Consider the kind of damage an employee could do from inside a business. Some employees have even used the Internet at work to sell pornographic material.

If you do not have any employees, you still need to back up your data and protect it against viruses and other potential invasions (see Chapter 12 for additional information).

Training Employees

Although the Internet is very easy to learn and many people already know how to use it, proper use of the Internet by your employees will require, at the very least, that you inform them clearly about:

- Company goals, objectives, policies, code of ethics, and conflict of interest
- Security, risks and policies for safeguarding your data

In addition, you must make sure they understand what you mean and the implications of failure to comply. Another consideration is making sure they know how to use and manage a computer properly. That may seem obvious, but in light of the fact that a majority of people use only about 10% of the full potential of their computers, it is easy to see how computers can be misused. Some people, although able to learn the basic operation of certain software, never quite grasp the logical organization of the computer and the information it contains. Some people have a real problem understanding how a computer is logically organized. Others suffer from profound insecurity, which leads them to accumulate an incredible number of obsolete files on the computer. Still others accumulate useless temporary files, which can completely use up available memory and lead to a computer crash.

Initial employee training sessions must be followed up by sessions to remind them of things they may have forgotten or did not completely understand. This is generally a good opportunity to verify what they know and to identify areas in which they need more training.

Training is an area that is easy to neglect, especially in view of everything that has to be done in a business, particularly a small one-person business. Time and money are the major factors that influence the amount and quality of training a business provides. However, training is a valuable investment, and neglecting it is never profitable.

Monitoring Employee Activity

If you have several employees, you may want to do a certain amount of monitoring when implementing the Internet in your business to see what's going on, particularly at the beginning of the implementation process. This is a good way to prevent problems and ensure that your profitability will not go down because of misuse by employees.

To that end, there is specialized software that can help you. The ethical side of the issue is not quite clear-cut yet, and the subject is still quite controversial. But the trend is toward giving the employer more leeway than less, especially in view of the fact that the employer generally bears most of the responsibility for the employees' behavior.

The Advantages of Using the Internet for Your Business

Connecting your company and personnel to the Internet has many advantages. Time and money saved, ease of use, ease of access and speed of access are all immediately apparent. Compatibility requirements are greatly reduced. The learning curve is decreased.

Employees can remain in touch when traveling abroad as well as when at home. The Internet makes telecommuting a lot easier. Employees can find information on just about any topic. A whole wealth of it is at the user's fingertips.

You can reach wider markets and allow customers worldwide to reach you easily. Time and money can also be saved through virtual meetings with people who are in different and/or remote locations.

You have access to a much larger market once you are on the Internet. The whole world has access to your products, in proportion to the access people have individually to the Internet. With today's courier services, your products can reach your customers worldwide in 24 or 48 hours. You are no longer restricted by intermediaries and agents. Customers obtain their stock rapidly, straight from the source.

Most of all, information is circulated extremely speedily and is widely distributed and available. With Internet technology evolving at mind-boggling speed, more and more services become available as the weeks and months go by.

The Challenges of Corporate Use

It is important to get to know your new market and what it wants. You have to discover your Internet customers' tastes, requirements, expectations and so on. Remember that this market has its unique characteristics and may have different requirements than what you are used to. The commercial side of the Internet is still young, and you have to approach it carefully and be well prepared.

How employees use their time can represent a challenge for your company's profitability. Indeed, how do you know what employees are doing while sitting at their computers? They could be doing almost anything related to their personal lives while surfing the Web.

They could be surfing a dating site, reading a magazine, looking at sewing patterns, chatting with friends or planning their next vacation. There is also fraudulent use of e-mail and file exchanges to consider. Your employees could be using your company's computers for dubious purposes. It is a good idea to obtain legal advise in terms of the extent of your responsibility in relation to your employees. Remember that legal responsibility may vary with geographical location. Evaluate the situation and see if you need to implement any special measures.

Make an inventory of the technical expertise you have in-house and determine the resources you can dedicate to Internet implementation. If you decide that you need outside resources, obtain estimates and evaluate total costs. Keep control of the process at all times.

8 Establishing and Strengthening Contact with Customers and Partners

The purpose of a business having a presence on the World Wide Web is to be recognized, to establish and increase its credibility and to increase its profitability. As discussed before, the Internet represents a formidable tool for making contact with customers or potential customers, if used well.

Corporate Image and Identity

The first step in establishing a strong presence is to clearly define your corporate identity, whatever the size of your business. Do you have a clearly defined corporate identity now? If so, is it appropriate for the Web, and can it be transferred to and/or adapted for that medium? If not, what kind of impression and image do you want to convey? Now is a good time to build a strong corporate identity and establish your business solidly in both the cyberworld and the real world.

Have you defined clearly what it is you want to do with and on the Internet? What exactly is your business and how do you want it to be perceived?

Your corporate identity includes your logo(s) and trademarks, how you present your company and the kind of message you communicate. The content (i.e., text and pictures you put up on your Web site) will determine the quality of your corporate image. The interaction you have with your customers also has an impact on your image. There are additional influential elements on the Internet that are not encountered in the real world.

For instance, being able to access your Web site easily and rapidly makes a difference to the visitor. A Web site that is not available or that takes forever to appear on the visitor's screen does not make a good impression and does not present a good image of your company. Also, a site that contains bugs (which happens frequently on certain sites) or is incompatible with the visitor's browser (e.g., HTML tags [see Chapter 9] that are not standard for all browsers and therefore work only with certain ones) will not look good either.

Another aspect is how the information is organized within your Web site. If your site has only a few pages, organizing them will be a relatively simple task. But the more information you have to present, the more pages you will have and the bigger a challenge organizing them will be. Make it easy for people to find what they are looking for. Also make sure that all hyperlinks within your site are working properly. If your Web page says "Click here for more information" but when people click all they get is an error message, that's a definite turn-off. If you are selling products, people must be able to find what they want fast. If you are offering information, it must be well organized and presented in a logical order.

The overall performance of your Web site is as important as the appearance of the pages (discussed in more detail in Chapter 11). All this adds a whole new dimension to doing business.

Your Domain Name

Now is a good time to decide what domain name you want and should use. Because the domain name becomes such an important part of corporate identity on the World Wide Web, it requires careful examination. There are two choices: having your own domain name officially registered or using one that is provided for free by your

Internet service provider (ISP). In order to understand the difference, let's look at how the Uniform Resource Locator (URL) or World Wide Web site address is assembled. A URL is made up of several parts; typically, it reads something like:

http://www.domainname.com

In this address, http:// indicates the protocol used. In the case of the World Wide Web, it is the HyperText Transfer Protocol.

Following http are three w's, which stand for World Wide Web. This sometimes varies and can be replaced by "w3" or other designations.

Next comes the second-level domain name. This is the name that you will register as your very own, and it will belong to you no matter where your Web site is hosted. In our example, it is "domainname," but it could be anything you want as long as it has not been taken by someone else.

The last part is the top-level domain name. It does not belong to you as such, as it is shared by many domain names, but it is attached to your domain name for as long as you have it. There are several possible extensions, among which is .com, the most widely used for commercial Web sites. The extension can also be a country code or an extension such as .net. You will get all the necessary information about domain names on the InterNIC Web site where you register your domain name. Your ISP can also register your domain name for you for a fee, but you should read InterNIC's information before you get involved with registration, as there are important considerations and things to watch when registering.

When an ISP provides a domain name to you for free (e.g., when you get free space for your personal Web site on an ISP's server), the ISP uses its own domain name and adds the name of your directory. In this case, your domain name would read something like:

http://www.ispname.com/directoryname

Obviously, this formula will not do much for your corporate identity; it is therefore recommended that you carefully pick a good domain name, as well as a second and third choice in case your first choice is already taken.

For more information about registering domain names, go to:

http://www.internic.net

Your Web Site as a Point of Contact

In addition to the above-mentioned capabilities, your Web site can be used to establish a more direct and interactive relationship with your customers and potential customers. For instance:

- You can ask them to provide you with specific information (e.g., their preferences, their habits, what they are looking for, what they would like, what they expect). You can identify several important trends among your clientele by obtaining that information. It is also more profitable to determine who your customers are and to tailor your offer to them.
- You can build special promotional events for your customers' benefit and organize them around the process of gathering the above information.
- You can use your Web site to provide customer service and technical assistance. You can also use it to give advice and suggestions.
- You can offer visitors an opportunity to chat together, either in real time or through a newsgroup or mailing list.
- You can choose to entertain them, in a way that promotes your business and/or specific products or services and that entices customers and potential customers to purchase from your Web site.
- You can provide information services in several formats: news posted and updated regularly on your Web pages, audio and/ or video broadcasting, push technology, bulletins, banners, messages, etc.
- You can implement a call center as part of your Web site. This is done through special software and implies that you have service reps available to take calls while on-line or to interact on-line with customers.
- You can provide visitors with a billboard or other services according to the type of business you have.

Market Segmentation

It is clear that it is not possible to do everything or to implement all services at once. An additional consideration is the growing trend toward market segmentation. The total Internet market is in reality a multitude of smaller and varied markets, like a mosaic made up of numerous pieces. In addition, people expect more personalized services and products. This trend is showing up in the real world as well as on the Internet, but it is probably more acute on the Internet because of everything the technology makes possible.

Hence, it is important to know which market segments you want to target first, second, third and so on. The Internet contains a wonderful and extensive array of statistical data about its structure, its services and its users. By doing some research, you will be able to gather enough information to draw a pretty good picture of the Internet population segments.

From there, by analyzing your products and their Internet potential, determine which segments you can serve initially and what you need to do to reach those customers. Prepare your plan accordingly. Then, plan for widening your market if you wish to do so. This can be done through higher volume, new products or by serving new segments.

The following URLs provide Internet demographics:

http://www.nua.ie/surveys
http://www-survey.cc.gatech.edu
http://www.gvu.gatech.edu/user_surveys

Customer Service

Customer service can be greatly improved and its costs dramatically reduced through the use of the Internet. The Internet offers easy, reliable and permanent access to current information about your products and services. For instance, you can offer instructions, with illustrations and photos, 24 hours a day, 7 days a week. This might allow you to eliminate costly 800 phone lines, expensive mailings and the personnel needed to accomplish those functions. Furthermore, the information can be updated very rapidly, so it is always current. This is especially useful in industries where technology changes rapidly.

Your customers can have access to this information whenever they want at their convenience, at no cost other than the cost of their own Internet service. You can also include an FAQ service, which is a series of frequently asked questions. This service has the advantage of freeing up the receptionist or technician who has to answer the same questions over and over.

You can offer advice, highlight new products or services, invite suggestions and e-mail messages through your Web site. Specification sheets can be included, along with illustrations, sketches, maps, plans, pictures, photos, etc. You can set up a newsgroup or chat and allow your technical people to interact with customers.

With customer service, you add one more function to your Web site — a certain degree of interaction with your customers. You will most likely receive specific requests from your customers, and you can evaluate what to add to your Web site based on the queries you receive. This means that someone will have to answer those requests promptly and make the necessary updates to your Web site.

True customer service requires a certain degree of interaction. Your customer service can either remain in its traditional format while being complemented by the Internet or can be completely taken over by the Internet, taking full advantage of this medium's features. However, the latter is probably more appropriate for businesses that are involved with computers or Internet services.

Some companies have set up real-time on-line services for their customers, where service reps answer customers' questions and give advice on-line, in real time, as customers browse the Web site. Some relatively new products allow businesses to do this. It is now possible to integrate a call center into your Web site, where customers navigating through the site can call while they are on-line and get help with problems or answers to questions. Some software allows on-line telephone calls; other software does something similar in the form of text that is posted on users' screens while they continue to browse the Web site. This adds a whole new dimension to on-line customer service.

Internet customer service is an excellent opportunity to invite customer feedback and to obtain it more easily and in a larger quantity than through traditional techniques, where there is no real motivation for the customer. It is a lot easier for a customer to give you feedback while he or she is surfing the Web and is just a mouse click away from answering a few short questions. Typing a few comments while cruising the Web requires less time than, for instance, reading a printed questionnaire, picking up a pen, filling in the answers and returning it by mail. You can also add incentives to your Web site and reward those who decide to give you some feedback. The reward can be a gift or even something that does not cost you anything, such as eligibility for rebates, special products or customized and/or restricted services on your Web site. Customers can obtain special advantages by providing feedback. You are limited only by your imagination!

Frequently asked questions and up-to-date specifications and product descriptions can be posted on the Internet in a more extensive manner than through standard printed material that is distributed to customers. References can be made to the Web site on instructions and other customer material, allowing customers to find immediately any additional information they need.

Customer service can have its own page or series of pages on the Web site. The location should be clearly identified to make it easy for customers to find. The following questions will help you identify where you stand in terms of customer service. The list of questions in the next section will help you determine your needs and budget for implementing electronic customer service.

To determine your customer service needs and requirements, answer the following questions:

1. What kind of customer service are you offering at the moment?
2. Do you have clear customer service policies?
3. Who is responsible for your customer service?
4. How is it done?
5. How much does it cost your company?
6. What kind of results are you getting from it (positive, none, negative)?
7. Is your actual service adequate for your needs?
8. Is it building a positive corporate image of your business in your customers' minds?
9. Does it support your marketing strategy and your sales?

Using the Internet for customer service can bring a business substantial savings, especially when it replaces 800 telephone lines and personnel. In some cases, customer service can be achieved with fewer people when done through the Internet than by phone. The more efficient the customer service on your Web site is, the less burdened the other customer services in your company will be. However, to be efficient, no additional burden must be placed on customers. It must all be transparent to the customer, as well as easy to use.

Obtaining Personal Information and Feedback from Customers

Given the particularities of the World Wide Web, it could prove very useful to be able to obtain information from people visiting your Web site as well as from customers. This raises a couple of issues. In order to obtain that information (and for it to be meaningful and useful), you need:

1. To reassure people about how the information is going to be used
2. To determine exactly who will have access to that information
3. A way to allow people to opt out if they do not wish to provide any information

For that information to be useful to you, you need:

4. To determine exactly what information you need
5. To have an effective way of collecting, sorting and storing that information
6. A method for analyzing the information
7. A form of output (e.g., reports, statistics, etc.)

It is a good idea to offer incentives to people in exchange for providing you with their personal information. Some types of incentives are more useful than others in making sure that the information provided is accurate. The fact is, you cannot easily verify the accuracy of the information provided electronically on the Internet. For instance, surveys reveal that over 50% of people have provided inaccurate information on the Web at one time or another. Be sure to take this into account when analyzing your data.

Customers can sometimes be reluctant to give personal information or to give it accurately. How you are going to collect the information, what you are going to do with it and what you will do to entice your customers to give it to you will definitely have an impact on your results.

To obtain customer feedback, you can:

1. Ask customers to send you e-mail through a clickable e-mail address posted on your Web page. This is probably not the most attractive method because customers have to initiate the action. In addition, they must compose a written message without necessarily knowing what to write or exactly what they want. Furthermore, they might forget to include important information in the message. But if you can find an incentive for them to do so, it will be to your benefit.

2. Ask customers to fill out a questionnaire. This makes it a lot easier for people to give you information, and it makes it easier for you to get exactly what you want. However, people might still be reluctant because of privacy issues, as discussed later in this chapter.

   In order to provide people with a questionnaire, you will have to include it in the Web page. You also need to program instructions, embedded in the HTML code of the page, regarding what you want done with the information provided by the visitor. This calls for a technical means such as CGI script, JavaScript, Java or other types of scripts. You will also probably need a database to store the information and some way to analyze it. In all cases, keep your questionnaire short in order to keep the visitor's interest and to ensure the entire questionnaire will be completed.

3. Offer incentives conditional upon correctly filling out the questionnaire. Incentives can take many forms. They can range from privileged access to certain reserved sections of your Web site to something like CyberGold, ClickRewards, E-centives or FreeRide. CyberGold is an actual cash payment made for visiting specific Web sites, whereas the other incentives are in the

form of points, discounts and frequent-flyer miles. Incentives can also be in the form of free subscriptions to publications and other attractive offers specifically targeted to your market.

For more information, go to:

http://www.cybergold.com
http://www.clickrewards.com
http://www.e-centives.com
http://www.freeride.com

Using Databases

When you set up a database, make sure it is compatible with the Internet, because not all databases are. Also make sure it does what you want it to do and that it produces the reports you need. Managing databases requires expertise; if you are not a specialist, do not expect to be able to do it by yourself.

A database can be used to process orders, but it should also be able to produce statistics that you can use to manage and grow the Internet portion of your business. It should be fully functional with your Web site and well protected. A database will also allow you to immediately return answers or feedback to customers upon receiving their queries. For instance, a database can receive a list of specifications or characteristics that a customer has checked on a form and then return to the customer suggestions for products, actions to take and other options. The flow of data back and forth enlivens the Web site and allows customization for the visitor. It could, for instance, allow you to present customers with various customized Web pages according to their individual specifications. This means that a different page could appear to different visitors who agree to interact with your Web site, allowing you to collect specific information at the same time. Various criteria can be used to customize the pages according to the type of business you have and what customer information you are seeking. Although this can be achieved to a certain extent with JavaScript and cookies, a database will allow a wider range of possibilities.

Databases can also be used to collect a variety of information provided by customers as well as to store their orders, among many other things.

Privacy Issues

The importance of security is explained in Chapter 12. However, equally important, from the customer's point of view, is the issue of privacy.

Privacy is among the important concerns of Internet users, and with good reason. It is impossible to guarantee 100% security or privacy, whether in the real world or on the Internet. However, the very nature of the Internet brings on new challenges because it provides new means of collecting information at speeds and in amounts never seen before. Also, the capacity for processing this information is also greatly enhanced by technology. This means that a Web site administrator must take special precautions when collecting people's personal data on the Internet. The crucial element, then, is the level of risk, which has to be kept at an acceptable level for the user. This means two things:

1. Proper security measures, including monitoring, verification and testing, to make sure that the data you collect is safe from misuse
2. Proper reassurance to the customers

Reassuring customers thus becomes an important marketing element and should be included in your marketing strategy. It is especially important if you collect sensitive information which could be detrimental to customers, and hence to your business, if disclosed. You need to tell customers how important it is for you to keep the information you collect from them private and what practical security measures you are taking to do that. Any meaningful technical description or reassurance should be communicated to them, as long as it does not jeopardize your security. Disclose to customers, in a simple way, everything you are doing to ensure confidentiality. If there are special logos or symbols that would reassure customers more effectively, use them. A good business practice is to become a member of a World Wide Web security-related organization or chamber of commerce.

The Netscape browser also has a small key or lock symbol at the bottom left of the browser window. During a normal browsing session, that symbol appears broken in half. However, in a site that uses secure data exchange, the two halves of the symbol reunite or the lock closes, thus indicating a secure session. Nothing prevents you from creating your own symbol to let your customers know that the personal information they are communicating to you is going to be kept confidential and that you are serious about the matter.

Reassurance can also be offered in the form of a pledge. The pledge can take whatever form you deem appropriate, but, most of all, it must represent what your customers need, want and expect.

If you plan to offer customer information to third parties, you have to obtain permission from your customers in advance and give them the opportunity to indicate whether or not they will allow you to communicate that information to outside parties. It is now unacceptable and sometimes illegal to divulge any personal information without a person's knowledge or consent. However, providing general statistics without any specifics falls into another category and, in this case, does not threaten privacy. For instance, you can compile figures from number of visits, age bracket and so on in order to build a profile for potential advertisers and communicate the results without compromising confidentiality.

What it comes down to is this: show a minimum of respect and consideration for your customers and it will pay off. Figure 8 will help you in making decisions regarding your options.

Integrated Search Feature

If your Web site contains a lot of data or a lot of pages, or if you have a database that stores your information, you will probably need to build a search feature to help visitors find the information they need within your Web site. This search tool differs from the search engines currently available on the World Wide Web in that it limits

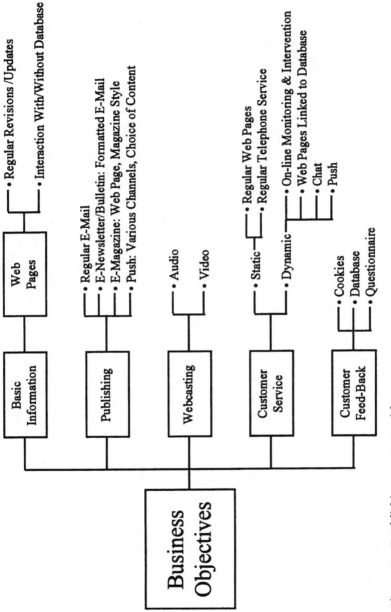

Figure 8 Establishing contact with your customers.

its search to the data contained in your Web site instead of on the entire Internet network.

Whenever you deal with customers, whether in real life or on the Internet, always take good care of them. Remember, you never get a second chance to make a good first impression.

9 Understanding the Technical Aspects of the Web Page

In a business, whenever you want to prepare information for a specific purpose, it needs to be converted to the format of the medium you select for the final result. For instance, if you prepare a brochure, you select and prepare what you want to say (i.e., the content), and then you prepare the way you will present that information (i.e., the format). The same principle applies to the Internet. The above example involves technical considerations; in the same manner, preparing a Web page also involves technical aspects.

When preparing a Web page, the main thing to keep in mind is your customers' limitations. Those limitations can be one or several of the following:

- Computer speed
- Computer capacity (RAM and hard disk)
- Size of the computer screen
- Browser software and version currently installed
- Speed of the telecommunication link
- Internet connection (i.e., through an Internet service provider [ISP], a network, etc.)

Computer speed will influence a user's level of receptivity. For instance, a slow computer means additional waiting time for the user, especially if your Web site has fancy features. Also, some of those features will not be accessible to the user.

Computer capacity puts limitations on the browser version that a user can install and on various plug-ins as well. For instance, people who still only have 4 or 8 Mb of RAM will face serious Web limitations and will not necessarily be able to do what they want. Certain plug-ins require 8 Mb of RAM to run properly, although most of them are not that hungry.

Size of the computer screen has an impact on your page design. For instance, if you design a large page, its appearance will not be as interesting for people who have a small screen — and there are a lot more small screens than large screens.

Browsers have been published in numerous versions. There are different World Wide Web browsers, and each browser has several versions. Although there is a certain level of standardization as far as tags are concerned, each publisher of a World Wide Web browser also has proprietary tags. Therefore, the way you prepare your page will make a difference in terms of what people see.

The speed of telecommunication links is another important consideration. How fast will the page download on users' screens? The more images or graphic elements you have, the more time it will take.

How users are connected to the Internet (i.e., through an ISP, a network, etc.) is another factor. For instance, some networks will not let users download Java applets; instead, they get error messages. Putting Java applets on your page will not do any good in this case, so you need alternatives.

In addition to customer limitations, you have to take into account the technical limitations (availability of bandwidth, bottlenecks, etc.) of the Internet and the World Wide Web. The good news is that you do not have to take into account which platform (i.e., Windows, Macintosh, UNIX, etc.) your customers are using.

The following section explains the basics of how Web pages are prepared, to allow you to understand what can and cannot be done. Even if you use automatic Web page composer software, it is still useful to understand the basics of HTML (HyperText Markup Language). Although the automatic software does most of the work, you may at some time want or need to get involved with some HTML tags for one reason or another.

Most Web pages are prepared with HTML. HTML consists of tags that tell the browser what information to show on the user's computer screen and how to display it.

HTML also allows text, graphic elements (images), pages and documents to be linked together. This means that everything you include in a Web page must be accompanied by the proper tag, whether or not it is hyperlinked to something. Preparing Web pages is called HTML authoring or Web design and not HTML programming because HTML is not a programming language in the conventional sense.

Basic Preparation of the Web Page

To prepare a Web page using HTML tags, you need an HTML editor. Netscape and Microsoft Explorer both have an integrated HTML editor, allowing you to prepare basic Web pages without the need to master the use of HTML tags. However, if you need fancier HTML, you will need specialized HTML editing software. You can find that kind of software on the Web. Some of it is sold, and some is free. Note that it is possible to manually prepare any HTML document, even the fancier ones, using a simple text editor, provided you use proper HTML tags.

Introduction to HTML

Most HTML tags have two parts; the first indicates the beginning and the second indicates the end of the action to be performed. Tags are always contained within < >. The format of the opening tag is

    <tag>

and the format of the closing tag is

    </tag>

Notice that the only difference between the two is the / inside the closing tag. Other than that, most beginning tags and closing tags are identical (i.e., the command to end an action is the same as the one to begin it but includes a /.

The basic tags are provided in this section. Note that the tags presented here represent only a partial list; a lot more tags and HTML specifications can be found at the Uniform Resource Locators (URLs) given at the end of this chapter. The tags themselves never appear on a Web page, unless there is an error in the HTML code. Only the text that appears between tags (most of them) is visible.

The tags that indicate the beginning and the end of a Web page are

<HTML></HTML>

The first tag appears at the beginning of a page and the second tag appears at the very end of that page, which means that everything else contained in the page will appear between those two tags.

The tags for the information that must be included in a Web page are

<Head>Information</Head>

These tags are not actually shown on the page. For instance, META tags (discussed in more detail later in this chapter) are included in this part.

The tags that show the title of your page in the browser's title bar at the top of the browsing window are

<Title>You Write Your Actual Title Here</Title>

Keep the title short. It should be between 5 and 15 words (maximum) and include the name of the organization and the product name, along with a short descriptive phrase. This will allow for more efficient indexing by the search engines.

The tags for the rest of the information contained within a Web page are

<Body>Text</Body>

All the other tags for text and images are contained within these two tags.

Headers

There are various HTML headers which show fonts in various sizes and formats. They are the titles of paragraphs within a page.

<H1>Header 1</H1>	will look something like	# Header 1
<H2>Header 2</H2>	will look something like	## Header 2
<H3>Header 3</H3>	will look something like	### Header 3
<H4>Header 4</H4>	will look something like	**Header 4**
<H5>Header 5</H5>	will look something like	**Header 5**
<H6>Header 6</H6>	will look something like	**Header 6**

Line and Paragraph Breaks

The tag for a line break is

The line break tag ends a line. There is no end tag for this break. The tag for a paragraph break is

<P>

There is no end tag for this break either. This break ends a line and adds a space before the next paragraph. Two <BR> equal one <P>.

Styles

The tags for showing text in bold are

<B>Text</B>

The tags for showing text in italic are

<I>Text</I>

The tags for underlining text are

<U>Text</U>

Alignment

The default alignment is left. Therefore, if alignment is not specified, the text is aligned left with a ragged right edge. The following tags are used for both text and images.

The tags to align elements on the left-hand side of the page are

    <LEFT>Text</LEFT>

The tags to align elements on the right-hand side of the page are

    <RIGHT>Text</RIGHT>

The tags to align elements in the center of the page are

    <CENTER>Text</CENTER>

The above tags are read by the major browsers; however, some of the other browsers will not read them properly. Again, test the various browsers.

Lists and Bullets

The tag to indicate the start of a list section is

    <UL>

There are different kind of lists, with and without bullets.

The tag for a bullet is

    <LI>

Each bullet in the list bears that tag. For this tag, the end tag

    </LI>

can always be omitted. For instance,

    <LI>   Bullet #1
    <LI>   Bullet #2
    <LI>   Bullet #3
    <LI>   Bullet #4

The tag to indicate the end of a bullet section is

</UL>

In the example shown here, the bullet section would have four bullets in all, but you can have as many as you want. Note that you can change the appearance of bullets. Additional types of lists can be found in HTML editor software as well as on HTML authoring Web sites.

Graphic Elements

The tag to show a horizontal line on a page is

<HR>

Unless there are other attributes, the line will be a narrow line in the same color as the background but with an embossed effect. It is possible to show lines of various widths by using specific tags.

The tag to insert an image in a page is

<IMG SRC="image.jpg">

The image will be aligned left by default.

There are numerous possibilities in terms of graphic elements. For instance, you can indicate the size of an image so as to wrap text around it. You can also choose to center an image or to align it flush right. An image can bear either the .jpg or .gif extension. For more details, see the section on images later in this chapter.

Hyperlinks

A clickable e-mail address would look something like:

<A HREF="mailto:dvallee@point-net.com"> dvallee@point-net.com </A>

These tags make the dvallee@point-net.com address (i.e., the address between the <A> tags) clickable in the text. This means that when a visitor clicks on it, an e-mail window will appear on the visitor's screen and he or she will be able to send an e-mail message automatically to that e-mail address, simply by typing the message in the window and clicking on "Send." The browser, if it has been set up properly, will automatically show the sender's address in the right place.

The text between the tags

<A HREF="Altpage.html"> Text</A>

has a hyperlink to another HTML page. Altpage.html would be replaced by anything you want to call the HTML page where the hyperlink leads.

In a real HTML page, all the above tags would normally be followed by the tags

</BODY> </HTML>

The end of the text is indicated by </BODY> and the end of the page is indicated by </HTML>.

A complete, very simple Web page would look something like:

<HTML> <HEAD> <TITLE>Your actual page title</TITLE>Plus any other head element such as META tags</HEAD>

<BODY>This is where to place your text. There will also be in this section:

<H1>A paragraph title</H1>

Then the paragraph itself in which you include images, bullets or whatever you need and <P>

<H1>A second paragraph Title</H1>

With the text of the second paragraph, and so on.

</BODY></HTML>

On the browser, the above would look something (but not exactly) like:

Your actual page title

This is where to place your text. There will also be in this section:

A paragraph title

Then the paragraph itself in which you include images, bullets or whatever you need and

A second paragraph title

With the text of the second paragraph, and so on.

Hyperlinks

A hyperlink in a Web page is an underlined word or group of words or an image which is defined by a hyperlink tag. In the Web page, the word or words are underlined and appear in a different color, while the image has a colored frame around it. When the mouse pointer comes upon that text or image, it changes into a hand to show that the user can click on that element. Clicking brings the user to another section of the page, another page in the Web site or another Web site.

The tag to establish a hyperlink is in the following form:

<A HREF="linkname.html">

The end tag is

</A>

The text appears between the tags. For instance, if your text is "See our mission" and it is hyperlinked to a page named "mission.html," the whole tag would be

<A HREF="linkname.html">See our mission</A>

Of course, you would need to have a file named mission.html in your Web site directory.

If an image is hyperlinked to another element, you simply indicate the file name where you want to send the hyperlink, just as you would for text. The only difference is that instead of the text being underlined, the image is surrounded by a colored frame. Therefore, the image name appears between the hyperlink tags.

As an example, let's use the image from the preceding section on graphic elements. That image was called image.jpg, which means that in the HTML page it would bear the tag

```
<IMG SRC="image.jpg">
```

Suppose you want to hyperlink this image to another page; that is, when users click on the image, they go to another page named page.html. The complete tag for the hyperlinked image would be the above tag plus the hyperlink tag:

```
<A HREF="page.html"><img src="image.jpg"></A>
```

Basically, that is all there is to a Web page. Of course, there are a lot more tags and HTML extensions available that create fancier displays and effects, but the basic principle is the same.

META Tags

In addition to the above, one other element that is crucial to your Web page is META tags. META tags allow search engines to identify a page and its content and display a short description in search results. Those tags do not alter the way a page looks because the information they contain is completely invisible on the page. However, that information is made available to search engines whenever they come upon your site.

A META tag is included within a <HEAD> tag, which means that you would find the META tag between <HEAD> and </HEAD>.

There are several META tags, but the most important ones are the description and the keywords META tags because those are the ones used by search engines to index your Web site. Those two META tags would read as follows:

```
<META NAME="keywords" CONTENT="list of keywords">
```

```
<META NAME="description" CONTENT="description of the Web site content">
```

and would appear on the page between the <HEAD> and </HEAD> tags.

The <META NAME="keywords"...> tag contains keywords by which search engines will find and index your Web site. This tag should contain several words (up to about 15) but should avoid repetition because certain engines stop indexing a site when they encounter repetition.

The <META NAME="description"...> tag contains the description of your Web site and should include up to 25 words (200 characters maximum). This is the summary that will appear in the search results of some search engines.

For more information about META tags, see:

http://www.webdeveloper.com/categories/html/html_metatags.html
http://searchenginewatch.internet.com/webmasters/meta.html
http://www.w3.org

Use the Proper Tags

When preparing a Web page, it is important to stick to standardized tags (there are many more standard tags in addition to the ones shown here). This means using tags that are officially recognized by the World Wide Web Consortium, or W3C, which is the governing body of the World Wide Web. Using standard tags ensures that your page will be correctly read by various browsers. There is currently strong competition between two browser publishers: Netscape Navigator and Communicator and Microsoft Internet Explorer. Each company has independently developed a set of tags that are proprietary to its browsers. This means that each browser has its own tags which sometimes offer interesting features but cannot be read by the other browser. If half of the Internet population cannot read your page, what's the point of using proprietary tags? Fortunately, there are a lot of standard tags, and there are enough to give you an interesting set of authoring options. Sticking to standard tags will help you avoid making a browser faux pas.

Another "foolproof" method is to stick to basic tags as much as possible. While it might be interesting to have fancy effects on a Web page, think about how many people out of your total number of visitors will be able to see them. Remember that a business cannot afford to alienate part of its clientele for the sake of using a few gimmicks.

Another precaution is not adopting new tags too early, before they are standardized. Whenever a new version of a browser comes out, it takes some time before users adopt it. Even if it is free, often the first version to come out is a beta version, which is risky to use because there are probably still some bugs in the program. This means a higher risk of browser malfunction, which is why a lot of people wait until the final version of a browser is ready and the bugs have been worked out. Some people wait even longer because if the browser they have is working well, they do not feel like going through the downloading and installation process.

A lot of excellent books on HTML authoring are available. If you decide to get into HTML seriously, it is essential that you get additional information, including some good books, that will reveal tricks of the trade. You can visit the following URLs, where all the necessary information about HTML is available for free:

http://www.w3.org   (World Wide Web Consortium)
http://www.dreamscape.com/frankvad/webmaster.html
http://www.iw.com/daily/tips/1998/06/2201-titletags.html

Images

Images and all graphic elements must be prepared carefully in order to appear properly and be effective on a Web page. Preparing an image for the Web requires special consideration because of bandwidth limitations and downloading time. The larger (both actual size and file size) your image, the more time it will take to appear on the user's screen. This does not mean that you cannot include a fairly large picture on your Web page, but it does mean that you have to make sure that the byte size of the image is kept to a minimum.

One way to do that is to reduce the number of colors that appear on the computer screen. Instead of several million or thousand, keep it to a maximum of 256 colors, which is generally sufficient for a good rendition on a computer screen. Remember that you are not printing a magazine page. Images with a lot of colors will be very large and very cumbersome to process, and the effect on the computer screen will not necessarily be superior.

It is also a good idea not to have too many images on the same page. If you must show a lot of images, prepare smaller versions, called thumbnails, that load rapidly, and make them clickable. If the user wants to see one of the images in a larger version, clicking on the thumbnail will call up the larger image on another page. A thumbnail is the same version of an image but in a very small format. This allows several images to be displayed on the same page without overburdening it. Making each thumbnail clickable allows users to bring up the larger image if and when they want to see it.

There are some graphic converters available on the Web that will specifically process an image to render it in an appropriate file size for the Internet. You can also use some basic image-processing software, such as Adobe Photoshop, to change the screen size and the format of a picture.

Images should be prepared in either GIF or JPEG formats. These are the two nonanimation formats for the World Wide Web. Almost any image format can be converted to GIF or JPEG. A GIF file is usually a bit smaller than a JPEG file, but JPEG offers slightly better quality. GIF is limited to a maximum of 256 colors and is appropriate for images with solid colors (i.e., with no shades in the colors). JPEG is better suited for images with shades (i.e., color or black-and-white photographs).

Images are named with the .gif or .jpg extension and must be placed in the same directory as your HTML pages; otherwise, the browser will not find them.

When hyperlinking an image to something, you will receive a prompt to type in an alternative text line. This is for those browsers that do not see images. In this case, the user will see a line of text that might say something like "Image of landscape" or whatever text you have typed in.

There are also thousands of prepared GIF and JPEG images available on the World Wide Web. Many are free, and others are sold. You can find them by doing a search with keywords such as "images," "pictures," "GIF" and "JPEG."

You can find more about images at a number of URLs. For information on image preparation, go to:

http://www.xs4all.nl/~joz/ftm.html

http://www.wizards.dupont.com/cristy/www/formats.html

http://www.matisse.net/files/formats.html

For image preparation software, visit

http://members.aol.com/htmlguru/transparent_images.html

http://www.aldridge.com/faq_gra.html

http://www2.ncsu.edu/bae/people/faculty/walker/hotlist/grahics.html

For image banks, see

http://www.clipart connection.com

http://www.nvtech.com

http://www.iconographics.com

http://www.eyewire.com/eyewire.html

Animated Images

It is possible to animate an image without using plug-ins, applets or video files by using the GIF89a format. The animation is somewhat more limited, but the format has the advantage of being quite small in size and not heavy for the Web page. The file is downloaded relatively fast and can be easily read by all browsers without the need for a plug-in because GIF89a uses the built-in browser resources. These animated images offer a way to easily add an interesting touch to your Web site, without making it heavy or slow.

A GIF89a image is made up of a single GIF file that displays multiple GIF images in sequence and according to the preprogrammed speed. The result is very similar to flip-book animation, except the images appear on the Web page as continuous animation, with the help of the GIF decoder which is already part of the browser. GIF89a files are self-contained and downloaded once, in the same manner as regular GIF and JPEG images. They are then played from the browser's cache.

Including one or more animated GIFs (but not too many) on your Web site represents an interesting alternative to other types of animation which sometimes have a rather high failure rate, due to the fact that they do not always work well with the browser. There are more conditions that they must meet in order to work well, thus increasing the chance of failure. Animated GIFs are almost foolproof in that regard.

You can find on the Web some GIF89a libraries that offer prepared animated GIFs for free. All you have to do is choose from among the selection the ones that are appropriate for your Web site, copy them (with the author's permission and, as required, with appropriate credit on your page) and include them in your Web page.

You can also prepare your own, in which case you need the images that will serve as a base for the animation, a bit like a storyboard. Then, you need a GIF builder program that will let you integrate those images into one file and make it ready for the Web. Of course, this means that you (or someone you designate) must have a minimum of artistic talent to prepare the original images.

You can find GIF preparation software on the Web for both IBM compatibles and Macs. Some useful URLs are

http://www.rogersgif.com/anitools.html (resource center for GIF animation)
http://www.webdiner.com/annexe/gif89/snowstp1.htm
http://member.aol.com/royale/gifanim.htm

Shockwave and Other Macromedia Tools

Shockwave animation is viewed with the Shockwave plug-in. The plug-in is free, but it requires around 8 Mb of RAM to run, in addition to the 10 to 15 Mb the browser needs to run and the RAM the system also needs to operate the computer. This can put quite a burden on the computer memory. It also means that customers may encounter difficulty if you put Shockwave on your pages with no other alternatives. This can be circumvented by offering an option with and without Shockwave. Shockwave is a very interesting feature, and the only thing that has prevented it from being widely used so far is the memory requirement. However, when a computer has enough RAM, Shockwave can bring very lively elements to your page.

Authoring a Shockwave file is somewhat more complex than a GIF89a file. It is done with the Shockwave software, made by Macromedia. Note that the same company has other feature programs that also do interesting things, such as Flash. For more information, go to:

http://www.macromedia.com

Java

Java is another possible option for animation. The visitor's browser downloads an applet from the Web site visited. This means the browser must (1) be capable of reading Java applets and (2) be set to accept them. Remember that Java applets are executable and therefore run the risk of viruses. Some users turn the Java reader off on their browsers in order to protect their computers from potential viruses.

To prepare an applet, Java software must be used, although some prepared applets are freely available on the Web. Again, beware of viruses. After preparing an applet, it needs to be stored on your Web site. Each time someone visits your Web site, the applet will be downloaded to the visitor's computer automatically, provided you have coded your HTML page to do so and provided the user has not urned the Java reader off.

Java is different than JavaScript. Java also allows you to create forms that interact with your database, among other things. Remember that Java is a programming language.

Image preparation is an art and should receive the attention it deserves. If you are new at it, you should take some time to research the subject and familiarize yourself with the use of a scanner and with graphic-processing software.

The Web contains a lot of free information regarding image preparation. A simple search will locate a lot of resources. Some URLs for information on Java are

http://www.symantec.com   Symantec
http://www.netscape.com   Netscape
http://www.javasoft.com
http://www.javaworld.com
http://www.digitalfocus.com/faq
http://www.siliceo.com/java.html

Naming Your Page

An HTML page is a computer file. This means that each Web page has its own name. Your Web site has a greeting page, which is the very first page people see when they arrive at your Web site. This page is commonly referred to as the Web site's "home page" on the World Wide Web.

Each Web page must have the .html extension on the server (or .htm for Windows NT servers) in order for the browser and the HTML editor to recognize it as a Web page. The home page for any Web site must be named "index.html". This tells the browser that it is the initial page of the Web site and the first place to go when the browser comes to the whole content of the Web site on the server. Because each Web site has its own address, each can have its own index.html with no problem.

The other Web pages can be named just about anything, followed by .html. The name can generally contain up to eight characters plus the .html extension. In cases where more than eight characters are used, groups of characters are sometimes separated by an underscore (_), depending on the system that operates the server. But you can never go wrong with eight characters. Note that the *file name* can be different than the *page title*. Page name and page title are two different things. The page name is the file name (i.e., the name the page has on the server), whereas the page title is the title that appears for that page in the browser title bar at the top of the browser window on the computer screen. The title is coded inside the Web page with the <TITLE> </TITLE> tags.

The HTML links you build into your Web page always refer to the file name of the page, which is the eight-character name followed by the .html extension (i.e., somename.html).

CGI

Using CGI (Common Gateway Interface) within your Web page allows you to collect information from visitors and send it wherever you want. It can also offer visitors a series of choices that are connected to a database for retrieval.

CGI requires programming skills and also requires participation from your ISP. By using CGI on your Web page, you place CGI scripts in that page that call up a CGI program on the server to accomplish specific things on that server. For instance, your CGI script can:

- Collect information from customers who fill out forms
- Validate certain fields in a form
- Send information to a database
- Retrieve information from a database
- Retrieve an appropriate answer or confirmation for a customer
- Retrieve specific information from a database according to a customer's specifications (e.g., show a customer products or information based on specific choices)

To find out more information about CGI, see Perl-related Web sites.

Java and JavaScript

Java and JavaScript require programming skills but do not generally require your ISP's intervention. These two options are not equally supported by all browsers, and older versions do not support them at all.

You can either program your applets yourself or use those that are readily available on the Internet for public use. Of course, this means that your Web site will not be the only one using those particular applets. Also, some applets may be viruses in disguise. If you decide to use existing applets, screen them carefully because applets are executable files. This is the main downside of Java, as mentioned earlier, because a lot of networks do not allow their users to download applets, which prevents your visitors from seeing your Web page properly.

JavaScript is not executable, as applets are. However, older versions of browsers will give error messages on some of the scripts. JavaScript is written into the HTML code of the Web page and is interpreted by the browser, so that network users who are not able to see applets will still have access to JavaScripts. JavaScripts tend to produce rather standard things in a page, but they can be useful in giving a page an interactive feeling.

There are several JavaScript tutorials on the World Wide Web:

http://www.desktoppublishing.com/java.html
http://www.webteacher.com/javatour.htm
http://www.jsworld.com

Cascading Style Sheets

Cascading style sheets (CSS) provide standard formatting for HTML pages without having to put individual tags in each page. It is possible to identify which fonts, colors and styles will appear in each page for paragraphs, titles, text and so on for the whole Web site. Thus, you can make a change once and it will be replicated on all the pages. If you have several pages, the advantage that CSS presents becomes obvious.

For more information about CSS, go to:

http://www.w3.org/pub/WWW/Style

Validating Your Web Pages

The last step before launching your Web site is to validate your Web pages. The purpose is to make sure that they will be read properly by most browsers. What good is it if half the Internet population cannot see them properly?

There are three ways to validate Web pages. The first is to test your Web site with several browsers. However, this may give only limited results because there are lots of different browsers and it is difficult to try them all manually or to have access to all of them.

The second method is to use special software or an Internet service, both of which usually cost something but offer good results. Some HTML authoring software has a built-in validating function, but make sure that it covers all types of browsers.

The third way is to use one of the free services available on the Internet, such as the following:

http://validator.w3.org/	World Wide Web Consortium Validator
http://www.webtechs.com/html-val-svc/	Web Tech's Validator
http://www.cs.duke.edu/~dsb/halfaq.html	Validator FAQ

10 Where to Start?

As a businessperson, you have specific results to achieve. You must, most of the time, attain maximum efficiency in the shortest period of time while meeting precise objectives and attaining maximum profitability. That is why getting involved with the Internet must be an integral part of your overall plan.

The Internet has been like a tidal wave, and it will have a critical impact on your business. You can either ride the wave or be swept away by it. Therefore, it is important to plan carefully before jumping in. Identify the potential the Internet has to offer your business, according to your particular situation: large, medium or small business; well established, start-up or in the critical years; local, national or international; retail or service; and the field in which you are operating.

The Internet is an extra business tool to help you meet your existing objectives as well as new objectives that can be added because of the very nature of the medium. It is a communication tool as much as it is a marketing tool. You have to integrate the Internet into your overall marketing plan to make sure its use is compatible with your other strategies, and adjust those strategies if necessary. It is a good idea to review your business objectives and see where the Internet can play a role in meeting them. You may also need to include in your plan of action additional objectives that are specific to the Internet.

Inventory of Computer Equipment and Software

Before implementing or changing anything, do the same as you would when considering any computer-related investment. Make an inventory of your existing computer equipment (use Form 1: Inventory of Computer Equipment) and software (use Form 2: Inventory of Computer Software). Implementing the Internet in your business operations gives you an excellent opportunity to "tidy up" the computers if you have not been doing so on a regular basis. We all have a tendency to clutter up our computers. Prepare backups of all important information and data. Get rid of the obsolete data. This will greatly facilitate things when installing new Internet software. Failure to clean up your machines could result in serious problems.

The information in Forms 1 and 2 will help you determine which machines are suitable to connect to the Internet and the upgrades needed. Personalize the forms according to your specific needs and use additional sheets as necessary. Also, make sure that all software is legal. Illegal copies can bring your business a lot of problems.

Setting Objectives

Make a list, if you do not already have one, of your existing business goals and objectives. It might be a good idea to review your business plan and make any necessary adjustment in light of the new business opportunities and markets offered through the Internet. Take a few moments to reflect on what kind of business development you want to achieve and what your possibilities are. A list of questions is provided below to help you.

The Internet can be used for a variety of purposes. After reviewing all the possibilities presented in the preceding chapters, you should have a pretty good idea of what you want to do with the medium.

Answer the following questions to help determine possible objectives and uses for the Internet:

1. Do you want to increase your business?
2. Do you want to widen the geographical area you serve?
3. Do you want to reach new markets?
4. Do you want to use the Internet for communication purposes?

Form 1
Inventory of Computer Equipment

	Computer 1	Computer 2	Computer 3	Computer 4	Computer 5
Type (Mac, IBM, etc.)	_____	_____	_____	_____	_____
Model (portable, desktop, server, etc.)	_____	_____	_____	_____	_____
Serial number	_____	_____	_____	_____	_____
RAM capacity	_____	_____	_____	_____	_____
Hard disk size	_____	_____	_____	_____	_____
Motherboard	_____	_____	_____	_____	_____
Operating system (indicate version number)	_____	_____	_____	_____	_____
Video card	_____	_____	_____	_____	_____
Audio card	_____	_____	_____	_____	_____
Monitor (VGA, SVGA)	_____	_____	_____	_____	_____
Monitor serial number	_____	_____	_____	_____	_____
Modem speed	_____	_____	_____	_____	_____
Modem type (voice or not)	_____	_____	_____	_____	_____
Modem serial number	_____	_____	_____	_____	_____
Mouse	_____	_____	_____	_____	_____
Speakers	_____	_____	_____	_____	_____
Microphone	_____	_____	_____	_____	_____
Printer type	_____	_____	_____	_____	_____
Resolution	_____	_____	_____	_____	_____
Serial number	_____	_____	_____	_____	_____

Form 1
Inventory of Computer Equipment (continued)

	Computer 1	Computer 2	Computer 3	Computer 4	Computer 5
CD-ROM	_____	_____	_____	_____	_____
Serial number	_____	_____	_____	_____	_____
Backup system	_____	_____	_____	_____	_____
Serial number	_____	_____	_____	_____	_____

Other Equipment

Scanner model _____

   Serial number _____

   Resolution _____

Laser printer model _____

   Serial number _____

   Resolution _____

Ink jet printer _____

   Serial number _____

   Resolution _____

Color printer model _____

   Serial number _____

   Resolution _____

Other _____

   Serial number _____

Other _____

   Serial number _____

Other _____

   Serial number _____

Form 2
Inventory of Computer Software

	Computer 1	Computer 2	Computer 3	Computer 4	Computer 5
Software #1	_____	_____	_____	_____	_____
Name and version	_____	_____	_____	_____	_____
Number of licenses	_____	_____	_____	_____	_____
Software #2	_____	_____	_____	_____	_____
Name and version	_____	_____	_____	_____	_____
Number of licenses	_____	_____	_____	_____	_____
Software #3	_____	_____	_____	_____	_____
Name and version	_____	_____	_____	_____	_____
Number of licenses	_____	_____	_____	_____	_____
Software #4	_____	_____	_____	_____	_____
Name and version	_____	_____	_____	_____	_____
Number of licenses	_____	_____	_____	_____	_____
Software #5	_____	_____	_____	_____	_____
Name and version	_____	_____	_____	_____	_____
Number of licenses	_____	_____	_____	_____	_____
Software #6	_____	_____	_____	_____	_____
Name and version	_____	_____	_____	_____	_____
Number of licenses	_____	_____	_____	_____	_____
Software #7	_____	_____	_____	_____	_____
Name and version	_____	_____	_____	_____	_____
Number of licenses	_____	_____	_____	_____	_____

5. Do you want to use the Internet for advertising purposes?
6. Do you want to use the Internet for customer service?
7. Do you want to use the Internet for interaction with your customers?
8. Do you want to make sales on the Internet?
9. Do you want to publish on the Internet?
10. Do you want to hold virtual meetings on the Internet?
11. How active do you want to be on the Internet?
12. What kind of resources can you dedicate to that activity?

When setting objectives, remember to take into account the resources, both financial and human, that you will need for the initial setup and maintenance. Determining how involved you want to become will determine the time and money you will have to invest.

It is best to start by reviewing your business plan and making a list of your objectives that is as complete as possible. The second step is to assess the cost of attaining your goals. Third, make a progressive plan to implement your goals that takes into account the rest of your business plan. Remember that if you enlist outside help (e.g., from consultants), you need to maintain control of the process. To do so, your goals have to be well defined and your objectives clear. Use Form 3 to prepare your list of objectives. The next section will help you to assess the resources you will need to meet your objectives.

Depending on which Internet services you decide to use and what you want your business to offer on the Internet, there are several options. After defining your objectives by using Form 3, you are ready to assess your needs in order to meet your objectives and to prepare an estimate of the cost. Remember that you do not have to implement all of the services at the same time. After preparing your list of objectives and assessing the costs, it is a good idea to decide at what rate you want the services to start being implemented on the Internet and prepare your plan accordingly.

Assessing Your Needs

First, decide if you want your own domain name and your own server. The pros and cons of having your own domain name and

Form 3
List of Internet Objectives

Make a list of your specific objectives. Write some objectives for the next six months, one year, two years and three years.

1. _____

_____

2. _____

_____

3. _____

_____

4. _____

_____

5. _____

_____

6. _____

_____

7. _____

_____

8. _____

_____

9. _____

_____

10. _____

_____

operating your own server were discussed earlier. If you decide to have your own domain name, do so without delay because there may be a waiting period to have it checked (the name may already be taken), registered and activated, depending on who you deal with to get registered. Some Internet providers now offer a ten-minute service to register a domain name, but be sure to check what the real time elapsed will be from the moment you choose your domain name until the moment it will be functional on the Internet. Depending on where you are located and the provider you work with, the time can vary, but the service is very fast if you do it directly with InterNIC, the official registration service for second-level domain names. (Recall that the top level is the extension at the end of a name, such as .com.) You must provide three choices for a domain name in case your first choice is not available.

As soon as these steps are completed and you receive confirmation of your domain name, you can start using it on the Internet. To do so, it must be installed on the server with its own identification and Internet Protocol address. You can ask any Internet service provider (ISP) to activate your domain name on its server so that you and your customers can start using it right away.

Then, decide what services you want to use and what services you want to offer. There are several possibilities. Let's take a closer look at each of them.

Increasing Your Business Share of the Market

Getting on the Internet does not guarantee that you will automatically increase your business volume. Even setting up a World Wide Web site will not automatically bring you more business if no one visits it. You have to promote your Web site along with the services and products you offer if you want to see an increase in your business.

If your goal is to increase your business through the Internet, you need to set specific and realistic objectives. The Internet is not a recipe for a miracle. Its use for commercial purposes is, in fact, a rather recent phenomenon, only a few years old. A lot has developed in the past few years, and the medium is evolving rapidly. There is much hype and many unrealistic expectations. Trends are only start-

Form 4
Plan for Increasing My Business

% of total business increase targeted _____

Product #1 to promote/sell on the Internet _____

Target for that product _____

% of increase from existing results _____

Internet services to be used for that purpose _____

Product #2 to promote/sell on the Internet _____

Target for that product _____

% of increase from existing results _____

Internet services to be used for that purpose _____

Product #3 to promote/sell on the Internet _____

Target for that product _____

% of increase from existing results _____

Internet services to be used for that purpose _____

Product #4 to promote/sell on the Internet _____

Target for that product _____

% of increase from existing results _____

Internet services to be used for that purpose _____

Service #1 to promote/sell on the Internet _____

Target for that service _____

% of increase from existing results _____

Internet services to be used for that purpose _____

Service #2 to promote/sell on the Internet _____

Target for that service _____

% of increase from existing results _____

Internet services to be used for that purpose _____

Service #3 to promote/sell on the Internet _____

Target for that service _____

% of increase from existing results _____

Internet services to be used for that purpose _____

ing to emerge, and knowledge about markets is still in the early stage. However, you can use whatever information is actually available to build a sound plan and even try a few innovative things.

As in any business area, to be successful you need a sound strategy that takes into account your actual situation in the market and your position in the industry. Then, you need to gather some data, both on the Internet and from your customers. A lot of information about your particular industry is available on the World Wide Web. As for your customers, you are the one who knows them best, or you should be. How long has it been since you were in touch with your customers to ask them what they think about your business and products? Even without the Internet, this should be done on a regular basis.

Are your customers accustomed to using the Internet? How many of your customers are using it at the moment? How comfortable are they with the medium? What do they use it for? What kind of services do they expect from you on the Internet? Are they purchasing things on the Internet? If your customers are not currently using the Internet, do they plan to use it in the near future?

Now, based on the list of objectives you prepared earlier, ask yourself what specific actions you can take that will allow you to meet those objectives. The answer will guide you in the first steps to marketing your business successfully on the Internet.

Penetrating New Markets

With the Internet, you will be in touch with part of your actual market because some of your customers, but most likely not all of them, are probably already using the Internet.

In addition to your existing clientele, the Internet also brings you a whole new market that can be anywhere in the world. You need to consider this seriously, even if your business does not offer products or services to all geographical regions. Suddenly having the whole world as a market may seem scary, but, fortunately, it is very improbable that you will receive a deluge of demands all of a sudden. The increase will most likely evolve gradually over time, unless a special event precipitates things, which is rather uncommon. Furthermore, remember that about 85% of Internet users are located in the United States.

You will probably see demand gradually increase over a period of time if you promote your Internet presence properly and consistently. However, you need to plan ahead for how you are going to meet the demand from new customers in general and the queries from places afar in particular. If you are set on serving only a specific geographical area, indicate so in a delicate and thoughtful manner on your Web site. Also, promote your Web site mainly by geographical reference in the search engine directories. Avoid alienating people who visit your site; keep the door open. You may discover new possibilities you had not thought of from the various requests you receive through the Internet. Of course, to receive those requests, you have to provide visitors with a means to easily reach you, such as a clickable e-mail address. The various methods of being in touch with your customer were explained in Chapter 8.

The Internet offers you a whole new range of possibilities for reaching markets you had not thought you could reach. Analyze carefully the feasibility of addressing those new markets and make a plan for what you would like your business to do in view of those new possibilities. Think about the steps you will take to do it and at what pace you will meet foreign demand. Remember to take into account the additional costs of serving foreign markets and to establish a time frame.

Of course, if you are already serving foreign markets, the Internet will make your business life a lot easier. Form 5 is a questionnaire to help you assess what you need in order to deal with foreign markets.

Using the Internet for Communication Purposes

Communication can be achieved in various ways:

- Sending and receiving e-mail messages
- On-line discussions (Internet Relay Chat)
- On-line conversations (Internet phone)
- On-line meetings (videoconferencing)

Form 5
New Market Penetration Plan

Which markets are you serving now? _____

What geographical areas are you covering? _____

Are you open to serving people in areas outside your existing territory? _____

Which markets do you want to add to your existing operations? _____

Define your time frame for serving those new markets. Have you established precise objectives to serve those markets? _____

Do you have everything you need to serve those markets (production capacity, delivery services, order-processing capacity, administrative personnel, shipping and handling personnel and facilities, storage facilities, service reps, agents, etc.)? _____

What do you need to add or acquire to serve those markets? _____

What is the cost of those additions? _____

What will you tell people in markets you are not ready to serve yet? (Remember to keep the door open for future business.) _____

How are you going to use the Internet to serve those markets (Web presence, service reps, agents, contact points, shipping, encryption, etc.)? _____

What other services will you need to serve those markets (shipping agreements, payment arrangements, customs brokers, etc.)? _____

What total extra expenses will be incurred to serve those markets? _____

- Electronic publishing
- Audio webcasting
- Video webcasting

At this point, you need to determine what means of communication your business is actually using, the time involved and the money spent. Make an objective assessment of what your business is actually doing with its communications, and then look at what the Internet can do to improve the speed and productivity and lower the costs. Look at the additional services you can offer customers with Internet technology. Also examine what the telecommunications costs associated with using the Internet will be (e.g., a high-speed link).

Telecommunication Needs Assessment

Depending on what you want to accomplish and how you want to do it, your needs will vary. The necessary facilities, equipment and services for each of the above options are described in the following sections.

Sending and Receiving Messages

Sending and receiving messages is the most basic service. You do not need your own server to do so. All you need is a basic telephone service line. Of course, you need to open an account with an ISP, choose your e-mail address, acquire e-mail software and connect your computer to your provider's server with a modem. The same has to be done for each person with whom you want to communicate, including any employees. It is possible to open one account with a provider and obtain several mailboxes for different users. Some providers offer interesting packages to small businesses. Just watch the total on-line time allowed before the provider starts to bill you by the minute. That kind of billing can be costly.

Sending and receiving messages consume very little time on the Internet. The only time you actually spend on-line is when you upload and download your messages. For instance, you can prepare the messages you want to send while you are off-line. When all your messages have been completed, you log on and send them as a batch. Then you download the messages you have received and log off. You can read the messages you received off-line and prepare your replies off-line as well. Done in that manner, e-mail requires very little time on-line.

Messages can now be sent to and received from wireless devices such as cellular and PCS phones as well as pagers. Of course, you have to plan and budget for those devices, as these types of operations generally require special equipment and services.

In assessing the costs of using the Internet for part of your communication needs, determine the following:

1. How many employees are there in your business?
2. How many of them need to communicate with one another?
3. What is the average frequency of their communication needs (hourly, daily, weekly, monthly)?
4. What communication tools and means are actually used in your business?

    ___ In person   ___ Internal mail for documents
    ___ Telephone   ___ Fax
    ___ Internal memos   ___ Internal e-mail
    ___ Meetings   ___ Cellular phone
    ___ Bulletins/newsletters   ___ Pager
    ___ Other   ___ Mobile phone

5. What is the monthly cost of each method? In time? In money?
6. Do your employees have to make long-distance phone calls?
7. How often?
8. What is your monthly charge for long-distance phone calls?
9. What is the geographical territory covered by your business?
10. Are your employees all in the same location to serve that territory or are they in various locations?
11. Do some of them travel?
12. What portion of your actual telecommunications can be done on the Internet?
13. What are the estimated monthly savings?
14. How many employees have access to a computer?
15. How many are computer literate?

16. Are the computers up to date?
17. Are they well managed?
18. Do they need to be upgraded?
19. Are they organized in a network?
20. Is your network equipped with a server?
21. How are you going to connect the network to the Internet as far as telecommunications and software are concerned?
22. How are you going to protect your network from the outside? What kind of security measures will you put in place?
23. What kind of measures do you have in place for inside protection?
24. If your computers are not part of a network, is each computer equipped with a modem? How many modems will you need to purchase?
25. Do you have enough phone line capacity for each person who will be using the Internet?
26. How many Internet accounts will you need?
27. What software will you implement in your business?
28. How many hours will each employee devote to Internet surfing or other Internet functions?
29. Are some of your employees already familiar with using the Internet?
30. Do you know exactly what you want your employees to do on the Internet?
31. How easy will it be to train employees to use the Internet efficiently?
32. Who will train them?
33. How efficiently will you be able to make sure that your employees use the Internet for business purposes only?
34. How will you prevent employees from using the Internet for illegitimate purposes (illegal acts, fraud, etc.)?
35. Are you going to use the Internet to communicate with your customers?
36. Who will be responsible for communications with customers?
37. What code of ethics and customer service policies will you implement for your business's Internet communications?

On-Line Discussions (Chat)

For on-line real-time discussions, you need client chat software. A couple of companies offer free client chat software.

An on-line discussion demands that all the communicating parties be logged onto the Internet at the same time because the written conversation takes place in real time. If your corresponding party is not available, you can log on and wait or you can try to find him or her. All you need to know is your correspondent's nickname or "nick." There is software that allows you to check if the person is on-line so as to reach your correspondent easily. You need to evaluate the software available on the market and decide which one meets your specific needs.

The main limitation is each party's typing speed, as the communication takes place in real time. There may also be lag time during some peak periods. The software allows you to participate in public discussions as well as to hold private discussions that other participants will not see. This flexibility allows you and your employees or customers to discuss matters privately. However, if what you discuss is really sensitive, you should upgrade your security level for those discussions. It is possible to do so through an intranet/extranet structure. Again, it depends on what you want to achieve. The security level will be different for a chat between one of your technical representatives and a customer compared to a chat between company executives.

Does your business need to operate an on-line chat? What could you achieve with a chat in terms of meeting your business goals? At what frequency will the chat be active? This means that someone from your business has to start the chat by opening a chat channel and then monitor and animate it until you decide to shut it off after a predetermined period of time. Note that you can spend anywhere from a few hours per day or week all the way up to full time on the chat function.

Remember that you can purchase chat server software or subscribe to a service that allows you to own your chat name and keep it even when your chat is not on.

Chat Budget Planning

One-time purchase

_____ chat software/subscription at $ _____ each = $ _____

Monthly expenses

_____ hours per month at $ _____ per hour = $ _____ per month (chat channel operator)

On-Line Conversations (Internet Telephone)

The same principle that applies to chat also applies to Internet telephone: two people who want to talk together must be present on the Internet at the same time. To hold an Internet telephone conversation, you need to acquire Internet telephone software.

The quality of the sound will probably not be as good as on a regular telephone. The speed of the modem and phone line will influence the quality level of the sound. Expect the sound to be of a lesser quality than on a regular telephone. Even though the sound is poorer quality, it is generally acceptable for a real-time conversation on the Internet.

Answer the following questions to determine how much you are going to use Internet telephone:

1. How reliable do you need your phone connection to be?
2. How clear do you need the sound of your phone conversation to be?
3. How often are you or your personnel going to use it?
4. Who is going to use it and when?

There is no monthly charge for this service, as it is used in conjunction with your regular Internet service and telephone line, but you may have to upgrade modem speed and telecommunication link.

Internet Telephone Budget Planning

One-time purchase

_____ Internet telephone software at $ _____ each = $ _____ total

On-Line Meetings (Videoconferencing)

Video on the Internet offers tremendous possibilities. Video is available for both downloading video files and viewing video images in real time. Video files should be kept to a minimum size and compressed to reduce downloading time. That is where video streaming comes into play. To use video streaming, you need to install the appropriate software on the server.

On the other hand, real-time video, called videoconferencing, allows you to chat live, in real time, with a person while seeing a live image of that person. The parties can see each other provided each has a video camera and video capability built into his or her computer, along with sufficient modem speed (33.6 Kbps).

Real-time video capability is not yet built into Web browsers. This means that in order to hold a virtual meeting, you need to acquire video software for each person, along with a camera and any necessary video card for each computer. You may also need to upgrade modems to get the necessary speed and transmission capability.

Evaluate how much you are currently spending on meeting and travel expenses. The following questions will help you:

1. Do you have employees in remote locations?
2. Do your employees at remote locations need to meet?
3. Do your personnel need to hold meeting with other companies in remote locations?
4. Would it be advantageous for you to be able to "meet" your customers on a regular basis through videoconferencing?
5. How many meetings must be held each month?
6. How much do those meetings cost?
7. What benefit will you gain by holding virtual meetings?
8. How much money do you estimate could be saved each month?
9. Are there other uses for videoconferencing in your business?
10. Do you see any added benefits of video on the Internet (e.g., distance learning and training)?

If you plan to use the Internet for training, your training program will need to be adapted.

1. What degree of adaptation will be required?
2. What are the costs related to these changes?

3. Who will perform the adaptation?
4. Will it be worth it?
5. What will you gain business wise?
6. What will you save?

There is no monthly charge for this service, but you may have to upgrade modem speed and telecommunication link.

Videoconferencing Budget Planning

One-time purchase

_____ video software at $ _____ each = $ _____

_____ cameras at $ _____ each = $ _____

_____ video cards at $ _____ each = $ _____

Electronic Publishing

Electronic publishing can be done in various manners, and there is all kinds of software to do it. The software produces various results, as described in Chapter 6. Electronic publishing can take a variety of forms; let's examine the options.

Newsletter

To use e-mail to reach your customers with, for example, an e-mail bulletin or newsletter, you can use exactly the same equipment, services and software as for regular e-mail service. Most e-mail software allows you to have an automatic distribution list, up to a certain number of subscribers. Over that, you will need to implement a more automated system, such as one that can process automatic registration and delivery.

What you need to budget for is the time of the person/people who will be responsible for preparing and sending the newsletter. Estimate the time involved each month for the following tasks:

- Planning content and publishing schedule
- Writing the newsletter

- Sending it out
- Receiving requests for subscription
- Registering subscribers and building the distribution list
- Correspondence with subscribers

You can use the LISTSERV service or a similar service when your distribution list increases to a size that is difficult to manage in the manner described above. LISTSERV can automate certain functions, such as subscriber registration. Ask your ISP what the cost of that service is, as you will need your provider's help to implement the LISTSERV service and there are usually charges. Note that some servers provide LISTSERV for free. There is also software on the market that allows you to achieve the same result.

To help prepare your newsletter, answer the following questions:

1. What is the purpose of publishing the newsletter?
2. What information and content do you want to transmit through the newsletter?
3. How long will each newsletter be?
4. How often will it be published?
5. To whom will it be sent? (Who is your target?)
6. Who will be responsible for the content?
7. Who will be responsible for the preparation?
8. Who will be responsible for the transmission?
9. Who will be responsible for answering subscribers' queries?

Newsletter Budget Planning

Monthly expenses

_____ hours per month at $_____ per hour = $_____ per month

Provider's charges: $_____ per month

Other charges: $_____ per month

Push Technology

If you decide to use the push technology, you need to acquire some software and hire someone who knows how to use it. You also need a plan to organize what you will send to customers, how often and so on. This information needs to be retrieved from a database, which requires that you link one you have and is compatible or set one up.

Push Budget Planning

Who will plan the push operations?

Who will prepare the material?

How often will you broadcast?

What software will you use?

Price of the software: $_____

How many channels will you need? $_____ per channel

Electronic Magazine

There are two options for publishing an electronic magazine: one is through HTML pages and the other is through PDF files.

HTML Pages

Option 1 is to use HTML pages to present an electronic version of a magazine. This means that Web pages are designed in a format similar to the pages of the magazine. This also means that all of the Web pages relating to the magazine itself have to be changed completely according to a regular schedule, just like the frequency with which a magazine is published.

This also means archiving previous issues to make available to your readership. Publishing an electronic magazine is as big a task as publishing a paper magazine. However, you save the printing and shipping costs and time.

Your magazine can be made available to all Internet users or on a subscription basis, either for a fee or for free. You can give access to everyone or have subscribers enter a password to access the magazine. The choice is yours. There are several magazines published on the Internet, and you can do a little research before setting up the kind of service you want to offer.

An interesting aspect of an electronic magazine is that you are not quite subject to the same technical considerations as for a printed magazine. For example, the total number of pages does not have to be divisible by eight, as is the case for print.

Electronic Magazine Budget Planning

1. Will your Web site include a section for an electronic magazine?

2. What will the size of the magazine be (how many pages)?

3. How often will it be published?

4. What pictures and graphic elements will be included?

5. How many graphic elements will there be per issue?

6. Who will prepare the logo, illustrations, graphic design and layout of the magazine?

7. Who will prepare the content and write the articles?

8. Who will author the HTML pages?

9. Who will scan the photos and pictures?

10. Who will load the pages on the server?

11. Cost of graphic elements: _____ pictures at $ _____ each = $ _____ per issue

12. Will previous issues be archived?

13. Will they be available on the Web site?

14. Who will organize and maintain the archive system?

15. What software will be used for:
    - Images
    - Drawing and illustrations
    - Layout
    - Content

PDF Files

Option 2 is to use PDF files (discussed in more detail in Chapter 6). PDF, which stands for Portable Document Format, allows you to show a page exactly as it is printed on paper, in a more controlled and precise manner. To prepare PDF pages, you need the Acrobat software that converts your pages to PDF files. The Acrobat software includes several modules, among which are the authoring program and the reader program.

Customers can obtain for free the client software to read the files, called Acrobat Reader, but the software that creates PDF files must be purchased. You will also need someone who knows how to use the software.

To help determine your needs and budget for publishing PDF documents, answer the following questions.

PDF Budget Planning

1. What will you use PDF for on your Web site?
   - Paperless proposals?
   - Operation manuals?
   - Newspapers?
   - Magazines?
   - White papers?

2. Will those files be linked to your regular Web site or electronic magazine?

3. Who will design the initial pages (in their original format)?

4. What is needed to design those pages (content, software, existing documents)?

5. Do existing documents need to be digitized? Who will scan the pages?

6. Who will convert the pages to PDF files?

7. Where will the PDF files be stored?

8. Price of Acrobat authoring software: $_____

9. Will you distribute the Acrobat Reader? What kind of setup will you use?

10. What is the estimated time to:
    - Design the pages: _____ hours per month at $_____ per hour = $_____ per month
    - Create the PDF files: _____ hours per month at $_____ per hour = $_____ per month

11. Who will manage the PDF files? _____ hours per month at $_____ per hour = $_____ per month

Audio Webcasting

Audio webcasting is already used by radio stations to broadcast programs on the Internet. You can use it to broadcast lectures and speeches from special events for the benefit of your employees. You can also offer your customers live audio information. You can organize special events around this medium. For instance, you can broadcast live conferences and symposia.

The customer needs to acquire the audio client software that is a plug-in for World Wide Web browsers. There is usually no charge for the receiver software. However, if you want to broadcast through your Web site, you need to install software that allows you to broadcast on your server or your ISP's server. This means that if you do not have your own server and are dealing with an ISP, you need to arrange that capability with your provider, which is likely to cost something, either a one-time fee, a monthly fee or both. Ask your provider what costs to expect.

Remember that you will actually be producing something similar to a radio show, and you need professional-quality material and content.

Form 6 will help you prepare a summary of your communication needs and expenses.

Audio Broadcasting Budget Planning

One-time fee

Broadcasting software: $ _____

Provider's installation fee: $ _____

Other costs: $ _____

Monthly expenses

Provider's charge: $ _____

Other: $ _____

_____ hours per month at $_____ per hour = $ _____ per month (production costs, hosts, guests, etc.)

Form 6
Summary of Communication Needs and Expenses

One-Time Purchase

_____ Computer(s)	at $_____	each =	$_____
_____ Modems	at $_____	each =	$_____
_____ Video cards	at $_____	each =	$_____
_____ Audio cards	at $_____	each =	$_____
_____ Connection software	at $_____	each =	$_____
_____ E-mail software	at $_____	each =	$_____
_____ Activation fees	at $_____	each =	$_____
_____ Web browser	at $_____	each =	$_____
_____ Phone software	at $_____	each =	$_____
_____ Video software	at $_____	each =	$_____
_____ Virus software	at $_____	each =	$_____
_____ Communication devices	at $_____	each =	$_____
_____ Employee monitoring	at $_____	each =	$_____
_____ Other software	at $_____	each =	$_____
Other equipment	at $_____	each =	$_____
_____ Other	at $_____	each =	$_____
_____ Other	at $_____	each =	$_____

Monthly Expenses

Equipment

_____ Phone lines	at $_____	per month =	$_____ per month
_____ Internet accounts	at $_____	per month =	$_____ per month

Human Resources

_____ Web administrator	at $_____	per month =	$_____ per month
_____ Programmer	at $_____	per month =	$_____ per month
_____ Customer service rep	at $_____	per month =	$_____ per month
_____ Technician	at $_____	per month =	$_____ per month
_____ Resource person	at $_____	per month =	$_____ per month
_____ Resource person	at $_____	per month =	$_____ per month
_____ Equipment rental	at $_____	per month =	$_____ per month
_____ Other	at $_____	per month =	$_____ per month
_____ Other	at $_____	per month =	$_____ per month
_____ Other	at $_____	per month =	$_____ per month

TOTAL Monthly Expenses $_____ **per month**

Advertising and Promoting
Your Business and Web Site

A variety of means can be used for advertising:

- Publishing
- Push technology
- Customer service and follow-up
- Product and service updates
- Seeking feedback from customers
- Banners
- Regular advertising

Having your own Web site and using it to advertise your business and products does not necessarily cost a fortune. It depends on how fancy you want to be and who prepares the site. Remember that the most important thing is to remain efficient and to easily and rapidly provide customers with the information they want.

Never lose sight of the fact that you have specific information to transmit, and you can transmit it in a variety of ways. For instance, with regular marketing, you can send out business cards, flyers and brochures. You can also purchase advertisements in local and national newspapers, in magazines and on radio and television. Each of these solutions has its own price range. The same is true for an Internet Web site. The price depends on the degree of refinement you want to include and the scope of advertising you use.

Some of the above options have already been covered (i.e., publishing). Each has its own price tag. An additional cost is personnel. The person or people responsible for your Web site will have to know your company well and be aware of your objectives and strategies in order to do a good job. Depending on the size of your company and your Web site, you may have to assign one person or a team to the tasks involved, which are to determine the content of your Web site according to your objectives and strategies, prepare and write the content, plan the look and the design of the pages, prepare the pages, maintain the Web site in good working order and update the information on a regular basis.

Let's discuss the various options available through a Web site.

Advertising Budget Planning

1. Who will prepare the marketing strategy?

2. What kind of additional advertising do you want to use?
   - Banner
   - Regular media
   - Customer service section
   - Feedback techniques
   - Updates
   - Other: _____

3. What kind of advertising is indicated for your company?

4. What is your cost for each of those services?

5. Who will manage the ad planning and preparation?
   _____ hours per month at $_____ per hour = $ _____ per month

6. Who will prepare the Web ads?

7. Who will prepare the regular ads?

8. Who will prepare the content?

9. Who will create the design?

10. Who will do the planning?

11. Who will do the updates?

12. Who will load the pages on the server?

Customer Service

As discussed in Chapter 8, a Web site is a very useful tool to offer enhanced customer service and to cut costs associated with that service. Your type of business may or may not be appropriate for offering customer service on a Web site. If it is, the possibilities are definitely interesting.

The requirement for the customer service function is that you must have clear customer service policies that are adapted to the Internet to the extent of the business you do on the Internet. Depending on the size of your company, the same person or the same team should take care of interaction with customers in order to maintain your desired level of customer service in a consistent manner.

Determine how many people are going to be assigned customer service responsibilities. Also decide what tools you will implement for customer service on your Web site.

Customer Service Budget Planning

1. Who will set the customer service policies in regard to the Web site?

2. Who will plan and prepare the content of the customer service section?

3. What kind of tools will you implement for customer service?
   - Call center
   - On-line representative
   - 800 telephone line
   - Other

4. Who will answer customer queries?

5. Who will follow up on the queries (customer service quality check)?

6. Who will make updates on the server in the customer service section?

7. Will you invite customer feedback?

8. Who will receive and process customer feedback? How will it be used?

9. Will you offer incentives in order to obtain feedback?

10. What is the estimated monthly cost for preparing and managing incentives? Estimate the time for each of the above functions each month:

    1. ____ hours per month at $____ per hour = $____ per month

    2. ____ hours per month at $____ per hour = $____ per month

    3. ____ hours per month at $____ per hour = $____ per month

    4. ____ hours per month at $____ per hour = $____ per month

    5. ____ hours per month at $____ per hour = $____ per month

    6. ____ hours per month at $____ per hour = $____ per month

    7. Monthly cost of incentives = $____ per month

    8. ____ software at $____ = $____

    9. ____ telecommunication costs at $____ per month = $____ per month

    10. ____ other costs at $____ per month = $____ per month

Updates

Plan the frequency and the scope of your updates. Determine who will oversee and prepare them. Designate a coordinator if updates involve several departments.

Web Site Budget Planning for Updates

1. How often will you need/want to update your Web site?

2. What means will you use to publicize your updates?
   - Changes indicated on Web pages
   - Special icons
   - E-mail personal messages
   - E-mail newsletter
   - Push technology
   - Other

3. Who will supervise/coordinate the updates?

4. Who will plan and prepare the updates?

5. What material will you need in order to prepare updates?

6. How much will it cost?

7. How much time will be required for the updates on a monthly basis?
   _____ hours per month at $_____ per hour = $_____ per month

Feedback

You can put up a Web site without ever having direct contact with your visitors. However, it is highly recommended, as a simple courtesy and to take advantage of a golden opportunity, that you have at least an e-mail address so that visitors or customers can get in touch with you. This is useful when they have questions or comments. There is no cost to implement this.

You can also have a higher degree of interactivity on your Web site. You can ask customers to fill out forms that are automatically sent to you when they are finished. This requires the use of other programming languages, either Common Gateway Interface (CGI), Java or something similar. This means that you need to install a few lines of code in your HTML page that call up a script on the server (either your own or your provider's). This script accomplishes specific tasks that meet your objectives. Talk to your provider about the exact cost because some providers will charge you for using the CGI script libraries or other types of scripts on their servers.

In addition to that cost, you might need some programming software and someone who knows about CGI, Perl or Java programming. Another thing to consider is where you will send the information collected. You could use simple CGI forms that send the content of the forms to your e-mail box. This means that for each form that is filled out, you receive an e-mail message that you need to interpret because CGI scripts are not complete messages. But that is a rather primitive solution, especially if you have a high volume of traffic (i.e., a lot of people who send forms to you). You will probably want to try a more refined solution. You will also need to find a way to manage, analyze and store the information received, most likely through a database.

Obtaining information from customers can be very useful if you are serious about developing your business on the Internet. That is why you need to plan carefully the kind of information you want to receive, the way you are going to obtain it and how you are going to process it. The positive aspect is that the information is obtained at a relatively low cost compared to traditional methods of data collection.

To help you determine your interactive form and script needs, define the information you want to obtain from your customers. Identify the questions you need to ask them in order to obtain that information.

Prepare a list of the forms you want on your Web site:

- Feedback forms
- Order forms
- Shopping forms
- Other forms

Answer the following questions:

1. Which software will you use to prepare those forms?
2. Who will do the programming (you or a specialist you hire)?

3. Where will you send the information collected?
4. Will you need a database?
5. Which database will you use?
6. Where will the database be stored?
7. How will it be linked with your forms?
8. What are the storing costs?
9. Who will program the database?
10. Who will manage and analyze the data?

Use the answers to the above questions to obtain a quote from your ISP or a reliable specialist, along with his or her recommendations.

Taking Orders Through Your Web Site

With the help of scripts, you can build an automatic ordering system for your customers. You can have on your Web page an order form for customers to indicate their choices and all the specifications for their orders, along with method of payment.

An important decision you will have to make is the method of payment that you will implement. One of the issues on the Internet nowadays is the security of the information transmitted and how comfortable customers are giving confidential information on the Web. Customers are willing to send their orders through the Internet, but they are still very reluctant to give a credit-card number or any other personal information. That problem can be circumvented in several manners: by using security-enhanced software, by establishing a phone line (800 number) that allows customers to call to give confidential and credit-card information, by offering to call customers back with order confirmation and to get their payment information, by implementing alternate payment methods such as CyberCash, by accepting money orders and checks by mail, by offering COD delivery, etc. Your ISP may offer a security payment service to handle financial transaction security for you. You will have to try a couple of methods and see which is the most appropriate for your business.

With all the security involved, electronic commerce can be costly, especially if you do not have a minimum number of transactions. Obtain a quote from a specialist as well as from your ISP to get an idea of the investment involved.

Budget Planning for Payment System

1. What are your banking fees for credit-card certification (initial registration)?

2. What are your banking fees for payment by credit card?

3. What are the ISP's fees for credit-card processing and security?

4. What are the fees for other Internet payment systems?

5. What software will you need for payments?

Determining Your Budget

The budget is an important part of your plan, as always. Just as you have an advertising budget, you should have a budget for the Internet as well because there are specific costs associated with its implementation and use.

The costs can be minimal or astronomic, depending on the way you plan to organize and use the Internet. How much you are going to use it is not necessarily a factor, depending on the types of services you plan to use. For instance, if you use the Internet for e-mail only, even if you and your employees use it extensively, the costs will be minimal. However, if you decide to set up your own server, the costs will increase rapidly. Of course, if you have several hundred thousand dollars at your disposal, that will not be a problem. Implementing your own server starts in the $15,000 to $20,000 range, not including labor. The good news is that you have a variety of options with different price tags that increase progressively as you add new requirements and specifications.

Even if you did not include the Internet in your operating budget, make a small allowance for it the moment you plan to start using it. From then on, add to the budget for the coming years, taking into account the kind of expansion you plan for the Internet. You can start simply with a few basic accounts that allow some of your personnel to send and receive e-mail and surf the Web. Then, you can set up your own Web site later. If your objective is to increase your business, you need to develop a sound and well-planned strategy and implementation plan as soon as possible. At the pace the Internet is evolving, it is to your benefit to ride the wave rather than be swallowed by it. If you surf the Web, you will soon realize that it is in your best interest to get involved as soon as possible if you want to reap the rewards.

Once you have determined your budget, price each service you want to utilize for your business. Then, make allowances for each one.

To help you, a list of possible costs and expenses for a number of options is included in the next section. Customize the forms according to the kind of setup you want. Don't be intimidated by the lists because I have tried to make them as complete as possible.

Studying Your Options

A number of options are compared in the following sections.

Option 1: Starting with Basic Internet Accounts

This option allows you to try the Internet. With this kind of service, you can log onto the Internet, send and receive e-mail and surf the World Wide Web as a visitor. You also have access to FTP (you will need FTP software), newsgroups, chat, video (software needed, camera optional), search engines and Internet phone (software needed). You can fill out forms, shop on-line and even set up a personal Web site if your ISP offers space on its server as part of the basic package.

Option 1 Budget Sheet

One-Time Expense		If You Set Up a	
Computer and cards purchase	_____	**Personal Web Site**	
Modem purchase	_____	FTP software	_____
Camera purchase	_____	HTML editor	_____
Telecommunication fees	_____	Good HTML book	_____
(phone line installation)	_____	(useful but not	
Software upgrades	_____	mandatory)	
Internet connection software	_____	Total one-time charges	_____
Web software	_____		

E-mail software   _____
(optional)
Chat software   _____
Phone software   _____
(optional)
Video software   _____
(optional)
ISP activation fees   _____
(if applicable)
Other   _____
Monthly Expense
Internet accounts   _____
Telephone line   _____
Other   _____
Other   _____
Other   _____
Total monthly charges _____

Option 2: Your Corporate Web Site with an Internet Provider

If you choose to install your Web site on a provider's server rather than use your own server, you greatly simplify your operations. The provider will give you full access to your Web site, not only as a visitor but also as an administrator, allowing you to make changes any time you want. This means that you prepare your Web pages and, when tested and ready, install them directly on the provider's server using FTP (discussed in Chapter 3).

If you choose to go with an ISP, a variety of costs can be involved. Some providers charge a setup fee, and others do not. Most allow you a certain number of megabytes of space on their server. Some add a traffic fee, and others do not. The traffic fee is usually what makes a Web site expensive if you have a lot of visitors. The more visitors, the higher the price you will pay. You will have to estimate the number of visitors you anticipate (be realistic) and evaluate how much it will cost you. Also, you will want to have proof of traffic and reports on visitor activity from the provider; the provider may charge you for those reports.

You will want to know what kind of activity is happening on your Web site. Indeed, you need to know if your Web site is visited at all and if the promotion efforts you have made to publicize your Web site are profitable. Another useful indicator is to know what people are doing once they log onto your home page. Are they going farther into your Web site (i.e., to other pages), or are they turning back and going elsewhere? How much time are they spending on each page? Which one is the most popular? Make sure the provider can give you that kind of information. Otherwise, think about purchasing software that can perform a site analysis.

Ask how much the provider will charge to host your Web site (most providers charge for commercial or corporate Web sites), if there is a setup fee, if there is a traffic fee (for the number of megabytes downloaded) and if there are any other fees. Ask if you can get reports and if the cost of reports is included in the prices quoted to you. Some providers will offer to take care of registering your domain name, also for a fee, but that fee does not necessarily include the fee for registering with the InterNIC. Ask for a complete picture. Because competition is so fierce, there may be hidden costs or there may be some fees that providers "forget" to include in their quotes.

Having an ISP host your Web site may represent an interesting and economical option if:

1. The ISP's rates are competitive
2. Your company is not too big
3. You want a relatively simple Web site operation

For instance, if you are going to need a database, you need to check carefully the kind of setup your ISP can provide, as well as the level of security and prices, and compare it with the costs you would incur operating your own server, as described in the next section.

Are you going to implement audio or video? How will you do it and what is the cost of the webcasting software to do it? Will your ISP charge you extra for those services (e.g., to host that software)?

The benefit of using an ISP's setup, as long as the operation is sound and well organized and managed, is that you can take advantage of a full operation while paying for only part of the costs because you are sharing it with the provider and other users. Below a certain level of Internet activity, this option can be worth it.

Option 2 Budget Sheet

One-Time Expense		Monthly Expense	
ISP's installation fees	$ _____	Internet accounts	$ _____
Camera purchase	$ _____	High-speed telecom.	$ _____
Scanner purchase	$ _____	Provider's additional	$ _____
Additional telecommunica-tion fees	$ _____	charges	
		Traffic fee	$ _____
Phone software	$ _____	CGI/Java/etc.	$ _____
Video software	$ _____	E-commerce electronic	$ _____
Webcasting/streaming software	$ _____	transaction fees	
		Database fees	$ _____
Publishing software	$ _____	Security fees	$ _____
Audio webcasting software	$ _____	LISTSERV fees	$ _____
Push software	$ _____	Audio broadcasting fees	$ _____
Training	$ _____	Video broadcasting fees	$ _____
E-commerce activation fees	$ _____	Push fees	$ _____
		Programming fees	$ _____
Forms preparation	$ _____	Report production fees	$ _____
Other	$ _____	Maintenance fees	$ _____
Option 1 one-time fees	$ _____	Domain yearly fee	$ _____
		Technical fees	$ _____
		Professional fees	$ _____
		Other	$ _____
Total one-time costs	$ _____	**Total monthly payment**	$ _____

Note that you will not necessarily need to pay for all of the above, depending on your implementation plan and the setup you choose.

Option 3: Setting Up Your Own Server

Setting up your own server may be more costly than using an ISP if your Web site is modest and your traffic relatively low. Even if you have a lot of traffic, being able to take advantage of your ISP's installation for 24-hour monitoring, maintenance, security and high-speed links may still be a good deal.

If you do have a lot of traffic, watch carefully the prices your ISP charges for traffic. Every time an Internet user visits your Web site, the Web page is downloaded to the user's computer. This produces traffic on the server and on the cables that link the various pieces of equipment. A lot of visitors means a lot of traffic. This is what ISPs usually base their fees on. They know how many pages from your site have been downloaded and charge you accordingly based on a monthly fee. Some offer very good deals and others are more expensive.

Also, if you need to use a database, you can choose to set up a server for that function while being linked to an ISP's server by a reasonably fast link (for instance, ISDN) and use the provider's installations for everything else.

Your Own Installations Directly Connected to the Internet

Having your own server and installations directly connected to the Internet means that you have to purchase your own equipment and hire qualified personnel to operate and maintain it. You will need a powerful and reliable telecommunication link between your server and the Internet network. You will also need to establish an account with a network service provides (NSP) in order to have access to the Internet network. This account is different from and more expensive than the account you would have with your regular ISP. In this case, you are not dealing with a "retail" Internet provider but rather with a "wholesale" Internet provider, the NSP. The types of services NSPs offer are for high-capacity traffic and are therefore more expensive than regular ISP subscriptions, although they might represent a lesser proportional expense that can be worth it if you have sufficient volume. The end result is the same: you are linked to the rest of the network. Having your own server eliminates one intermediary between you and the network but puts on your shoulders a whole range of responsibilities regarding your Web operation.

Another cost to factor in is labor. If you have Internet and Web installations on your premises, you will need constant (24 hours a day, 7 days a week) monitoring and regular intervention to ensure they are in good working order. This means you need specialists to monitor the system and to do any necessary intervention, including occasional repairs. Problems do happen once in a while. Your equipment has to be in good working order at all times and your Web site must be available. Downtime must be kept to a minimum; between 1 and 5% downtime per month is considered acceptable.

Last, but not least, is the cost for protection. You have to protect the information that your server contains as well as any interactivity and electronic transactions that take place between your customers and your business. All kinds of things can happen. A virus can shut your system down and destroy the entire content of your server. Hackers can attempt to invade your system. This means that, on top of potential technical problems, you need to monitor for unauthorized intrusions by hackers and crackers and be able to intervene and take appropriate measures to foil the attempts and maintain your security. You need to install proper security to protect electronic commerce on your Web site. Imagine what would happen if customers gave you their credit-card numbers and they were stolen from you?

Security can vary in price, again according to the type of setup you have. You can cut costs by using an ISP's services. Some ISPs offer to process financial transactions for their subscribers. It is worth asking providers for quotes on those kinds of services before getting involved with the setup. Remember that providers have to offer those services and protect themselves, so they already incur those costs. It does not cost them that much more to offer their facilities to their customers.

A midway solution is to have your own equipment but to install it on your ISP's premises. This is usually less costly than having equipment that is independently linked to the network. Again, you have to get prices from ISPs and equipment suppliers in your area. The competition is fierce among ISPs, and you can sometimes find a good deal. Furthermore, you can benefit from the protection already installed by your provider.

If you are considering the above option, you need to obtain additional information, along with quotes from specialists and ISPs. If you decide to operate your own Internet installation, you will need a team of people to maintain both hardware and software as well as the content of your Web site. Systems go down, telecommunication links go down and peripheral equipment (modems, routers, etc.) does as well. A system failure requires someone on site for immediate intervention. Pieces of equipment need to be repaired or replaced, which means that you need backup equipment to get back on the network immediately. You can choose to hire personnel on a permanent shift basis or to have some kind of alarm with technicians on call.

If you are considering this option, you definitely need help from Internet professionals.

Checklist for Option 3: Obtaining Quotes from Professionals

- Prepare a list of necessary hardware equipment
- Prepare a list of necessary software
- Prepare a list of necessary Internet link(s) with the rest of the network
- Prepare a list of necessary telecommunication lines to connect with the rest of the network
- Obtain prices to get connected to the network
- Obtain prices for technical help for server operation and maintenance
- Domain name registration fee (InterNIC)

Making an Informed Decision

If you are considering serious involvement with the Internet, you need to define:

1. What your objectives are
2. What your existing business setup is
3. What you need to do to bring your existing installations up to Internet operational status

4. Your options and how much each will cost
5. A time frame for meeting your objectives

Then, you need to prepare a plan with specific guidelines and follow its implementation closely.

Hiring Consultants

Regardless of the option you choose, you can proceed by yourself or you can outsource the job to consultants. If you decide to go with consultants, first prepare one or two scenarios that describe exactly what you want, along with your requirements, expected results and deadlines, as well as any specifications, requirements or other relevant information. Gather as much information as you can.

Ask for written proposals that are specific enough to avoid any gray areas that could jeopardize your project and that tell you exactly what you are getting into. Remember that it will be difficult for consultants to be specific if you are not or if you do not know what you want.

Then, when you have made your choice, prepare written agreements that outline everyone's responsibilities and obligations (remember that you will also have a role to play), as well as the fees to be paid and a payment schedule.

IV Offering Your Products on the Internet

11 Preparing Your Own Web Site

Although preparing a Web site entails much more than technical considerations, the technical aspects are important, and that is why this chapter is devoted to them. For a Web site to be successful, however, there are other important considerations, such as planning, content and organization of the information.

People and Technology

The content and the way it is organized are too often neglected. A lot of companies make the mistake of assigning all their Web site responsibilities to technical people. Technical people are excellent for taking care of technical aspects; however, technicians who also have expertise in marketing, management and content preparation are rare. This often results in Web sites that fail to raise visitors' interest, in spite of good technical features. These sites either lack interesting content from a Web surfer's point of view or are poorly designed, even though they use top technology; that is, they are designed in a way that makes it difficult and time consuming for people to find the information they need.

Using all the latest Web technology does not necessarily mean having a competitive edge on the Internet and the World Wide Web. In fact, early adoption of new standards and technological advances might even cut you off from part of your clientele if you do not also offer simpler alternatives on your Web site. There is always a delay

187

before a majority of users adopt the latest technology. Some like to play it safe and keep the older versions of their browsers or plug-ins until they are sure the newer ones work well. Others just don't have the time to install upgrades and therefore don't get around to it until later. In other instances, people are restricted to using an older version of software because of business network requirements. Also, remember that new software often places additional demands on the hardware. If people have to purchase a new computer to meet minimum software RAM and speed requirements, they may think twice before doing so.

Customer Expectations First

Another thing to consider is your customers' expectations. Your Web site will not use the same approach if you address teenagers versus businesspeople. Teens appreciate a lot of lively graphics and are not intimidated by new technologies. Businesspeople, on the other hand, prefer a faster, no-nonsense Web site that goes straight to the point and where they can immediately find what they are looking for.

Knowing what you want to achieve will help you determine and design the structure of your site. Organizing the information well and logically serves a dual purpose: it gives visitors what they need and want rapidly, while retaining their interest, and it helps you manage your site and everything it contains efficiently and smoothly.

Emphasize Content

Content is very important because that is what gives value to your Web site and what will attract people to it. Content requires thorough planning, preparation and review. Design is then organized around the content according to the goals to be achieved. Prepare a list of all the documents you want to install on your Web site. Prepare a list of services you want to offer through the site. Then, design the architecture to accomplish it (i.e., establish the relationship between each element and its role in the overall structure). Most of all, avoid making people go round and round and coming back to the same documents over and over again.

If you are going to hire a technical expert to prepare your Web site, do not expect him or her to be equally qualified to design the content and the layout. They are two different kinds of expertise altogether.

Preparing a plan or a "map" of the site should be the very first step, even before getting involved with the technical aspects. This map can also be used to help customers navigate through the Web site. Once you know what you want to present on the Web, it will be easy to explore various technical options that can deliver the desired results. Mapping your Web site will show you if it has the efficiency you want it to have. It will also show you the potential it has for expansion and development. Organizing Web pages is like organizing files in a cabinet or books and documents in a library.

Updating your Web site will be easier to plan for and to perform if you follow a plan. Having a map of your Web site structure will allow you to plan and implement changes in an organized and well-balanced manner for maximum effect. Furthermore, there is an aspect of reliability to maintain within the site. You want to provide your customers with points of reference and/or a framework on which they can rely. If you provide a service that people come to know and expect, it must be there, and always in the same location, when they try to access it. There is no point in changing its location just for the sake of change. Changes should be meaningful and serve a specific purpose. A Web site contains things that change and things that do not. The things that do not change represent the anchor of your site, and the things that change should be just enough to keep your site lively and your customers' interest high.

What Type of Site?

The type of business you are doing on the Web will have an impact on the balance between novelty and reference, between static and dynamic, between text and graphics and so on. That brings us to static versus dynamic Web sites. If you have surfed the Web, you have certainly come across both types of Web sites. Static sites are limited in their action and mostly remain the same, sort of like a permanent, immobile reference. Sites that offer plain text with little or no opportunity for feedback or customer contact fall into that category.

These types of sites have their use and should be mostly reserved for reference material. A static Web site is not effective for generating sales or business transactions. Given the very dynamic nature of the World Wide Web and its users, Web sites should be as dynamic as possible because there is a lot of competition for visitors' attention. Web surfers must be enticed to visit your site and are always just a click away from leaving it and going elsewhere.

As a general rule, about one-third of Internet users give up on a search after about 10 to 20 minutes and another quarter give up after 20 to 30 minutes. The rest give up after 5 to 10 minutes. Your Web site must therefore be fast, its content must be well organized and the overall operation must be efficient. This means excellent planning and organization. Keep in mind how browsers interact with Web pages and what the technical constraints of the World Wide Web are. Select graphic elements carefully. Remember that a picture is worth a thousand words, so make the most of it.

If your Web site has a lot of information pages, arrange them so that they can be found easily. You can use a directory, a table of contents or even an integrated search feature. At all times, imagine yourself as one of your visitors and think about what you would like to find, what you would expect and how you would like it to be.

If you outsource Web page preparation, your plan will help you keep contractors focused on what you want done and will help you follow the project to ensure it evolves as planned and according to schedule. It will also help you keep costs under control. You will become immediately aware of any deviation and will be able to make any necessary adjustment in an informed way and according to the "big picture."

How Much Interactivity?

The degree of interactivity visitors will have with your business through your Web site will depend on the amount of time you or your personnel can devote to it, as well as the technical resources you have at your disposal. More precisely, you cannot implement truly interactive (i.e., customized) pages if you cannot afford an information computer system. That means a system that runs a database to store your information and includes high-speed telecommunication links as well as personnel to install, service, maintain and update the system.

However, if you have the time and expertise or can afford to pay someone, you can implement simpler or more readily available solutions, such as a chat or a newsgroup that will allow visitors to exchange information on specific topics in relation to your business. You can use such a forum to offer advice, thereby showcasing your expertise and your business services.

Have You Chosen Your Information System?

Two options are available: your Internet service provider's (ISP's) system and your own system. Using an ISP allows you to introduce your Web site on the Internet at a low cost. You can always transfer your site to your own system should the need arise.

Speed is of the utmost importance. The system you choose must provide fast access through high-speed links. This is not the part of the system that connects you to an ISP with an ordinary telephone line, a modem and a personal computer but rather the part that connects the ISP's system with the rest of the Internet. It should be at least a T1 telecommunication link or better if possible (see Chapter 15 for telecommunication specifications). If there is any serious traffic to and from your Web site, a telecommunication link less than that will be painfully slow for your visitors.

The Composition and Structure of Your Web Pages

You need to take into account how you are going to prepare your pages in terms of what you put into them, how you organize the information and the images you use to avoid pages that take too long to download. There are ways to prepare your information to make sure that your pages are not overly heavy in terms of bandwidth.

At this point, your domain name, whether your own or your provider's, should have been selected and identified on the system.

Also, a directory (linked to your domain name) must be created on the server hosting your Web site, to receive and store your Web pages. Your ISP or system manager will give you an FTP access authorization, along with a user name and password. You need the FTP information system address as well as a user name and password to access your directory. That allows you to transfer the content of your Web pages on the information system, in a directory on the computer server to which your domain name will be linked.

Determining Content

What do you have to say? What do you want to communicate? When you have prepared your content, you are ready to organize it into a Web site. The following few questions will help you in preparing your Web site:

1. Will you use your Web site to inform customers only?
2. Will you use it for customer service?
3. Will you use it to address specific customer needs?
4. Will you use it to serve internal business needs?
5. If so, will it be used to distribute business information to your entire organization?
6. What will people find out about your business when they first access your Web site?
7. What do you want them to find out?
8. Will they find a fast Web site with pages that load rapidly?
9. Will they find the information they need?
10. Will they find it easily?
11. Will they find a user-friendly site?
12. Will they be confronted with numerous and annoying attempts to install cookies?

Hierarchy of Information

Information should be organized for maximum efficiency from the user's point of view. Users must be able to navigate at will and easily find what they are looking for. This means organizing the information in a logical and intuitive manner. That is an art in itself.

The first page will bear the file name index.html. From that page, there will be several links leading to a primary, secondary and maybe tertiary level. You should not go farther than three levels because it is very annoying to users to have to click endlessly, deep into a Web site. Some sites have more than six levels until users reach any significant information. Visitors end up not knowing where they are anymore. Most visitors will go to another site before getting to the information. This is a fact of cyberlife. Rather than adding levels, add horizontal features. For instance, start with something basic, such as the hierarchy in Figure 9. Then, instead of adding deeper levels, as in Figure 10, opt for something that looks like Figure 11.

A home page with only a logo and "Enter" that a visitor must click on in order to proceed is quite annoying. Remember that in order to get there, users have already clicked on a link or typed your URL. What's the point of asking them to click yet another time to enter your site? This is definitely a turn-off and is enough to make them click again, but to go elsewhere.

Also, avoid links that make the user go around in circles. Clicking on links only to come back to where you were a few minutes ago is also annoying. Some sites have limited information and replicate references everywhere in the site, constantly bringing people back to the same content. If you do not have a lot of information, don't

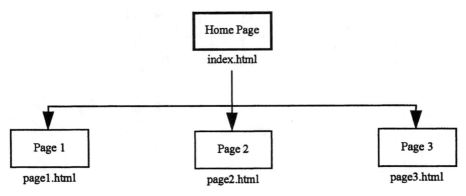

Figure 9   Web site hierarchy.

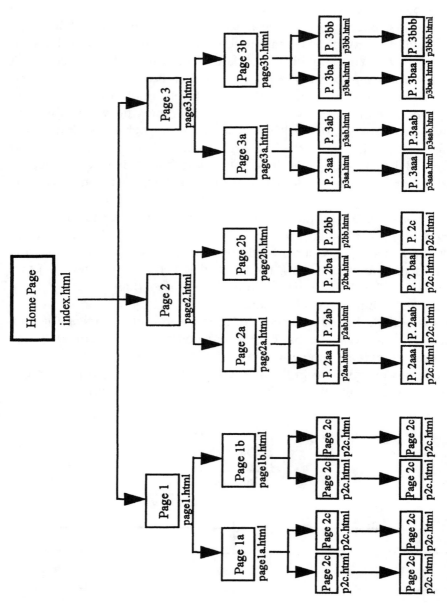

Figure 10 Hierarchy to be avoided.

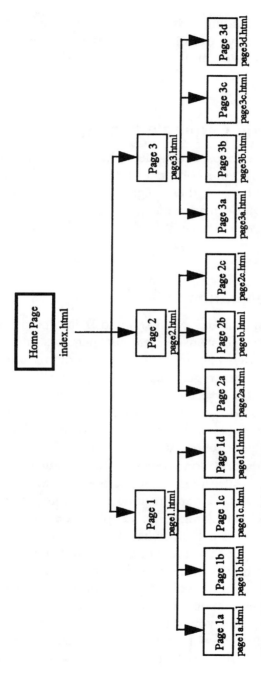

Figure 11 Recommended hierarchy.

multiply the pages leading to it. This is bad for your corporate image. The structure will vary according to your type of business, what you want to do on the Web and the information you have available for use on your Web site.

Web Design and Corporate Image

You probably have logos and trademarks that you will want to use in order to reinforce your corporate image and build your credibility. The first step is to have them digitized. If you do not have any corporate identification mark, this is the time to start thinking about creating one that will positively identify your business in customers' minds.

Web Page Preparation

You can start with a modest Web site and build upon it as time goes by and as your business on the Internet increases and evolves. The Internet is a very dynamic and interactive medium, and it is recommended that you make regular updates to your Web site to avoid a static look. The main objective is to bring customers to your site on a regular basis. To do that, you must offer them something new and different that they want, on a regular basis. This does not mean that you must change your whole Web site regularly. All you need to do is add some new information or make a few changes and update the graphic elements or the presentation once in a while. Rather than launching a huge Web site and making no changes for a while, start smaller and build onto it regularly. People expect change from one visit to the next, so give them what they expect.

You have two options in preparing and maintaining your Web site: you can do it in-house or hire someone who knows the various programming languages involved in a Web site operation. Some knowledge of programming languages will be necessary according to the level of refinement you want to give your Web site.

If you choose to use your own personnel, make sure your employees have the necessary knowledge to do a good job. Remember that it is not only a programming job: it is also a design job, a content production job and a marketing job. If you choose to hire Internet professionals, you can easily find graphic designers who are knowledgeable in HTML authoring, but it is uncommon to find someone who has the ability to produce good content *and* handle the marketing as well.

Installation of Your Web Site

Loading your Web pages on the server requires the use of FTP and FTP software. The FTP software allows you to connect to the server that will host your Web pages. If you use an ISP's server, you will be given authorized access to your own directory on the server that will host your Web site. The ISP must also provide you with a user name (also called a user ID or login) and a password to access the directory. No one should have access to your directory other than you or the person you designate to maintain it. Your ISP should give you the following information, which you will enter in the appropriate window of the FTP software:

1. FTP address
2. User name
3. Password
4. Path to directory

User name and password are either chosen by you or given to you by the ISP. The path is the location of your directory on the ISP's server. This directory can even be a subdirectory somewhere in a reserved section of the server. Usually, this section will contain many Web sites, but each will have its own directory and will be accessed only by its owner. This path is the exact location of your Web site on the server and follows the same principles as any other path (e.g., the path of your personal files on your own computer).

The first step is to open the FTP software and enter the FTP address, your user name and the password. It is best not to share your user ID and password with anyone, but if you do, make sure you choose responsible and competent people who are able to take good care of your Web site. FTP access should be restricted to specialists because you do not want just anyone to be able to modify the appearance and content of your Web site or damage it if they do not know what they are doing.

FTP is done in the same manner as surfing the Web. After connecting to your ISP, instead of opening the browser software, you open the FTP software. The following is an an example of an FTP session (the screens will vary according to the FTP software used):

1. Open the FTP software and log on (i.e., enter the FTP address, user name and password in the appropriate fields and click "OK" or "Done") (Figure 12).
2. Select the directory you want to work with on the remote server (the ISP's server) and indicate what kind of files you want to transfer (text or image).
3. Tell the software if you want to retrieve from or put a file into your directory (Figure 13).
4. Click on the proper icon to complete the transfer. Confirmation will be posted on your screen (Figure 14).

Transferring your HTML pages and the GIF/JPEG images requires only a few seconds. A lot more time is involved in preparing the pages than in transferring them to the server.

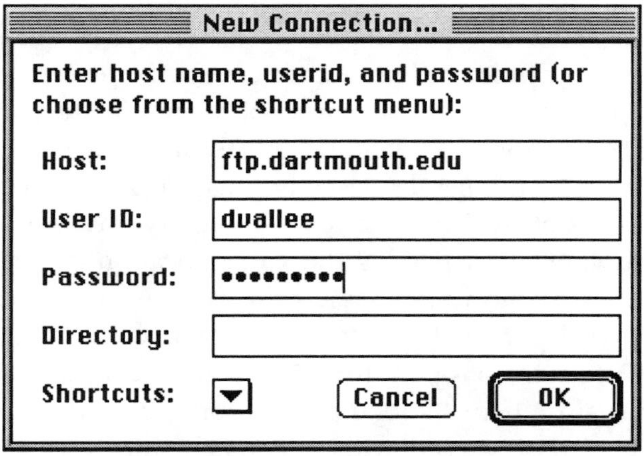

Figure 12   Example of the first window for an FTP access session.

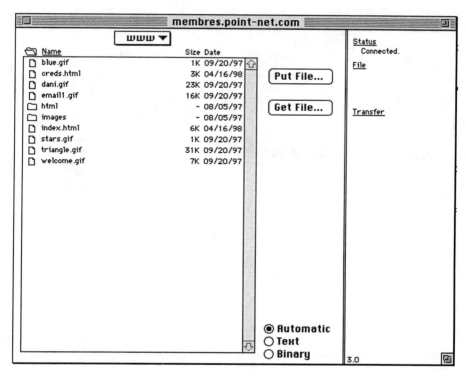

Figure 13 Arriving at your Web site with FTP software.

Updating the Web Site

You can update your Web site by altering your HTML documents or by creating new, additional ones. You can add text or images, make changes, add new pages, change or add links, etc. When you transfer a new Web page to your Web site through FTP, your computer sends a copy of the new Web page, which is an HTML file that you have prepared on your computer, to the server where your Web site is hosted. This means that all original Web pages remain on your computer, and you can work on them and update them anytime you want.

After you have updated the Web pages on your computer, all you have to do is repeat the FTP process described above. Transferring a page again with the same file name on the server will simply crush

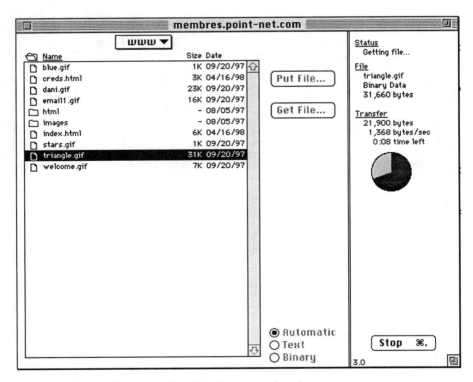

Figure 14   The file triangle.gif is being updated.

the initial page and replace it with the newer version. Do not change the computer file name for a given page unless you also change that name in all the links that lead to the actual page. Otherwise, some links will be out of working order, and all your visitors will see is a "404" error message ("File Not Found") for a nonexistent page.

Checking the validity of links is a relatively simple task when your site has only a few pages, but it soon becomes a challenge as the number of pages increases. There is now on the market software that will check all links automatically within a Web site. This can be particularly useful for large Web sites because it is always a turn-off when customers encounter bad links.

FTP software is readily available on the Internet. Several resources for FTP software are provided in Chapter 15.

Managing the Web Site

Several aspects are involved in managing your Web site, including technical administrative considerations, as well as marketing, sales and customer service. In the ideal situation, the Web manager will have a basic knowledge of the technical aspects along with strong management skills and marketing knowledge. He or she will occasionally be assisted by technical people on an as-needed basis.

Web site management includes:

- Negotiating with the ISP concerning requirements pertaining to your Web site (i.e., disk space, reliability, downtime and special needs such as CGI libraries, database implementation, security, etc.)
- Promoting the Web site
- Ensuring the availability of the Web site
- Negotiating with the ISP for reports and statistics
- Negotiating with the ISP concerning security, monitoring, special password authentication, etc.
- Monitoring the amount of traffic or number of hits the site receives
- Answering customer queries
- Maintaining statistics on time spent by visitors to your Web site as well as time spent on each page
- Identifying the most popular and least popular pages
- Identifying potential opportunities
- Testing new technology and assessing its potential for Web site implementation
- Analysis and recommendation for future Web development

Managing the Web site also includes testing the site and its links and soliciting opinions and suggestions from Web surfers.

In summary, when preparing your Web site:

1. Have clear objectives
2. Determine which technology you need to implement, along with the phases in which it will be implemented
3. Know your customers

4. Offer them what they want
5. Include basic information that visitors can find right away
6. Prepare rich content and good design
7. Avoid bad links or defective pages
8. Be thorough
9. Keep total control over the project, whether you do it in-house or outsource it

For additional information on preparing Web pages, go to:

http://www.webmaster-resources.com
http://www.poorrichard.com
http://www.zeldman.com/faq.html
http://www.andyweb.com
http://www.geocities.com/SiliconValley/Pines/4845
http://info.med.yale.edu/cain/manual
http://www.professorpete.com
http://www.pageresource.com
http://members.aol.com/itzjmp/webpage_links.html

12 Security and Protection

Protecting Your Data

When interacting with the Internet, protection takes on a whole new dimension and impacts several areas of your business. Those areas are

1. Your data
2. Your equipment
3. Your customers
4. Your employees

Your data can be the target of theft, alteration, industrial espionage, viruses and other kinds of destruction such as flood and fire. This can occur through the Internet, a local network, a diskette or locally on a machine itself.

Your equipment can be damaged by external factors, such as people or accidents, or it can simply break down. The physical location where your equipment is kept might be struck by disaster. Portable equipment can be stolen or destroyed while on the road.

Your customers can be victimized as a result of doing business with you if their personal or financial information escapes your custody and is disclosed to unauthorized parties. Security breaches can happen during information exchange or once information has been transferred to your database.

Employees can fail to follow elementary precautions; for instance, they can turn off antivirus software or share passwords. You or your employees can unknowingly or willingly disclose your trade secrets or confidential data. Your data can also be damaged by unintentional or intentional infection from viruses or other damaging agents. Employees can engage in industrial espionage or revenge.

Whether or not you use the Internet, all of the above can happen anytime within your regular business operations. No one is exempt from theft or a natural disaster. In the real world, you can take precautions to protect yourself and your business. In the cyberworld, you can do the same in order to greatly reduce the risks. Just as you would in the real world, you can minimize the risks in the cyberworld.

The cyberworld is like a parallel universe where most of the real-world rules apply, plus a few special ones. In the real world, if you do business on a large scale, you need more protection. On the Internet, you definitely do business on a large scale; because your exposure is greater, you also need good protection. Industry statistics are quite astonishing. It is estimated that less than 5% of attacks are detected and a little over 25% of those are reported. This highlights how little attention is paid to security, as well as how important it is to act now. Most of the time, lack of security can be attributed to ignorance or lack of understanding of its role as well as the possible consequences of a breach of security. When one does not have sufficient knowledge about a topic, especially a technical one, that area becomes a nebulous, intangible issue and is not addressed properly. If one does not know where to start or what to look for, addressing security is not an easy task.

However, as much attention should be devoted to security as to any other technical aspect. Just as you would hire a specialist to take care of specific technical aspects, you should not hesitate to do the same for security.

What Do You Need to Protect?

First, you must protect your data. The first step is to make regular backups of everything that is important and that can have an impact on your business operations in case of loss. The reason this point is so important is that, all too often, there is a total lack of backups or they are done inadequately in small and medium-size businesses.

The ideal backup system should be easily accessible when needed and should include more than one backup. Multiple backups should be updated on a rotational basis. If you have a limited amount of data, you can use a system comprised of three different backups; every time you do a backup, you update the oldest of the three. That way, you have some peace of mind if one of the backups is damaged or nonoperational. The backups can be done on cartridges or other media.

Prepare a first backup and put it in a safe place, off your business premises. What is the point of doing a backup and keeping it in the same location as your computer? In case of fire, both will be destroyed. Next time you are scheduled to do a backup, prepare a second one, then a third. If you lose one of the backups, you have the other ones to fall back on. Try the most recent one; if it doesn't work, try the next most recent. Sometimes the support used for backup can be defective, which is why you need more than one. Also, if one of your backups is stored in a location that is damaged, you still have the other two. At worst, you will lose the data accumulated during the time period between two backups; you would have to be very unlucky to lose more than that. In principle, the period of time you establish between backups represents your maximum potential loss. Therefore, if you cannot afford to lose more than one day's or one week's worth of data, set up your backup schedule accordingly.

Backups can be done in a variety of ways and with various degrees of sophistication, ranging from simple diskettes to larger, more powerful and automated systems. It depends on your needs, the quantity of data, how vital the data are to your business operations and what impact loss of the data would have on your business and your customers. If you have a lot of data, you will need a larger system that makes automatic backups at fixed intervals. This usually means that your computer or server will be unavailable for the period of time necessary to perform the backup. Some companies specialize in backing up data. Backups can also now be done over the Internet, which can present certain advantages. For more information about Internet backups, go to:

http://www.back-up.com

Always keep at least one backup in a location other than your business premises. If anything serious happens, your precious data will be safe elsewhere.

Viruses

Other things can also damage your data. For instance, viruses can do a lot of damage over a short period of time. When dealing with the Internet, you should always have the latest antivirus program installed on your computer. Also, keep the program active while the computer is on. An antivirus program that only inspects your files and computer content once when you start up the computer is not sufficient because you can do a whole day's worth of damage before a virus is detected. If you send out files on the Internet or on diskettes, you can infect a lot of other computers before you realize you have a virus on yours.

Viruses are small programs that replicate themselves and can execute various tasks on your computer against your will and outside your control. Some viruses have delayed actions. Some are very destructive and can wipe out everything on your computer. Some are simply annoying and slow your computer down. Some act inconspicuously and can be there for a long time before you notice them. If your antivirus software is up to date and running in the background, you will be immediately notified if any virus attempts to infiltrate your files. The newer antivirus software can detect new viruses before they have been identified.

It used to be that IBM-compatible viruses could not infect Macintosh computers and vice versa, but that is no longer true with the appearance of macroviruses. Macroviruses are viruses that are specific to text files, such as Microsoft Word and WordPerfect files, and take the form of macrocommands. Depending on the type of computer you have, you may not even realize that it has been infected by a macrovirus. The reason is that macroviruses are very discreet in their action. For instance, they usually slow down a computer, but if your computer is fast, it will not slow down enough for you to notice. Unless you have a Macintosh, which shows a different icon for an infected file, you might not know you have one and pass it on to a lot of people.

It has been estimated that from 1998 on, 60% of virus contamination will be the result of macroviruses. This is a serious threat and it can easily spread.

Some viruses infect Excel files, but they are not as common as viruses that infect text files. However, regular e-mail messages in themselves do not carry any viruses unless they also carry an attached file that is infected. As long as you do not open that file, your computer will not be infected.

Having a good antivirus program and updating it regularly is essential because new viruses appear regularly and spread rapidly over the Internet. Describing all the viruses that exist would take a whole book in itself, but it is definitely worthwhile for you to gather some basic information on how to recognize a virus and what to do if your computer is infected. For more information, go to:

http://www.symantec.com/avcenter/index.html	Norton Anti-Virus
http://www.nai.com/default_mcafee.asp	MacAfee Virus Scan
http://www.drsolomon.com	Dr. Solomon's Software

There are also a multitude of World Wide Web sites that offer advice or discuss viruses and related topics. You can access many of these sites by doing a search with one of the search engines.

Trojan Horses

Trojan horses are not usually classified as viruses because they do not replicate themselves. However, if they become widely distributed, they can in certain cases be considered viruses. Trojan horses are small programs designed to perform specific tasks that are more or less disruptive or destructive on a computer. They can also allow other people to access your computer or certain parts of your data without your knowledge, with the intent of stealing and/or modifying the data. They can be set up for the purpose of collecting data for later retrieval or to automatically send data to a specific person, and they can also be quite destructive. Trojan horses are scripts, often encountered in chats. For instance, if someone asks you to type a certain set of commands during a chat, they may be able to steal passwords and other data. Trojan horses can also masquerade as something desirable that you download and install on your system (e.g., e-mail software that really does perform an e-mail function).

For software protection against Trojan horses, visit the Web sites listed above that provide antivirus software.

Hackers and Crackers

Generally speaking, hackers are people who break into computer systems with the intent of doing some damage, in the form of either data theft or destruction. Even if you only use a personal computer to log onto the Internet, you can be the target of hackers. For instance, while involved in a chat, a hacker might ask you to type a precise string of text that would allow him or her to take control of your computer. That person could then access all your files and do whatever he or she wants — and there is nothing you can do about it. You might not even realize what is going on until it's too late.

In the same manner, if your network is connected to the Internet, it can be the target of hackers or crackers. The difference between hackers and crackers (criminal hackers) is that hackers are generally low- to average-skilled, rather inexperienced wanna-bes, whereas crackers are highly skilled and experienced professionals. Crackers usually go after important and valuable targets, whereas hackers will attack just about anything for the fun of it. For instance, crackers will not usually go after a single credit-card number but instead will try to break into the server that holds hundreds of thousands of credit-card numbers. Note that you can be the target of hackers from the outside as well as from inside your business. Hackers inside a business are often disgruntled or greedy employees who decide to steal information.

Telecommunications can also be breached. Any authorized telecommunication line that links your data and the outside network can be the target of unauthorized interception. Also, unauthorized links (such as employees plugging into the regular telephone line with an unprotected modem and therefore bypassing your protection) can put your business at risk.

The agents of security breaches outside of your business are

1. Electronic transmission of data
2. Hackers and crackers
3. Industrial spies and thieves

This is why you must carefully assess the situation in terms of your risks, your setup and your degree of vulnerability. After doing so, set up your security system and its physical arrangements and establish a clear and strong policy that will provide you and your employees with guidelines in order to safeguard the security of your data.

Precautions to Take in Protecting Against External Factors

The first basic precaution you can take if you operate a network that is linked to the Internet is to install good antivirus software on all computers. Establish a procedure to keep the software up to date and permanently on alert. It should not be turned off after computer startup. It should be left on so that it can warn you immediately should a virus attempt to infiltrate the system, whether through the Internet, a diskette or other means. Establish a policy for data exchange, especially concerning foreign diskettes.

Be alert to laptop theft. Airports in particular are popular locations for laptop theft. While the laptop owner is being distracted by one or more individuals, another one leaves with the computer. All laptops should be password protected, so that if you do lose a laptop, you will be less exposed to data theft.

Protecting Passwords

Passwords is an issue that is often discussed, with good reason. Password security is among the most neglected aspects in businesses. Weak passwords, password sharing and identical multiple passwords are common occurrences. By applying basic principles, it is possible to improve the situation a great deal.

Passwords should be chosen in an intelligent manner. Passwords that are easy to guess do little good. Passwords should be changed regularly and should not be divulged for any reason. Several persons should not share the same password. Employees should be instructed to follow these rules. A password should also be protected by encryption during transmission on the Internet. The matter should be taken seriously, because a password is the first thing hackers encounter.

Firewalls

If your network is connected to the Internet, you should install a firewall. If you have a Web server, think about installing a firewall between the Web server and the rest of your network. That way, if the Web server is compromised, the rest of your network will not be.

In certain instances, your Internet service provider (ISP) will provide security; if not, you need to address it yourself. For instance, if your network is directly connected to your ISP, you may have the option of using the ISP's firewall. Make sure the ISP has appropriate and safe installations because a badly configured firewall is not much help. If your network is connected directly to the Internet, you will need to set up your own security installations.

A firewall, which is either software or a combination of software and hardware (e.g., a proxy server with security software), will allow only authorized users to access your network from the outside while denying access to unauthorized users. However, to be truly effective, the firewall must be properly designed and configured in order to eliminate any security holes that might be the result of inadequate setup, which is fairly common. For this, you will need professional advice.

A firewall installation can include a screening router and a bastion host. As soon as you have more than one machine connected to the Internet, you need a router for packet distribution, which is the distribution of information between each computer and the rest of the Internet. The router takes care of the order in which the information is sent back and forth. The bastion host is an additional element that can ensure that packets meet certain criteria for transmission that cannot be met by the router. If you are considering installing a firewall, look into these issues as well.

Encryption

Encryption is a process by which information is scrambled using a mathematical formula. In order to unscramble the information, the recipient must have the proper key to the mathematical formula. Two kinds of encryption methods exist: private key encryption and public key encryption. Private key encryption is a method whereby both the sender and the recipient of a message share a single common key. That key is used to encrypt as well as decrypt the message. Public key encryption uses two keys: a public key that is available to the general public and a private key that is known only by the private key user. Both keys work together, and anyone can use the public key to encrypt data. However, only the private key holder can decrypt the data with the corresponding private key. Alternatively, the public key can be used by anyone to decrypt data, but only if it was encrypted by the corresponding private key. This would be used, for example, to authenticate the identity of a person.

There are several levels of encryption. On the Internet, the most common are 56 bits and 128 bits (a bit is the smallest unit of data used by a computer and is represented either by 1 or 0). From a business transaction standpoint, 128-bit encryption is far safer than 56 bits, but it is not available commercially. Indeed, 128-bit encryption has been classified for national defense purposes as ammunition and is therefore banned for export outside the United States. Regulations have been relaxed for 56-bit encryption, although it is still classified as ammunition to a certain extent. This represents a major stumbling block for the widespread use of electronic commerce that relies on high-level encryption for the security of electronic commercial transactions.

Whether you are operating a network or simply surfing the World Wide Web, you can use encryption. For instance, you can use PGP (which stands for pretty good privacy) to send and receive encrypted mail or for private Internet telephone conversations. PGP relies on public key encryption. It can be obtained from MIT at:

http://web.mit.edu/network/pgp.html

If you have a large budget and have installed security on your network, it may be a good idea to have specialists test it for possible loopholes. These specialists are legitimate professional hackers. Several companies offer such a service. The advantage is that these specialists keep on top of what is going on in the field at all times. Even if you hire Internet and computer specialists, they cannot know everything and have a lot of other topics to keep up with. They will have basic knowledge of security, but that may not be enough to render your installation hacker-proof. People who have to keep up with the rapid evolution of the Internet will not be able to devote 100% of their time to security matters, as specialists will. A thorough security evaluation will reveal what your regular personnel may have missed.

Overall, your plan should include the following:

1. A complete evaluation of your data, both the quantity and its worth.
2. Knowledge about the kind of setup you have. Know your equipment and your network. Make sure no alterations are made without your knowledge.
3. Keeping informed about what is going on and what could happen.
4. A procedure for properly implementing appropriate measures as soon as a problem is detected and informing your employees about it. You and your employees should know exactly what to do in the case of a security breach. Reacting appropriately will prevent further loss or damage.

Mirror Sites

Mirror sites are Web sites that are duplicated on computers in remote locations to distribute traffic and to ensure nonstop availability of certain data and material. Mirror sites are often used for certain high-traffic Web sites and for FTP sites that distribute software in high demand. ISPs sometimes have that kind of installation on their premises, which allows another server to take over immediately if one stops being operational. If you want to make sure that your Web site is available at all times, this can be an interesting option to discuss with your ISP.

Protecting Your Domain Name

Domain names are the object of a battle because their status is still not completely defined in relation to trademarks. Because the World Wide Web is a new phenomenon, legal status has not quite been defined completely. The way things currently work, if you register a domain name that does not already exist, it is yours. Of course, large companies have been quick to register all their trademarks as domain names to avoid court battles. Lawsuits have already been filed for trademark infringement, and in a couple of cases ownership of a domain name has reverted to the owner of the trademark.

In any case, according to InterNIC, the governing body of domain name registration, a domain name must be actively in use and a Web site must be up and running with that particular domain name in order for it to be valid. The policy is "use it or lose it." Failure to use a domain name can and eventually will lead to its acquisition by someone else. If you are thinking about registering your domain name, arrange to have at least one Web page with that domain name, even if your site is not in use yet or officially on-line, to ensure that you will still have your domain name when you are ready to use it.

Trademarks

The reverse can also happen. A domain name can be registered as a trademark by someone who does not own the domain. A domain name and a trademark are two different things. If you think that there is a chance that your domain name can become a trademark and be used as such, you should register it as a trademark as well. Some unscrupulous people have in the past registered trademarks only to resell them later to their rightful owners. Remember that court battles are expensive, and determining the rightful owner of a trademark is a matter of demonstrating the earliest and most extensive use of the trademark. Keep all your documents that demonstrate use of a trademark from early on, just in case. Samples with dates and locations can be very useful if you ever have to demonstrate use, but prevention is even better.

Furthermore, there will soon be an extensive increase in domain name extensions. At the moment, the most widely used domain name extension is .com, which is for commercial domains. However, due to a shortage of names with the .com extension, implementation of several new extensions in the near future has been proposed. Among the new extensions are .firm, .shop, .tour, .kids, .nom, .rec, .art and .web. There will probably be even more new extensions in the coming years.

This means that anyone would be able to register your domain name with another extension. Force of habit will probably mean that users will try a domain name with the .com extension first, but that could very well change in the future. It is not yet clear if registration of a trademark will prevent use of the same domain name with an alternative extension. A way to protect domain names is needed because even with a trademark, you may still have to go to court, and going to court is not necessarily an effective solution for the short term. It takes a long time before a matter is resolved, thus leaving ample opportunity for damage in the meantime. This can have serious effects, especially for small and medium-size businesses, in addition to the related legal costs.

Copyrights

Copyrights are another concern. There has initially been lose utilization of material that is available on the Internet, but it seems that the same laws that apply to any printed material also apply to the Internet. However, remember that a copyright applies to the format rather than the content. Ideas cannot be copyrighted unless they are patented. Generally speaking, two people can write about the same topic if they present it in a different format and if the text is different. No one can reproduce your sentences, but other people can write about the same subject as much as they want. The burden of proving copyright infringement always lies with the original author, which takes time and money to pursue. In the same vein, you must be careful not to infringe on copyrights owned by others.

The best position for a business is to always stay one step ahead. People who copy your material will never be able to get ahead of you.

For interesting guidelines as to what is permitted and what is not, see:

http://lcweb.loc.gov/copyright	Library of Congress
http://www1.uspto.gov	U.S. Patent Office
http://www.nolo.com/nn75.html	The copyright section of a self-help law center
http://www.delphi.com/pubweb/copyright.html	Delphi's copyright section

Protecting Your Web Site

Protecting your Web site is very important because a lot of people can see it in a very short period of time. The potential for damage is great unless you take the necessary precautions.

First of all, do not give FTP access to just anyone. Make sure that all the people who have authorization to make changes know what they are doing and are reliable. You want to have complete control over your Web site at all times and closely follow what is going on. Also, make sure that your ISP provides sufficient protection for your site. (For instance, it is sometimes possible to make changes directly from a browser, without using FTP.)

Additional Precautions

You do not want any offensive content that may result in lawsuits. You do not want a disgruntled employee to be able to set up a virus in Java applets that can be downloaded from your site. You do not want any offers that are detrimental to your business made to customers on your Web site. You do not want pornographic or other objectionable material to appear on the site, even temporarily or as a bad joke.

This means that no one should be able to change the content of your Web site from the outside. Your Web site must be protected from within as well as from the outside. If your ISP has not informed you of security measures, now is a good time to inquire. If you set up your own installation, prepare a plan that details what kind of data, if any, you will be acquiring from customers and what data you will have to protect. Also assess what will be needed in order to ensure maximum security.

Plan how you will intervene immediately in the event of an incident. Think about possible security breaches and devise a procedure for your employees to follow should one happen. Knowing what to do will limit the damage tremendously.

Protecting Electronic Transactions

An electronic transaction must be encrypted to be safely performed on the Internet. Cryptography has been available for years. Financial institutions use it for automatic teller machines.

Several packages are available for protecting electronic transactions on the Internet. Some are in the form of commercial software that uses encryption methods; others are in the form of third-party services. Some are packaged as a complete solution. Your ISP probably has its own setup and can offer you that type of service.

The main option for transaction security on the Internet is Secure Sockets Layer (SSL), created by Netscape, which is a layer protocol that provides authentication and confidentiality applications. In order to be effective, security should always include several layers. The more layers there are, the more secure the system will be.

If you do not plan to operate your own server, you will want to look into your ISP's installations first. This may be among the most affordable solutions.

Checking Your Provider's Protection

Do not hesitate to ask your ISP about security measures. As a business user, you are entitled to know how secure your Web site and any electronic transactions are. It would be very bad marketing for your ISP to refuse to give you that kind of information and would constitute sufficient justification for switching providers. When inquiring, you will probably have to ask several questions in order to get a complete picture.

Finally, if you are operating your own server, there is software that will assess security on NT servers. For more information, go to:

http://www.net-guards.com	NetGuard
http://www.iss.net	Internet Security Systems
http://www.securitydynamics.com	Kane Security Analyst

In addition, a pool of knowledge about security issues is available from the SANS Institute, a cooperative and research organization in which more than 62,000 specialists (system administrators and network security professionals) participate in order to share their experience in security matters. The SANS Institute Web site offers many interesting topics and tools, such as security assessment tools:

http://www.sans.org

There are also several sites that are resource centers for all kinds of security topics and resources:

http://www.w3.org/Security/Faq	World Wide Web Consortium Security FAQ
http://www.faqs.org/faqs/ computer-security	Computer security index
http://www.cert.org	CERT Coordination Center
http://ciac.llnl.gov/ciac/ CIACHome.html	Computer incident advisory capability
http://www.ncsa.com	International computer security association
http://theory.lcs.mit.edu/~rivest/ crypto-security.html	Page on cryptography and security
http://www.cis.ohio-state.edu/ hypertext/faq/bngusenet/comp/ security/top.html	Usenet FAQ on security

13 Finding the Right Provider

Finding the right Internet service provider (ISP) is important for your business. Reliability, security and professionalism are among the most important criteria but are not the only ones. In the past few years, a wave of new ISPs have appeared and disappeared all over North America and throughout the world. There has also been a lot of consolidation among ISPs, with some larger ones buying small ones.

Because of extremely aggressive competition, some ISPs have sold their services at a loss, which contributes to the number of ISPs that have gone out of business. This is an important consideration for your business. What would happen if your ISP suddenly went out of business without any warning, taking your Web site and part of your order information and transactions with it. What kind of effect would that have on your results? Also, the fact the your Web site would be out of commission for a few days or longer — while you find another ISP ready to host your Web site, reach an agreement with the new ISP and transfer the address of your domain name — can have important repercussions in terms of your profitability. These issues may seem trivial when you first put up a Web site, but they will rapidly become major concerns after a while, when your Web site is working at full speed and is quite profitable.

Estimating Your Traffic

Because ISPs often charge fees based on traffic at a specific Web site, you need to estimate how much traffic your Web site will generate.

219

Each time a visitor looks at one of your Web pages, the complete content (text and images) of that page is downloaded on his or her computer. For instance, if your HTML page is 46 k plus one 12-k image, a total of 58 k is downloaded on a visitor's computer. If 100 people look at that page, your traffic is 5,800 k or 5.8 Mb. If 100 people each look at 10 pages of a similar size, your traffic is 58 Mb.

To estimate your monthly traffic, identify the size of your pages and estimate your monthly number of visitors. Estimate the average number of pages each visitor will look at and multiply by the size of the pages:

Average size per Web page (including images, etc.)

× Average number of pages visited per visitor

× Number of visitors per month

= Total traffic (in bytes)

This will give you an idea of your monthly traffic and will soon be confirmed by your ISP's traffic report. ISPs have various packages for different traffic rates. Choose the package that is appropriate for your situation and make any adjustment as your traffic increases.

Your Provider's Server

This assumes that you have decided to use an ISP's services. In this case, you need to rent space on an ISP's server; therefore, you need to choose an ISP. Before deciding on an ISP, make a list of the features you want to include in your Web site as well as your requirements. This is necessary because not all ISPs offer all services. This list should include the essentials according to what you plan to do:

- The total disk space you need for your Web site, both actual and future
- The number of Internet access accounts and e-mail accounts you need
- FTP access (to transfer your Web pages to your Web site)

- The traffic you anticipate
- The kind of link speed to the Internet network your site will need (in direct relation to the traffic)
- Other services that will be needed, other than Web hosting:
  - ☐ CGI support and access
  - ☐ Special mail and mailing list services
  - ☐ Database warehousing
  - ☐ Multimedia support (audio/video)
  - ☐ Anonymous FTP site (to make downloads available to customers)
- Support for Java and multimedia
- Electronic commerce and security features:
  - ☐ Secure forms
  - ☐ Shopping carts
  - ☐ Electronic transaction processing (including credit cards)
- The kind of technical support you will need and availability schedule
- Daily logs and other Web reports and analysis services you will need

You may also need the following services if you cannot easily manage them yourself:

- Domain name registration
- Creation and preparation of Web pages
- Web site management services

After preparing your list of requirements, verify the solvency of the ISP outfit in which you are considering investing your efforts. As discussed earlier, you want an ISP that is going to be in business for as long as you are in order to avoid prolonged Web site downtime.

Verify how the ISP's server responds (i.e., availability and speed) by accessing the ISP's own Web site. All ISPs have Web sites, and you can get a good idea of how they are organized by looking at their material. You will also be able to ascertain their service and installation efficiency.

Also verify the services an ISP offers and compare them with your needs, and get a price for each service. Then, prepare an estimate of the total cost.

ISP Shopping List

- Total space needed for your Web site, both actual and future: _____ Mb
- Price: $_____ per Mb
- Number of e-mail accounts: _____
- FTP access (to load your Web pages on the site): ☐ Yes ☐ No
- Anonymous FTP site (for making downloads available to customers): ☐ Yes ☐ No
- CGI support and access: ☐ Yes ☐ No
- Cost for access to CGI library: $_____
- Traffic allowed per month before additional charges are billed: _____
- Cost for extra traffic: $_____
- Services offered, other than Web hosting (electronic commerce, LISTSERV, special mailing lists, etc.): _____
- Cost for those services: $_____
- Link speed to the Internet network: _____
- Support for Java and multimedia: ☐ Yes ☐ No Cost: $_____
- Security features (secure forms, shopping carts, electronic transactions, etc.): _____
- Cost for security features: $_____
- Technical support and availability schedule: _____
- Cost for technical support: $_____ per month
- Daily logs and other Web reports and analysis services: ☐ Yes ☐ No
- Cost for reports: $_____ per month
- Domain name registration: ☐ Yes ☐ No Cost: $_____
- Domain name yearly fee: $_____
- Web page creation services: ☐ Yes ☐ No Cost: $_____
- Web site management services: ☐ Yes ☐ No Cost: $_____ per month
- Setup fee details: _____
- Monthly operation fee details: _____

Your Own Information Server

It may be possible to install your own server on your ISP's premises. This means that you install your server close to the ISP's server to which it will be linked. Your ISP should be able to help you with this kind of installation. One advantage of such an installation is that your data are not part of the ISP's server, and the benefit may be more capacity. Another advantage is that you can benefit from the ISP's security features and high-speed links that will be shared with other Web operators, thus reducing the costs while maintaining server integrity. This could be an interesting solution if, for instance, you want to maintain a separate database for processing your orders.

Ask if your ISP offers this kind of service and what the costs are. Your ISP will be able to give you any specific technical requirements. Also ask for alternatives and their costs, so that you can assess your options and make a decision.

The Agreement with the ISP

It is essential that you have a written agreement with your ISP. This is to ensure that the terms are clear and can be referenced in the future. The agreement should protect both parties (i.e., your business as well as the ISP). Do not enter into a one-sided agreement, whether it pertains to the Internet or anything else.

If your ISP provides the agreement, take a good look at it. Read each sentence carefully and think about what it means for your business. If you do not like a statement, it is probably not good for you.

Make sure you have some leeway and that you are not bound in an unreasonable manner. For instance, you can add a clause stating that the agreement is not transferable, in which case you will have some room to maneuver in the event your ISP is bought by another company. Also, avoid a contract that covers a long period of time, given the volatility of the market. There is so much movement in the ISP world that there is no way to tell which ones will be around in the next few years. A lot of ISPs go out of business and others are bought. The situation should quiet down in the next few years, but there will still be some moving and shaking for a while.

Establishing a Relationship with the Provider

Good collaboration is essential in maintaining a successful Web site. This means that you must be able to reach your ISP's support people when you need them. If it takes a few days to get in touch with them to solve a problem or get an answer, you will have a very bumpy ride.

It is therefore advisable to make sure you can establish a close and harmonious relationship, in order to obtain complete collaboration as soon as you need it. Remember that not doing so could have a detrimental effect on your Web site sooner than you think.

Installing Your Internet Services and Web Services

Once your Web pages have been prepared and tested, installing your Web site should be a fairly simple process using FTP, as explained earlier. However, if you are completely new at it, you may need some assistance the first time.

Technical Support

If you need help installing your Web site, make sure that your ISP's support people are available to help you when you need it. For instance, if you want to implement a special service or feature for which you will need technical assistance, you must be able to obtain it. Technical support includes several other aspects, among which is production of appropriate reports and statistics in order to assess the level of activity and see what works and what does not. Another consideration is ensuring that your Web site is functional at all times.

For help in finding the right provider, go to:

http://thelist.internet.com   The List

14 Maintenance

Maintaining your Web site and Internet activities involves both hardware and software.

The Hardware

A lot of the hardware can be monitored by special software that will warn you in case of equipment failure or potential defects. If you are dealing with an ISP, most or part of the hardware maintenance will be taken care of by the ISP's technical team.

If you are operating your own equipment, you will need to have reliable technical support that will provide you with the necessary assistance on an emergency basis, along with regular maintenance programs. This requires skilled help.

In addition, there is a minimum of maintenance to do on the PCs you use in your business, the ones you or your employees use to log onto the Internet, prepare the Web pages and perform other Internet-related tasks. Hard disks should be scanned on a regular basis to check that they are in good working order and defragmented to optimize their performance.

You also need to make sure that ventilation openings on the machines are not blocked by stacks of paper or other material, which can cause computers to overheat and break down. (To be on the safe side, leave one foot of free space around a machine.) Cables must be well connected and connections protected from dust. Avoid coffee spills and objects falling onto keyboards. When keyboards are not working anymore, they must be replaced.

If you have a network that is connected to the Internet, arrange to have the activity monitored so you know what is going on. In addition to security, verify to what extent your resources are used to make sure you can keep up with demand. Look at peak periods and determine if you have sufficient resources to serve the traffic flow at peak times as well as during quiet periods.

The Web Site

If you deal with an Internet service provider (ISP), obtain activity reports for your Web site. These reports should provide you with information about:

- How many visitors your Web site gets during various periods of time (e.g., at a specific time of day or on various days during the week)
- Which pages are the most visited and the traffic flow in various parts of the Web site
- The time each visitor spends on various pages
- General information about visitors (e.g., where they are from, based on ISP addresses)
- Percentage of use of bandwidth (e.g., what portion of the capacity of your available bandwidth is used, especially during peak periods, so that you can have more bandwidth allocated to your site if necessary)

Make sure that you can obtain technical assistance from your ISP when you need it. Verify the level of safety and redundancy your ISP has implemented. Create a schedule for accessing your Web site at regular intervals to make sure it is up and running. If anything happens, you will know about it right away and will be able to check out why and solve the problem. Inquire about the usual downtime the ISP needs for regular maintenance every month. The normal rate is between 1 and 5%. Make sure there is sufficient bandwidth to accommodate peak periods of traffic. How reliable are your ISP's services? If utilization of the ISP's resources is close to maximum most of the time, the ISP has the responsibility to upgrade equipment and/ or telecommunication capacities. A professional and serious ISP will not wait to be asked to do so; most of them will act before they reach that point.

If you are dealing with an ISP whose service is unreliable, consider alternatives immediately. It is important for your customers to be able to access your Web site when they need or want to.

Before installing an HTML page on the server, verify that the page is properly coded. Test it with several different browsers or have it checked by one of the Web services. Establish a method to check the links in your Web pages. As your site grows and you make changes and updates, keeping all the links perfectly operational will become increasingly challenging. If a customer clicks on a link, it means that his or her interest has been aroused. Getting an error message is frustrating, and getting several during a visit is a turn-off. When that happens, you have lost a golden opportunity to establish a relationship with a customer. Multiply that by the number of people who visit your site and have the same experience before the situation comes to your attention and the importance of updating links becomes obvious. Evaluate whether you need to invest in software that checks all the links in your site and identifies any links or files that are missing or nonoperational. This kind of software may be necessary when your Web site grows to multiple pages. Similar services can also be found on the World Wide Web. For more information, go to:

http://validator.w3.org	World Wide Web Consortium Validator
http://www.websitegarage.com	Web Site Garage
http://www.tetranetsoftware.com	Linkbot and Linkbot Express (Tetranet)

Also pay attention to the hierarchy of the pages so that visitors do not drown in endless clicking before getting anywhere. Immediately replace pages that are ignored or reposition them in the hierarchy.

Prepare a maintenance plan and schedule that covers your complete Internet operation, from PCs to Web servers (including any databases or other elements) to ensure that any weak link is strengthened and/or corrected and that every element is kept in good working order and remains efficient and properly operating.

Reports

Analyze your ISP's or system reports on a regular basis. Depending on the format in which they are presented to you, you may need software to interpret the results. Reports are a key element in your Web maintenance.

Being in business and remaining competitive means a constant renewal, either of product lines or services offered. That is why there should be regular updates of what your business is offering. Even in the service sector, you need a certain amount of renewal and novelty to maintain customers' interest. Informing your customers about those updates can sometimes be expensive and time consuming, which is why many businesses do not actively inform their customers about them. However, doing so generally proves to be worthwhile in terms of both corporate image and business results.

To that end, a Web site can be very useful and effective because changes and updates can be made rapidly and viewed by a maximum number of people in a very short period of time. Remember that your Web site also needs regular updating to remain interesting. It will be particularly effective if you can build a loyal following of customers who regularly visit your Web site. If you offer them what they need (i.e., specific information they are looking for on a regular basis), they will be aware that they can get the information anytime and regularly on your Web site. They can get it at their convenience, even outside of business hours, whether they are at their usual place of business, traveling or at home. They can spend as much time as they want and access as much information as they need. It is at their disposal 24 hours a day, 7 days a week.

You can put your updates just about anywhere on your Web site. Be consistent so that people know where to find what they are looking for and can find it rapidly. You can also use an electronic newsletter to indicate updates and invite your customers to visit your Web site for more information. You can put a teaser in your newsletter and tell customers that more extensive explanations can be found on your Web site. Use a "New" icon (some are flashing icons) on Web pages to indicate new material. Create a section for news and new features. Plan your updates so that you get the greatest effect out of them. Dress them up as much as you can so that each time you introduce one, it will have maximum impact.

You can also use the push technology to deliver tailored information automatically to customers.

Create an implementation plan and a development plan. Integrate updating into your plan, and follow the plan in order to meet objectives. The important thing is to monitor operations closely and make any necessary adjustment.

15 Computer Equipment, Telecommunication and Software

As has been highlighted so far, there are three main areas to be considered when getting involved with the Internet:

1. **Hardware**, which encompasses user PCs as well as other hardware used in setting up local networks and connecting to the Internet
2. **Telecommunication**, which encompasses all the links between PCs and servers throughout the entire network
3. **Software**, which is used to send, receive and manage various tasks over the network and on a user's computer

Hardware

Hardware includes personal computers as well as servers, routers, aggregators and repeaters. Appropriate hardware must be available on both

1. The user's end
2. The Internet network end

The User's End

The user's end requires a personal computer and a modem, used to log onto the Internet. The setup is relatively simple and is all a user needs to access the Internet.

Random Access Memory

A personal computer will need a minimum of 8 Mb of RAM (random access memory) and preferably 16 to 20 Mb or more to be able to use the latest World Wide Web browsers along with their plug-ins.

Remember that newer operating systems (Windows, Mac OS, etc.) require between 5 and 10 Mb of RAM to operate, and the newer versions of browsers require between 10 and 15 Mb of RAM to run properly. This means that a user with less than 20 Mb of RAM will have to use an older browser that require less RAM (2 to 4 Mb) to run.

Also keep in mind that if you want to use certain plug-ins, which are added to your browser, you will need extra RAM. Some plug-ins are more RAM hungry, depending on what they do. For instance, if you use Shockwave, you will need an extra 8 Mb. For Internet telephone, you will need around 5 Mb. Carefully assess your RAM requirements in view of what you want to do on the Internet.

Hard Disk

The size of the hard disk you need depends on the storage requirements of the software you use and the kind of documents you produce with that software.

It is not uncommon to see browsers that require over 10 Mb of disk space for storage, excluding plug-ins. (Plug-ins are usually small in size in terms of storage.) Furthermore, some larger applications, such as Microsoft Office, require over 75 Mb just for storage.

If you are going to produce graphic files, movies or multimedia, you will need a lot of storage space because graphic files are very large. Analyze your needs and determine your storage space adequately to avoid a shortage when you least expect it.

Speed

The speed of your computer is another consideration. Depending on how you use your computer, you may need more disk speed or higher processing capability. Software manufacturers usually include minimum requirements in their basic computer manuals. Do not hesitate to upgrade your computer if you think you need to do so.

The Internet Network

If you are planning to produce Web content for the Internet, you may need additional equipment if you do not use an Internet service provider (ISP).

Servers

A server is a computer that stores and runs server programs that manage information. A server is usually a central computer to which several client computers are connected. It can be the central part of a local area network or can be a computer owned by an ISP to which individual outside computers connect to access the Internet. A server is a multi-user, multi-task computer.

A server can be used for storing and transmitting Web pages, for storing and operating databases, as a proxy server to act as a security intermediary between the Internet and users, as a firewall (a firewall can also be software) or as a gateway to receive and forward packets from one network to another.

Modems

A modem, which stands for modulator/demodulator, is a device that allows one computer to "talk" to another computer through a telephone line. A computer is connected to a modem with a special wire which in turn is connected to a telephone outlet with a telephone wire. An appropriate telecommunication program must be installed on the computer to operate the modem properly and allow communication with the telephone network. Some modems have voice transmission capability, and others do not. If you are going to use a modem for Internet telephone or other audio functions, make sure that the modem has the appropriate capacity.

Certain modems are now available to provide analog channel bonding. This means using two regular telephone lines on which two bonding modems are installed to provide twice the regular speed. However, you will need to check with your ISP to make sure this kind of installation is compatible with its services as well as yours.

For more information about this kind of equipment, see the following Web site, which contains a complete resource center about all brands and types of modems:

http://www.modemhelp.com

Routers

A router is a device (this task can also be performed by software) that routes packets (units of data) to their final destination. A router is needed when several sources of transmission send packets through one conduit.

Aggregators

An aggregator is a device that concentrates transmissions. This can save bandwidth and make the overall rate of transmission faster.

Hub

A hub is a point of convergence of data that is equipped with some kind of switch that will redirect the data toward its destination. A hub can include a router.

Telecommunication Links

Telecommunication links are strategic for Internet use. The following types of telecommunication links are discussed in this section:

1. Between a personal computer and the Internet network.
2. Between a server or an ISP and the Internet network. If your PC is connected to a local network, you will probably connect to the Internet through a server. This server will in turn be connected to an ISP or to a network service provider. A server usually means higher traffic, which in turn calls for higher speed links.

Regular Telephone Lines

A basic telephone line, made with a pair of copper wires, is the most widely used option for basic and individual Internet accounts. A regular telephone line will generally allow a maximum speed of between 25 and 30 Kbps but can go up to 56 Kbps. All you need is a compatible modem of the desired speed (28.8 or 33.3 Kbps) that plugs into your telephone outlet.

Cable Connections

It is possible to use a television cable connection (i.e., the coaxial cable that brings cable channels to your television) to access the Internet. Note that not all cable infrastructure is able to support two-way communication. In certain setups, users can use the coaxial cable to download from the Internet but have to use a regular telephone line to send out data.

In any case, cable transmission typically allows more data to be transmitted from the Internet than the other way around. Since it takes more bandwidth to download Web pages to a computer than it takes to handle user requests to get those pages, this is not necessarily a downside. A cable connection requires the use of a special cable modem; the speed may vary from 56 to 512 megabits per second (Mbps).

USB

USB, which stands for universal serial bus, is an interface for computers. It is not a telecommunication link as such between a computer and the Internet, but it is a link between a computer and its peripherals. It allows you to easily hook up to your computer such devices as a printer, digital scanner, keyboard, mouse, joystick, telephone, digital camera, audio player, tape and floppy drives, CD-ROM drive and so on. The transmission speed is 12 Mbps. USB will offer interesting possibilities in the near future as it accommodates a new generation of peripherals such as MPEG-2 video products and allows as many as 127 peripherals to be connected to a computer at the same time.

For more information about USB, go to:

http://www.usb.org
http://www.whatis.com/usb.htm
http://www.intel.com/design/usb

DSL and Its Variations

DSL, which stands for Digital Subscriber Line, is a technology for using regular telephone lines at higher speeds. It is sometimes called xDSL; the prefix is used to identify the type of DSL. DSL technology allows several options, among which are ADSL, CDSL, DSL Lite, HDSL, IDSL, RADSL, SDSL, UDSL and VDSL. The most commonly discussed is ADSL, which stands for Asymmetrical Digital Subscriber Line.

Your regular telephone line can provide you with ADSL service. ADSL allows the use of existing copper phone lines to transmit digital information at high speed. The asymmetry resides in the fact that ADSL uses the larger part of the channel to transmit downstream (i.e., from the server and the Internet to the user) and a small part for the opposite direction (i.e., from the user to the server and on to the Internet). This is the same principle that applies to coaxial cable (cable television links), which is ADSL's main competitor. ADSL speed runs between 1.544 and 8 Mbps. There are also other versions of DSL, and each has its own specifications and requirements, some of which are typically European. The two main limitations of ADSL are the maximum distance a user can be from the central office of the telephone company and the kinds of cables that are available for the connection between the telephone company and the user's location.

For more information, go to:

http://www.whatis.com/xdsl.htm
http://www.whatis.com/dsl.htm#adsl

IDSL

IDSL usually designates ISDN DSL and is closer to ISDN data rates (see next section).

ISDN

ISDN, which stands for Integrated Services Digital Network, also uses regular copper wires for data transmission but can also use other media. This kind of installation requires a special adapter in lieu of a modem, sometimes called an ISDN modem, for a speed of up to 128 Kbps. If you opt for this solution, your ISP needs to provide you with special installations that will allow you a high-speed ISDN connection to its server.

To that end, your telephone company provides you with ISDN service that has two 64-Kbps channels for a total of 128 Kbps. You can either use one of the 64-Kbps channels and keep the other one free for incoming and outgoing regular telephone calls and faxes, or you can use both channels for maximum speed. If you use this service, your ISP will also need to have an ISDN adapter installed on its premises and will probably charge you more for the service. This service is available mostly in urban areas, and its price can be steep for small businesses. However, experience with ISDN has been a bit uneven and varies greatly from one location to another and from one telephone company to another. Your best bet, as a businessperson, is to talk to people in your area who have tried it and see what kind of service they got.

Note that a faster telecommunication installations does not automatically guarantee maximum speed because a lot of things have an impact on data transmission speed: ISP connection speed to the Internet network, Web servers, network congestion, bottlenecks in certain places on the network, etc.

For more information, go to:

http://www.whatis.com/isdn.htm

T1 and T3

A T-carrier system is a high-capacity cable installed by a telephone company. T1 provides a speed of 1.544 to 3.152 Mbps and is commonly used by Internet providers for their connection to the Internet, although some providers use a T3 line, which is faster.

The T3 line works on the same principle as the T1 but at a speed of 44.736 Mbps.

For more information about T1 and T3, go to:

http://www.whatis.com/tcarrier.htm

Satellite and Wireless Communication

Another option that is slowly emerging is wireless and satellite communication. This type of connection is available for both PCs and servers. At present, these technologies have not quite attained their full potential yet and still have certain limitations. However, they are very promising because of what they have to offer.

Wireless

It is now possible to connect a notebook computer to the Internet with the help of wireless communication. However, this requires the use of a special modem, called a PC card, that will compensate for the variation to which data are subjected through wireless transmissions. Regular modems are too sensitive to withstand such variation and will shut off automatically as soon as a variation occurs. PC cards can be used as modems to make the necessary corrections.

Wireless technology also allows small hand-held devices to send and receive e-mail and surf the Web.

For more information about PC cards and their standards, refer to:

http://www.whatis.com/pcmcia.htm
http://www.pc-card.com

For information about wireless, go to:

http://www.uwcc.org
http://www.wow-com.com/consumer
http://www.att.com/business_wireless

Satellite

Satellite communication allows access to the Internet, but that kind of access is expensive and still has some limitations for the common user. Satellite links can team up with other technologies such as the Global Positioning System (GPS). Special applications have been developed around this technology. For instance delivery companies have implemented such systems to allow them to track deliveries and to rapidly assign new deliveries and pickups. Looking into something like that may be worthwhile if your business needs call for it. Of course, the technology has a price tag, both for hardware and telecommunication services, but it can be worth it if it can be used for several business applications. Satellite communication also requires the use of a dish/directional antenna that must be directed at the satellite and follow its path in the sky. However, this is the way of the future. Some day you will be able to surf the Web from a beach anywhere in the world.

For more dreaming, go to:

http://www.msua.org/mobile.htm
http://www.TBS-satellite.com

Software

Software is a general term that designates a series of programs that are used to operate successive tasks on a computer and peripherals. The primary type of software is operating systems and the secondary type is application software. An operating system is installed on a computer and is at the heart of its operation. The main focus of this discussion is application software because, although all computers require an operating system, it is transparent when using the Internet.

Application software is the tools used to perform diversified tasks, by and for users, on the Internet.

For Internet purposes, there are two categories of application software: the user's software and the administrator's software. The user's software is comprised of all the software a user needs to connect to the Internet, surf the World Wide Web, download files, view video, listen to audio and perform other similar tasks specific to individual needs.

The first type of user software is **connection software**. It is used by a computer to connect to an ISP or the Internet through a modem. Each platform has its own connection software, and in some cases, several types of connection software are available for one platform. That kind of software can be obtained either from an ISP or through the Internet. It is also available as Internet connection packages that are sold in computer stores and outlets. Some new computers come equipped with it.

The second category is **browser software**. There are several browser packages on the market, and there are several plug-ins as well. Plug-ins that work with one browser will not necessarily work with the others, but the most popular browsers are able to use most of the popular plug-ins.

The two main browsers are Netscape's Navigator and Communicator and Microsoft's Internet Explorer. They are both available for free and are frequently already installed on new computers. For an up-to-date list of available browsers and their compatibility with various platforms, see:

http://browserwatch.internet.com/browsers-full.html

Plug-ins for World Wide Web Browsers

There are many plug-ins available for World Wide Web browsers. A list is provided below, but remember that by the time you read this, there will probably be some new ones. The list is by no means exhaustive. Also note that not all of the plug-ins work with all browsers and/or platforms. It is best to check which ones your particular browser and platform can accept. Note that both Netscape's and

Microsoft's browsers come with many preinstalled plug-ins, and others can be added as you need them.

- **3D and animation**
  AnimaFlex (RubberFlex Software)
  AuraLine (NEC Systems Laboratory)
  ClickToons (Music Pen, Inc.)
  Cosmo Player (Silicon Graphics, Inc.)
  Cult3D (Cycore Computers)
  CyberAge Raider (CyberAge Communications)
  DeepV (Heads Off)
  Enliven Viewer (Narrative Communications)
  Entrance (Cybercore Systems)
  Flash Player (Macromedia)
  Gig Plug-in (Generic Logic)
  HyperStudio (Roger Wagner Publishing)
  Icon Author (Aimtech)
  iRapid (Emultek)
  Jutvision (Visdyn Software Corporation)
  Live Picture Viewer (Live Picture)
  mBed (mBed Software)
  Media Controller 7 (7th Level, Inc.)
  Media Conveyor Player (Digital Evolution)
  MegaView Plug-in (MegaBitz Engineering)
  MetaStream Viewer Plugin (MetaCreations Corporation)
  Mirage (Clearsand Corporation)
  OnLive! Traveler (OnLive! Technologies)
  OpenPix Viewer (Hewlett-Packard)
  Proroplay (Altia)
  Quick3D (Plastic Thought)
  RealView (Datapath Limited)
  Scream (Saved by Technology)
  Shockwave (Macromedia)
  Sizzler (Totally Hip Software)
  Sony Community Place (Sony)
  Terrain.net plug-in (Cayenne Software)
  Viscape (Superscape)
  WebGlide Player (WebGlide)

WebXpresso (Dataviews)
Whurlplug (Apple)
Wirl Virtual Reality Browser (VREAM)
Worldview (Intervista Software)
Xswallow (Colan McNamara)

For more information about the above plug-ins, go to:

http://home.netscape.com/plugins/3d_and_animation.html

- **Audio and video**
  Apple Quicktime 3 Plug-in (Apple Computer, Inc.)
  Bamba (IBM)
  Beatnick (Headspace)
  ChaTV (Pseudo Programs, Inc.)
  CineWeb (Digigami)
  COM One Video Plug-in (COM One)
  Crescendo (LiveUpdate)
  Digital Sound & Music Interface for OS/2 (Julien Pierre)
  Echospeech (Echo Speech)
  InterVU Player (InterVU)
  IP/TV (Precept)
  Koan Plugin (SSEYO)
  Liquid MusicPlayer (Liquid Audio)
  Maczilla (Knowledge Engineering)
  MidPlug (Yamaha MidPlug)
  MIO (Asahikasei Jyoho System Co.)
  Modplug Plugin (Olivier Lapicque)
  MpegTV Plug-in (MpegTV, LLC)
  MusicGenie (SuperPlanet, Inc.)
  NET TOOB Stream 3.x (Duplexx Software, Inc.)
  OnLive! Talker (OnLive! Technologies)
  PanoramIX (IBM)
  PhoneFree (Big Bits Software)
  QuickFlick (Practoce Corporation)
  RapidTransit (Fastman)
  RealPlayer (RealNetworks)
  T.A.G.Player (Digital Renaissance)

Talker (MVP Solutions)
TrueSpeech Player Plug-in (DSP Group)
Ump (Umpire)
VDO Live (VDOnet)
ViewMovie QuickTime (Ivan Cavero Belaunde)
VivoActive Player (Vivo Software)
VOSAIC Mediaclient (VOSAIC)
WebTracks (Wildcat Canyon Software)

For more information about the above plug-ins, go to:

http://home.netscape.com/plugins/audio-video.html

■ **Business and utilities**
Acrobat Reader (Adobe)
Autodesk MapGuide (Autodesk)
Belarc Advisor (Belarc)
Browse and Zip (Canyon Software)
Calendar Quick (Logic Pulse)
Carbon Copy/Net (Microcom)
Celo Digital Signature (Celo Communications)
Chemscape Chime (MDL Information Systems)
Citrix WinFrame Client (Citrix)
Cryptolink Agent (1st Stop Software Corporation)
CustomMenu (Yellow River Software, Inc.)
CyberCash Wallet (CyberCash)
DemoNow (InstallShield Software Corporation)
Demo-X (DemoShield Corporation)
Dynadoc (DynaLab Encorporated)
Earthtime (Strafish Software)
Envoy (Tumbleweed Software)
Formatta Web Filler 97 (Formatta Corporation)
FormLock (General Network Services)
Formula One/Net (Visual Components)
ichat Plug-in (ichat)
InstallFrom TheWeb (InstallShield Software Corporation)
IntelliTrip (TheTrip.com)
Intermind Communicator (Intermind)

ISYS HindSite (ISYS/Odyssey Development)
JetForm WebFiller (JetForm Corporation)
KEYVIEW (Verity)
LABTECHnet (LABTECH)
Look@Me (Netopia)
METIS Model Browser (METIS SOLUTIONS)
NetJumper (NetJumper)
Network Ease for Applets (Visual Edge Software Ltd.)
NetZip 6.0 (Software Builders International)
NobleNet Web Opener (NobleNet, Inc.)
OmniForm Internet Filler (Caere)
Panorama Viewer (SoftQuad)
PC-Install (20/20 Software)
PenOp Plug-in (PenOp)
Quick View Plus (Inso Corporation)
Raosoft Database grid plug-in (Raosoft, Inc.)
Rapid Plug-In (Emultek)
ScriptActive (Ncompass)
SecureWeb Documents (Terisa)
Slingshot (CSK Software)
SwiftView (Northern Development Group, Inc.)
Tcl/Tk Plug-in (Sun Microsystems)
techexplorer Hypermedia Browser (IBM)
WebTerm Toolbox (White Pine Software)
Web Turbo (Netmetrics Corporation)

For more information about the above plug-ins, go to:

http://home.netscape.com/plugins/business_and_utilities.html

- **Image viewers**
  4U2C (Summus, Ltd.)
  Acordex ViewTiff (Cordant Imaging Systems)
  BubbleViewer (IPIX)
  CE Internet Plugin (Compression Engines)
  CMX Viewer (Corel Corporation)
  CPC View (Cartesian Products)
  CSView 150 (CSU Software Solutions)
  CyberSleuth (Signum Technologies)

DepthCharge Stereoscopic Image Viewer (Vrex, Inc.)
DjVu (Cloned) (AT&T Labs)
Dr. DWG NetView (Dr. DWG)
ELT/Net (Paragon Imaging)
GrafixView (InfoMill Limited)
ImagN' Netscape Java Plug-in (Pegasus Software LLC)
InterCAP Inline (InterCAP Graphics Systems)
IPIX Viewer (Interactive Pictures Corporation)
Lightning Strike (Infinop)
LuRaWave (LuRaTech)
MetaWeb CGM Viewer (Ematek/HSI)
MrSID Online Viewer (LizardTech, Inc.)
Pagis XIFF Viewer Plug-In (ScanSoft, Inc./Xerox)
Pantone WebImage Viewer (Pantone, Inc.)
Pegasus Plug-in (Pegasus Imaging)
picture-in-motion (K.C. Multimedia)
PNG Live (Siegel & Gale)
RasterNet (Snowbound Software Corporation)
Smoothmove (Infinite Pictures)
Surround Video (Black Diamond)
SVF (Softsource)
ThingViewer (Parable)
TIFF Surfer (VisionShape)
TruDef (TruDef Technologies)
Vdraft (Softsource)
ViewDirector Prizm (TMSSequoia)
Visual WebMap (Project Development)
Watermark WebSeries Viewer (FileNet)
Wavelet Internet Plugin (ALGO VISION Multimediale GmbH)
WebDocs (Advance Solutions Group, Inc.)
WHIP! (AutoDesk)
Xara (Xara)
XIF Plug In (Xerox Scansoft)

For more information about the above plug-ins, go to:

http://home.netscape.com/plugins/image_viewers.html

■ **Presentations**
  Astound Web Player (Gold Disk, Inc.)
  Billboard 97 (Xtratek)
  Corel Presentations Show It! (Corel)
  KIT-Plug-In (Deutsche Telekom Online Service GmbH)
  Lotus Web Screen Show Player (Lotus)
  Neuron (Asymetrix)
  OpSession (NetManage)
  PointPlus (Net-Scene)
  PowerPoint Animation Player & Publisher (Microsoft)

For more information about the above plug-ins, go to:

http://home.netscape.com/plugins/presentations.html

There are myriad other plug-ins which serve various purposes. For more information, go to:

http://home.netscape.com/plugins/plug-in_extras.html

For more information about plug-ins in general, see:

http://home.netscape.com/plugins/index.html

With all the plug-ins that exist and that are being developed, it can be challenging to keep up with product information. If you choose to provide a service through a specific plug-in in your Web site, remember to keep in mind the actual and potential popularity of that service and the availability of the plug-in. What will visitors have to do to acquire the plug-in? Does it come already installed in most browsers? Is it readily available and easy to obtain? Is it available for the most popular platforms or is it only available on one of them? Simplicity of downloading and installation as well as downloading time are other important considerations.

Will visitors be sufficiently motivated by what you are offering to download the plug-in? Will you put a link on your Web site to make it easy for visitors to download the plug-in? Which plug-ins do most Web surfers already have installed with their browsers? Can they access your particular service with "standard" plug-ins? If so, you have a better chance of attracting a wider audience than if you decide to use an unknown plug-in. Using an unknown plug-in can, however, be counterbalanced by strong interest from your audience and a strong drive on your part to make the plug-in better known. Decide if that is your goal and if it is worth it in view of your objectives.

Database, SQL

SQL, which stands for Structured Query Language, is used for programming updates and for retrieval of data from databases in the form of interactive queries. SQL works with such tools as Microsoft Access, Foxpro, Oracle, Sybase and IBM DB2.

Monitoring Software

Monitoring software encompass several categories:

- Use of computer resources and activity on the server (system monitoring software, system enhancement software and network monitoring software)
- Security (authentication and encryption software, firewall software)
- Employee activity on the Internet

You may need one or more of the above types of software. For up-to-date information on this type of software, go to:

http://www.alw.nih.gov/Security/security-prog.html

You can also perform a search using one of the search engines and find a tremendous amount of information about this topic.

Virus Protection

To find information about virus protection and software, go to:

http://www.symantec.com/avcenter/index.html   Norton Anti-Virus
http://www.mcafee.com   MacAfee Virus Scan
http://www.nai.com/default_mcafee.asp   MacAfee Virus Scan

http://www.drsolomon.com	Dr. Solomon's Software
http://www.thunderbyte.com	ThunderBYT Corporation
http://www.leprechaun.com.au	Leprechaun Software

HTML Editors

HTML editors are used to prepare Web pages. For more information, go to:

http://www.sq.com/products/hotmetal/hm-ftp.htm	SoftQuad
http://www.sausage.com/soft1.htm	Sausage Software
http://www.dexnet.com/homesite.html	Nick Bradbury
http://www.nesbitt.com	Ken Nesbitt
http://www.coffeecup.com/editor	Internet Cafe
http://www.aolpress.com/press/index.html	America Online
http://nt.infoflex.com.au/flexed/flexed.htm	Infoflex Software
http://www.allaire.com	Allaire Corporation (homesite)

Graphics Software

http://www.ausmall.com.au/freesoft/freesofta.htm

FTP Software

http://www.dartmouth.edu/pages/softdev/fetch.html	Fetch
http://www.ftpro.com	WS_FTP Pro
http://cuteftp.com	CuteFTP

E-Mail Management and Filters

http://www.eudora.com	Eudora from Qualcomm
http://www.banyan.com/products/beyondmail.html	BeyondMail from Banyan

Document Management Software

http://www.blueridge.com
http://www.xerox/scansoft
http://www.eastmansoftware.com
http://www.lotus.com
http://www.infologics.com
http://www.aviatorsoftware.com
http://www.imageedition.com
http://www.laserfiche.com
http://www.mindworks.com
http://www.bscw.gmd.de
http://www.computhink.com
http://www.imt.net/~jrmints/denhome.htm
http://www.compinfo.co.uk/index.htm
http://www.archivebuilders.com
http://www.isysdev.com

Telnet Software

http://www.metrowerks.com/tcpip/spec/telnet.html   Code Warrior
http://www.cstone.net/~rbraun/mac/telnet   NCSA Telnet

As an additional pointer, the following Web site contains an incredible number of references and software available for downloading, for all platforms:

http://www.tucows.com   Tucows

V World Wide Web Marketing

16 Promoting Your Web Site

The Need to Promote the Web Site

To increase traffic on your Web site, you will need to promote it. There are several ways to let Internet users know that your site exists. However, merely setting up a Web site will not automatically bring in a lot of visitors and generate a lot of orders for your business.

Advertising on the Internet is mainly achieved by creating your own and using other World Wide Web sites. On your own site, you are not limited in any way in the size, appearance, content and frequency of your own ads. You can also advertise elsewhere on the Internet; for example, you can purchase space, usually in the form of banners, in highly visible places. That is usually expensive and may or may not bring a lot of visitors to your Web site with just the click of a mouse.

Existing or potential customers have to be able to find you easily (i.e., find your Uniform Resource Locator [URL] or Web site address link). Purchasing space on the Web without putting up a Web site is a total waste of money. The same holds true if you do not have an e-mail address. People who are navigating the Web expect to be able to get more information and contact you through the Internet immediately. Your Web site has a permanent address and can be listed with or found by the various search engines. That allows people looking for you to find you. Including your URL and e-mail address on your business stationary makes it even easier for people to get in touch with you.

253

Remember that your Web site should not be pure advertising because that would neither be suited to the Web mentality nor well received by Internet users. Web sites that are nothing but advertising billboards are not very successful. Web surfers expect useful information and entertainment for free. Advertising has to be done in a subtle and informative way and has to be intermixed with other functions in order to reach your target audience.

Advertising on the Internet covers, therefore, the advertising you do on your own site as well as elsewhere on the Internet. The content of your Web site will cover many aspects, and you want to be sure that it showcases your business. You need to have a marketing strategy for the Web site itself, and that strategy must be integrated into your overall marketing plan. The Web site should support the other marketing activities and vice versa.

There are basically two main types of target clientele you want to reach: your existing customers and potential customers. Existing customers can also be informed about your Web site through regular advertising and promotional tools, among which are business cards, letterhead, brochures and other promotional literature. The trend is to include both e-mail address and URL on corporate stationary. This makes it easy for customers to reach you on the Internet.

You can organize a special event around the official launch of your Web site. For instance, you can rent a room for the event and invite existing customers to attend. Arrange to have a large screen or monitor available that will be hooked up to a computer that will be used to surf the Web live and demonstrate your World Wide Web site for everyone to see. This can be achieved with a portable computer and a projector, as long as you have access to a telephone line. If you cannot have access to a live Internet connection or a telephone line at the event, it is still possible to display your Web site on a laptop and simulate a live World Wide Web site visit without anyone knowing the difference.

Use this opportunity to organize a lively session that will be memorable for the guests. Make sure that what you show will entice customers to visit your Web site and do business with you.

Organizing a public event allows you to reach both existing customers and potential customers, as well as those that are on-line and those that are not. It is a great opportunity to position yourself and your business by promoting the fact that you keep up with technology in your business operations to better serve your customers.

Registering the Web Site with Search Engine Services

When Internet users are on the Internet and looking for your World Wide Web site but do not know its URL address, the main way they find it is by using search engines. The proper use of META tags has a direct influence on whether those search engines properly identify and catalog your Web site.

Some search engines require that you register your site with them. When you register with one of the search engines, take the time to carefully pick each category where your site should be listed and register in each one. A search engine will not automatically register your Web site in all categories that pertain to your activities. Registration is free in most cases, but individually registering with each of the search engines can be time consuming. There are services on the Web that will register your site with all the major search engines for a fee, but you don't have to pay if you do it yourself. If one of your employees is doing it, you are already paying, so make sure that employee knows what he or she is doing.

Search engines are very useful, but they list hundreds of thousands of Web sites, among which are hundreds of sites similar to yours or identified as such even if they are not really the same type. It can be quite a challenge for someone to find your Web site in that jungle and even more challenging to make your Web site stand out from the crowd.

To register with search engines, you can visit each one individually, click on the "Add URL" button and follow the instructions provided at each site. Each search engine has a page explaining the search method along with how to properly register a Web site. The other option is to use a specialized service, some of which are free, that will register your Web site with several search engines in one operation. Be aware, however, that they may not do as good a job as you in picking the categories where you Web site should be listed.

Either way, after waiting the appropriate time to allow for the registration process (which is particular to each search engine), verify with each search engine that your site has indeed been registered. There is a delay before your site actually becomes listed, and some search engines have criteria about whether or not they will list a site and therefore need time to make a decision. You also need to keep up with the occasional new search engines that are created. You may have to renew your registration occasionally, as some search engines may drop your URL link for one reason or another. For instance, some of the search engines perform checks to see whether the site is up. If your server is on downtime while that check is being done, or if there is a telecommunication problem or network failure in a certain geographical area, your link may disappear from that search engine listing.

For tips about promoting your Web site with search engines, see each search engine registration guideline section as well as the following URL:

http://www.webdeveloper.com/categories/management/
management _search_engine_tips.html

Banners

Some Web sites offer to sell you advertising space in the form of banners. This is found mostly on high-traffic Web sites that attract lots of visitors over short periods of time. While this may represent an interesting avenues in some instances, it may also not necessarily be the most effective way of advertising for your particular business. It depends on the working relationship that can be established between your business and the advertising site and the interest you can generate to make people click on the banner.

So far, it seems that banners have a rather low rate of response overall. Web surfers do not want to leave the site they just reached as soon as they arrive, only to find themselves on another site of secondary interest to them, such as the advertiser's. That is why new banners are being designed that let visitors browse and even buy without leaving the initial target site. These types of banners are more promising but are also more expensive than regular ones, so you need to figure out if they are within your budget and if they meet your objectives. For more information about these banners, refer to:

http://www.narrative.com

Mutual Links

A mutual link is an agreement with another Web site to add a link that leads to your site while you add a reciprocal link to your site. An advertisement or a link on somebody else's well-visited Web site can certainly bring you a lot of business, but it can also have no impact, depending on the popularity of the other site. This is a widespread practice, but the performance of this type of arrangement is not easily measured. Of course, the more sites that are linked to yours, the more successful this technique will be. Its popularity is due to the fact that it does not cost anything for the parties involved, as the arrangement is mutual.

Affiliate Programs

As described in Chapter 5, nothing prevents you from setting up your own affiliate program by which you give other sites a commission on your sales. You could have other Web sites set up links leading to your Web site and pay a commission for each sale you make when customers come from those sites.

The fact is, the cost of doing so is rather low when compared to traditional marketing methods. It is especially worth it if you have a high volume to move. So far, this kind of arrangement has been very popular and seems to be gaining a stronghold among the Internet community. It is a win–win situation in that anyone with a Web site can put up a link and get paid without spending any additional effort or time. The number of links from other sites is practically infinite, thus increasing exposure and potential transactions exponentially.

Traditional Advertising

Your can advertise your Web site in regular promotional materials, including magazine ads, newspaper ads and brochures. You can either mention your Web site URL address or you can include in your ads a sample of what can be found on your Web site.

Printed literature is still quite popular, and it is probably a good idea to continue using it within your overall marketing strategy. In addition to printed magazines and newspaper, where you would usually advertise in relation to your specialty, you can use magazines and newspapers that are related to the Internet. These magazines and newspapers are read by a lot of Internet users who may not otherwise see your ads and who might easily become new customers.

Business Cards and Letterhead

Including your e-mail address and World Wide Web site URL on business cards and letterhead is definitely a plus, and companies are doing so increasingly. If you have a Web site, include this information on your next order of letterhead and business cards. Nowadays, printing your e-mail address on business cards minimizes having to play telephone tag and increases the speed and efficiency with which people can get in touch with you.

Having that information on your letterhead also shows that you are well organized and can use technology efficiently. It is also a good reference for your customers, who can then reach you at their leisure, outside of business hours.

Magazines, Newsletters, Bulletins, Brochures and Other Promotional Material

Magazines

When advertising in printed magazines, take the opportunity to also advertise your World Wide Web site. Magazines are a good source of reference for URL visits. Printing one or more pages or sections of your Web site can add a new angle to your regular advertising. Many companies now successfully use that concept.

Some printed magazines will also mention a Web site for free if it is of interest to their readers. For instance, if your Web site offers something of value to a magazine's readership, that can be an incentive for the magazine to discuss it in the context of an article. Also, some Internet magazines are on the lookout for special Web sites to mention in their pages even if that business is not directly related to the Internet; the fact that you are using the Internet gives them an opportunity to demonstrate the use of the World Wide Web in conducting business.

There may also be electronic magazines that discuss topics related to your business activities. If an electronic magazine talks about your business, chances are it will put a link from its site to yours, which could represent a big boost for your Web site.

Of course, to take advantage of all this, your Web site and the way you use it must be innovative and present interesting new ideas and options for the magazine readers.

Newsletters and Bulletins

Newsletters and bulletins can be used in two ways: you can publish them yourself or you can use existing ones as a promotional vehicle. Newsletters and bulletins are published in electronic format as well as printed format.

Some marketing newsletters are regularly published on the Internet and sent to subscribers who want to be kept informed of what's going on in certain fields or new things happening on the Internet and the World Wide Web. Some of them will talk about you or your business for free, and others will charge you a fee.

In addition, you can publish your own newsletter to keep subscribers informed of various developments and news in your field of expertise while discussing your products in an informative manner. This gives you an opportunity to establish credibility in your field and position yourself and your business as a resource, should readers need your type of services or products.

Remember to keep it informative and avoid "pushy" advertising. Also make it available to subscribers as a choice. If you send it out unsolicited, it could be considered as spam.

Brochures

You can feature your World Wide Web site in your brochures by mentioning its URL address and the e-mail address to reach your business. This is a nice complement to the other information about your business included in a brochure. The advantage of doing this is that you can offer a lot more information in a Web site than in a brochure. Including a reference to your Web site in a brochure allows people to find immediately any additional information they are looking for, quietly and at their convenience, without the need to phone during business hours. Of course, your Web site must live up to the task, so take that into consideration when preparing it and make sure people will find what they are looking for. A well-designed Web site will get people ready for the next step, which is the actual business transaction or purchase. People like to be reassured before making a commitment, and the process is the same for a sale. If your Web site is able to give people the reassurance they need, it will be very effective.

If your business has a strong foothold on the Web, you can build your brochures and other promotional material around your Web site. Some brochures are replicas of the Web site and a direct invitation to visit the Web site, and everything it has to offer, rather than visiting the physical premises. Again, it all depends on how your business is set up.

Public Events and Trade Shows

When participating in exhibitions and trade shows, use the opportunity to publicize and demonstrate your Web site live. For instance, you can set up a computer in your booth and allow people attending the trade show to visit your Web site while visiting your booth. You can also organize live presentations around Web surfing and the use of the Internet, presenting your Web site and the services and convenience it offers. Take the opportunity a trade show presents to offer special promotions, such as a free subscription to an electronic newsletter or some other incentive. This can allow you to obtain certain information about the trade show visitors, such as the percentage of visitors who use the Internet. That will give you an idea of the potential your business has on the Internet. Hand out brochures advertising your Web site and its advantages: information, customer service, 24-hour availability, on-line ordering, product specifications and so on.

When participating in a trade show as an exhibitor, always set objectives ahead of time and prepare a plan that details how those objectives are going to be met through the event. By doing so, you will obtain profitable results from your investment because these events are usually expensive once all the costs have been factored in.

Prepare a strategy for your overall promotional activities. List your strengths and your objectives. Identify specific value-added benefits and bank on them to get as much free publicity as you can. Determine which promotional tools are best in order to meet your goals. Establish interaction among the various options and use every available possibility. Make the most out of your marketing efforts.

17 Taking Care of Business

Your Web site is a source of activity and requires attention and maintenance on a regular basis. Once it is up and running, it needs to remain "lively" if you want to retain your visitors'/customers' attention. A static Web site that contains only a few pages that are put up and never touched again will not attract a lot of interest and recurring visits once people have seen it. If nothing changes, people will not return unless they use your site only for ordering products they need and know will be there. Even so, you will want to offer them new products and direct their attention to special features, promotions or services you offer.

For instance, if you owned a store, you would change the interior decor, the displays, the product positioning and the window displays every so often. This is necessary to keep the customers' interest and to entice them to return to your premises to see what's new and make additional purchases. The same principle applies to a Web site.

Updating the Web Site

The importance of updating your Web site has already been discussed, but it cannot be stressed too much. Prepare a plan that details what you want customers and potential customers to see on your Web site. Plan your updates and do them on a regular basis. A plan

263

has several purposes. The first is to render the making of changes more even and harmonious. There may be periods when you have more changes than at other times, but that should be the exception. It is not a good idea to have a very slow period after a very intensive one. If you increase the pace of your changes, try to maintain that pace for a while and avoid a seesaw effect. A plan will help you accomplish this.

Also, it will help you identify instances where you need extra help or outside intervention. For instance, if you think you will need someone's input at a given moment, you can enlist that person's help in advance. The results will be far better than waiting until the last minute.

You do not need to make major changes regularly. A few new items that are well positioned will make your pages appear dynamic and will maintain interest. Add some news, and find one or two features that are of particular interest to visitors.

Again, check your links. Make sure all the files are present on the server. Also make sure your image files are on the server, in the same directory as your HTML pages, so that the broken icon does not show up on your page instead of your actual image.

Answering Queries Promptly, Processing and Filling Orders

In addition to the above, you will receive e-mail queries from visitors which you will need to answer and orders from customers which you will need to fill. It is important to follow up promptly, just as you would in a regular commercial business. Do not leave customers wondering whether or not an order has gone through, and do not give the appearance of a deserted Web site by not answering questions from visitors.

If you receive an e-mail query, either answer it promptly or send an e-mail acknowledgment to let the person know that you have received the query and will take care of it diligently. Do the same when filling orders. You can acknowledge an order and confirm that it will be taken care of shortly. Indicate to customers the total cost and the time frame in which they will receive their products or services. Failure to do so can and most likely will have serious consequences for the success of your Web site.

Monitoring Web Site Activity

To know what's happening within your site, you need to monitor what's going on. Find an effective way to follow the level of activity on your Web site. You can get your Internet service provider's support, or you can program your site yourself using cookies and appropriate software.

Monitoring will ensure that you can correct and improve any weak location within the site. You will be able to invest further in the pages that are very popular and delete or modify those in which people have no interest. A Web site can soon represent a sizable investment, and it is to your advantage to get the most out of it.

Monitoring your site will help you to plan for the next step and will guide you as to which direction you should take in order to improve your site and maintain and increase its profitability.

Dealing with Complaints

If you get a complaint, make sure to do something about it. Although it is impossible to please everyone, take time to carefully assess any complaint and find a way to address it that will be satisfactory to your customer. Be creative and always take customer service seriously. As vocal as people can be in the real world, they can be a thousandfold more vocal in the cyberworld. Among other things, people go to newsgroups and chats to complain about a company if something negative happens. Given the volume of Internet users that can be reached with those tools in a short period of time, the kind of damage that can be done is obvious. This can and has been devastating for some companies. That kind of damage is extremely costly and difficult to repair. Properly taking care of a complaint takes a lot less time and effort and costs a lot less.

Automatic Update Notification

You have the option of sending automatic updates to your customers, according to their areas of interest. These updates can take many forms. Plan which ones are the most appropriate for your involvement with the Internet, for the scale and type of your business and for your budget.

These reminders can be simple e-mail, newsletters, or fancier means using push technology to deliver customized material. Sending interesting material to your customers and potential customers will show them that you care about them and are equipped to meet their needs.

Integrated Search Feature

If you have a lot of data that can be searched on your Web site, sooner or later you will need to integrate a search engine within your site. This will make it easier for people to find what they are looking for. However, a Web site that presents only a window in which a keyword is typed is not very accommodating for the visitor. Figuring out what keyword to use in relation to your database can be challenging for the person doing the search.

Find a way to at least give some hints as to what your database may contain. This practice is good marketing; it will inspire people and will entice them to spend more time on your site. Try to enliven the search by offering various options. Provide links or an overview of the content. Give themes, ideas and suggestions.

Don't Overextend Yourself

Avoid getting in over your head when operating your Web site. This can happen if you do not prepare and plan carefully. If you prepare objectives, a schedule of what you want to do and an estimate of the costs, you will be able to do what you want in an organized manner, as well as meet your goals. This will contribute to the professional image of your Web site. There is no point in starting out strong only to flicker out later.

Beware of the Idle Web Site!

Above all, don't neglect your Web site once you have set it up. An idle Web site will make you look like you are out of business or will give the impression that your business is not doing too well. That is the last thing you want to do with a brand new Web site. Avoid losing the potential the Internet offers your business.

18 Business Ethics

Company Ethics for Employees

Why should you care about business ethics? You should care because lack of ethics can seriously threaten the progress and profitability of your business. Some strong values should be integrated into the business process right from the start. This applies equally whether you have a one-person operation or a business with a large number of employees.

Whether or not you have employees, you need a code of ethics to define the way your customers are going to be taken care of. This is especially important if you do have employees; if your business has no code of ethics, employees can use the excuse that they did not know they were doing something harmful to your company's image or credibility, whether done intentionally or not.

The code of ethics is a good basis for explaining clearly to employees what you expect from them on several levels: in relation to your customers but also your confidential information, your equipment, their behavior off premises when representing your business and so on. In the same manner, behavior with Internet customers should be governed by your code of ethics, as should what your employees do on the Internet.

Employees can do various things when using the Internet. They can transmit data, some of which may be confidential and require special processing before being sent. You may not want other data to be transmitted outside of your business at all. Employees can visit questionable Web sites and make transactions that could harm your business reputation or for which you are liable. A clearly formulated code of ethics plays an important role in preventing unethical or illegal activities. Employees need to know the type of behavior you expect from them while conducting business operations and while they are using the Internet on behalf of your business. They need you to outline their business responsibilities.

If you already have a code of ethics, you need to add a section governing the Internet and its use. If you do not already have a code of ethics, this is a good opportunity to prepare one because if you are doing business, you need one.

Ethics affect several aspects of a business: employee behavior, communication between employees and with customers, employee attitude, values and principles, working ambiance, business performance and results, respect and self-worth, disclosure of information and compliance with financial and legal requirements.

Ethics play a role in your employees' well-being, which directly affects their work performance and their relationship with customers (Figure 15). Ethics also affect business practices, corporate politics, procedures, regulations, rules and corporate image. As far as the Internet is concerned, issues that are governed by ethics include:

- Corporate credibility and reputation on the Internet and the World Wide Web
- Professional conduct in Internet dealings
- Dealing with customers
- Profitability
- Security (telecommunications, information, data, software)
- Use/misuse of company time while using the Internet
- Handling company assets/misuse of proprietary information (data protection and transmission)

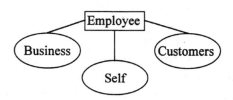

Figure 15   Employees' well-being affects their personal behavior, which in turn has an impact on the business operations and on the customers.

- Conflicts of interest
- Export control (encryption issues)
- Financial reporting (e-commerce fraud, etc.)
- Reporting misconduct of other employees and attitude toward those individuals
- Hiring practices (jobs posted and material sent by candidates on the Internet)
- Sexual harassment (through e-mail)
- Dealing with suppliers (suppliers' compliance to your procedures and regulations)
- Dealing with competitors
- Dealing with representatives and distributors
- Use of trademarks and copyrighted material, both yours and that of others
- Use of employee personal and medical records (confidential intranet issues)
- Advertising statements
- Foreign business practices
- Bribery (gifts, favors, etc.)

Internet Ethics Toward Customers

Define how you want your employees to treat your Internet customers. A set of procedures will guide your employees in the way they answer queries and process requests or orders. Prevention is always better than having to repair an unfortunate situation, and prevention takes less effort than repair does. Remember that in the real world, one unhappy customer will let at least 15 others know about his or her dissatisfaction. In the cyberworld, you can multiply that number almost exponentially because the Internet opens up new channels through which people can communicate their dissatisfaction instantaneously. For instance, a dissatisfied customer can let hundreds and even thousands of people on chat channels know that he or she is not satisfied and has been wronged (or so that person feels). An unhappy customer can also put your Web site on various blacklists, which may not always check out the facts.

A simple code of ethics will prevent a lot of problems if you take the time to systematically examine it with each new employee and if you ask your existing employees to review it at regular intervals. In your code of ethics, do not forget to deal with all regular business situations as well as those that are particular to the Internet, such as spam.

The following procedure will help you prepare the Internet portion of your code of ethics:

1. Establish policies and guidelines, as well as a mechanism by which they will be implemented.
2. Assess the risks to your business and the risk factors that are specific to your situation and employees on the Internet.
3. Identify vulnerabilities (i.e., "what if" situations) and how likely they are to occur.
4. Compare the above with your written code of ethics, if you already have one, and assess compliance.
5. Compare written policies with implicit rules (i.e., ones that are formally read and signed by employees versus ones that you assume are understood by employees).
6. Make adjustments if necessary.
7. Prepare an implementation plan; provide your employees with:
   - Information
   - Training
   - Review and follow-up
   - Supervision
8. Monitor and evaluate.

Remember that ethics are more critical on the Internet because customers are still wary of doing business electronically instead of face to face. Therefore, you have to make a special effort to demonstrate to your customers that you have high ethical standards and that you will live up to your promises. This will make the difference between success and failure on the Internet.

For more information on business ethics, go to:

http://www.kpmg.ca/ethics/vl/98ethcse.htm
http://www.usserve.us.kpmg.com/ethics

Also remember that a fresh search on the subject with a search engine will bring you up-to-date references.

Employee Training

Employee training is frequently a neglected aspect in small and medium-size businesses. However, it is an important aspect for every business as it has a direct impact on a company's performance and results.

Neglecting training will slow your operations and cost you money because of mistakes, time lost searching for information and blindly trying solutions and methods. Even if you operate your business by yourself, you need to stay on top of your specialty as well as acquire additional complementary skills. Also, taking some training once in a while is an excellent way to acquire new knowledge, renew your inspiration and motivation and make new business contacts.

If you want your employees to perform according to your specifications, you need to train them. You cannot expect them to know what you have not taught them. Even the most competent employees will still need a minimum of instructions, particularly those that pertain to your specific business operations. This should include your code of ethics and your conflict of interest policies and guidelines.

Even if employees tell you that they already know what you want to teach them, review with them their level of knowledge. Often, there are at least some details they do not know or aspects they have neglected or overlooked.

Training can sometimes seem to be costly, but if you make careful calculations, you will see that you will soon recoup anything you invest. If you choose your training program carefully, it will be a real investment for your business.

The Internet brings on new aspects of performing tasks and operating equipment. In addition, there are numerous possibilities and options in regard to hardware, software, setups and so on. It is practically impossible to know everything; you have to determine what your employees need to know to implement and operate this new approach in your business. If you have prepared a good plan, you will easily be able to identify the knowledge that is needed and choose the training accordingly. Of course, this also applies to you personally.

If you have several employees, organize tasks and training according to your objectives. Assess each employee's knowledge and determine what he or she needs to learn. If you are going to offer employees training, they need to have the necessary motivation to learn if you want the training to be productive. Training employees who are not interested in learning is a waste of time and money.

Any training program should be structured in a way that allows you to meet your corporate objectives. If you are running your company by yourself and decide to register with outside training programs, make sure that you will learn things that you can apply immediately in your business. If you have a training program prepared for your employees, get involved in the design to make sure it does for your employees what you expect it to do. Set precise objectives for the people who will prepare the program and make sure they stick to them.

Take advantage of the training opportunities the Internet offers. You can organize a tailored training program on the Internet, using the available technology in a cost-efficient manner.

Remember that the Internet is a highly technical medium, and if you want your business to evolve with it, you will need someone who maintains some level of technical proficiency in order to be able to keep up with that evolution. In addition, remember that training in relation to the Internet is still in a relatively disorganized state and will probably remain so for a while. The Internet encompasses so many different technical possibilities that keeping current on everything is virtually a full-time job. That is why you need to know the direction you want to take with it and steer your business and employees in that direction.

VI The Future and the Evolution of Your Business on the Internet

19 Making Your Business Evolve on the Internet

If you are not already involved with the Internet, this book has just started to show you what the Internet can bring to your business and the potential it has for your business growth.

As soon as you get involved with the Internet, it will open up new areas for your business. If you want to prosper from it, you need to keep on top of things. To gain some perspective, look at your business from a global point of view. There is a lot of talk about globalization, but does it apply to your business?

The New Economy

What is the new economy, and how is it going to affect your business? The Internet is an ideal tool to position your business in the global market. It opens up a whole new and very wide market if you know how to use the medium effectively. The new economy has developed around high technology and telecommunication. It is based mainly on new technologies, on information itself and on the transmission of that information. It is based on information goods as opposed to industrial goods. For instance, software, music, movies and electronic books and magazines are information goods. Furthermore, even where merchandise is sold, information becomes an important part of the total value of products, and that phenomenon is more acute on the Internet.

277

When applied to the Internet, the new economy brings an extra dimension — the Network Economy. The Network Economy is based on principles that directly contradict traditional economic principles and requires special attention from businesspeople. Up to now, scarcity has increased the value and price of goods. Think about old coins, precious stones, gold, works of art, etc. In the Network Economy, this is directly contradicted by the fact that plenitude increases value. This can be quite a shock to businesspeople who have not followed closely the recent evolution of business-related Internet developments. Making a product widely and freely available has proved a major asset for several companies in that it has secured a large portion of a given market. Consider World Wide Web browsers, portals and search engines. Those companies have seen the price of their stock skyrocket. It is an incomprehensible phenomenon even to the most seasoned financial analysts.

Another important aspect is networking. Networking has always existed in business. However, in the cyberworld, networking takes on new dimensions and is applied on a wider scale. We have seen similar phenomena before, without necessarily realizing it, because they were integrated into business operations in such a slow and gradual manner that they were almost imperceptible. Consider the example of the telephone. What would business be like without a telephone? When we purchase telephone service, we buy a phone and obtain the service for a few dollars. But the service takes on its real value when we consider the links it allows us to establish with millions of other telephones and subscribers. The fax machine has played a similar role. With the Internet, the networking experience is enhanced in that each participant can and does enrich the whole network with real input in a more or less extensive and sometimes unusual manner. The value of the network components increases exponentially as the square of the number of participants because the results are compounded by the amount of input.

A unique effect of the Internet is the fact that the more available something is, the cheaper it becomes, even to the point of being free in many cases, and the more value it has. This goes totally against traditional business principles and represents a major challenge for traditional thinkers. There is a definite risk for businesses that do not take into account this new axiom. If they do not pay attention, they will be at a serious disadvantage over a short period of time. The traditional commercial market as we know it is at risk of shrinking in the near future.

In view of all this, there is now competition where we never thought there would be any, and new markets have opened up where it was not possible to go before. Boundaries are slowly disappearing with this new electronic commercial structure; some attempts have been made to control it, but with mitigated success. The new economy affects a lot of businesses in that it is changing the rules of the business game.

This new concept is not always clear in people's minds, and a lot of people are not yet aware of it. That factor is compounded by the turmoil brought on by the changes and the level of adaptation to which businesses must adjust in order to keep up with those changes. In periods of important change, there is always some turmoil before things settle down, and the faster change happens, the more disoriented people become. In order to survive, a business must adapt. To adapt, businesspeople must know what is going on and keep informed.

Business structures are changing in an irreversible way. Long-term stability, whether in a business or a career, is becoming a thing of the past. Business success will still be achieved, but will be rather short-lived; business will have to repeat the process that led to success, but in another niche, another market or another sector and on a more regular basis. Emphasis will shift as businesses reorganize and produce in different ways. The most precious commodity will be brain power. That trend can already be seen in the newest companies whose main assets are their high-technology specialists and employees.

The Actual Growth of the Internet Throughout the World

The Internet has undergone and is still experiencing tremendous growth. People are getting involved with the technology at an increasing pace and new markets are adopting it. For instance, the teenage market is already a very active segment, as youngsters are not intimidated by the technology. An increasing number of seniors are also taming the Internet and using it to their benefit.

Electronic commerce will continue to grow, and although not all figures agree as to its exact future growth rate, the consensus is that it will experience fast growth over the next few years, displacing the traditional economy to some extent. The World Wide Web has had tremendous growth as well. Let's look at some recent trends:

Internet users	1993: 3 million 1998: 145 million
Domain names	1998: over 4.5 million, with a weekly growth rate of over 65,000
World Wide Web pages	1996: 72 million 1998: 320 million
Internet annual traffic growth rate	700%
Advertising growth rate	Among the 20 leading ad-supported World Wide Web sites, there has been an average increase of over 175% in revenues between 1997 and 1998
Electronic commerce	In 1998, Cisco's sales were $5 billion and Dell Computer's sales were over $6 million per day

The above figures show the extent to which the Internet is a phenomenon unlike anything we have seen.

Evolution of Various Existing and New Services

There are a tremendous number of options and services already available on and for the Internet. The number of plug-ins that are available for World Wide Web browsers is just one example. The Internet is a universal medium open to everyone, and it contains a lot of free resources. The fact that thousands and even hundreds of thousands of people are working on their own to develop new things for the Internet means that the number of options is sure to multiply.

However, those efforts are not necessarily coordinated, and only the forces of the market will determine which ones will succeed and which will disappear. Making decisions and selections in that context is not an easy task for the businessperson. Some mistakes are bound to be made once in a while, because of the relative instability of the market, especially if one focuses too much on details and loses sight of the "big picture." One must therefore study the matter carefully because making too many wrong decisions can seriously affect a business.

To make informed decisions, you need to look at what is going on now and at future trends. You can still try a few things without incurring significant losses, because a lot of the options are not very expensive. Offer various options to your customers and see which ones they prefer and which ones they adopt. Keep informed and look around. Study the freely available statistics and trends and get personally involved with the Internet to get a good feel for it. Explore new markets and experiment before implementing.

Checking the Profitability of Serving Foreign Markets

If you are thinking about serving new markets, you need to assess whether it will be profitable. In business, expansion is not automatically profitable. It depends on how it is done. The Internet can certainly expand the geographical territory you can serve, provided your service or product can be widely distributed. For instance, a dentist would not necessarily expand his or her territory through the Internet, but the concentration of his or her clientele in a given area could be expanded with that medium. On the other hand, if a business sells high volumes of merchandise, the Internet will allow it to reach a far wider area.

If you are considering the whole world as your playground, make some calculations to determine what it will cost you to serve new markets. Foreign markets often have different constraints and requirements than one's home turf. In certain cases, you bypass intermediaries and sell directly to the consumer. In other cases, you might be subjected to new rules and regulations as they will surely appear over time in relation to electronic commerce. For instance, Europe's privacy regulations could represent a major obstacle for North American businesses. It is a matter of studying your market, the same as you would do for any basic business operation. Roll up your sleeves and get down to analyzing the mechanisms and details that pertain to your Internet project. Look at how much it will cost and what your profit margin will be. Also look at what it will cost customers. Will it be worth it from the customer's point of view? Are you going to be competitive in those markets?

Plan for the Internet Evolution of Your Business

Just as you would plan your business expansion carefully in the real world, you must do the same for the Internet. Remember that expansion is one of the most common reasons for business failure. That is because uncontrolled expansion is very costly and the costs are sometimes too much for a business to bear, even over a short period of time. With the Internet, that factor may be compounded. In addition to regular expansion costs, an additional factor is the required investment in technological products. Make sure you understand the implications of the new technologies you are planning to implement and what their total cost will be in the end.

If you have prepared a good business plan, you will have forecasted your business growth. If your results differ from what you anticipated, assess the impact on your business operations. This is most effectively done through the operating budget. Comparing the operating budget to actual results is the most effective way to manage your business and its growth.

Gradually Adding Services on Your World Wide Web Site

If you prepare your plan carefully, you will be able to determine which services you can implement first and schedule further implementation. Include in your plan what measures you will put in place that will allow you to follow new technological developments, how you will assess their value for your business and how and when you

User

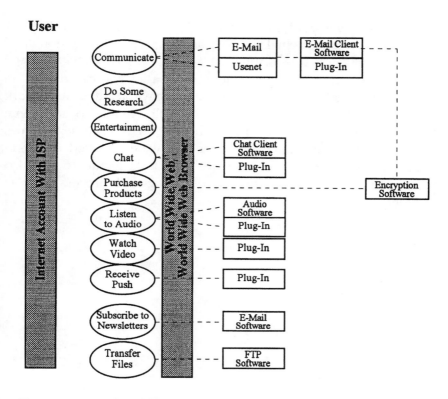

Content Producer / Merchant

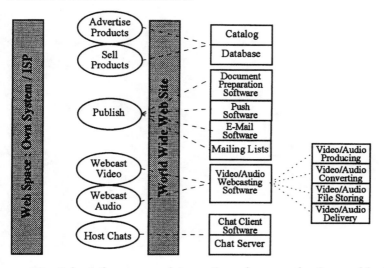

Figure 16 Select the appropriate options for your business objectives.

will implement some of them in the future. Plan for an Internet budget and phase in actual as well as future implementation in a sustainable and profitable manner.

If you have a limited budget, there is still a lot you can do on the Internet. Start modestly with basic but effective features and work your way up. As you make money, you will be able to add some fancier functions and services. Establish the cost of each service and plan for its implementation. The forms that were included earlier in this book are designed to help you with this task. Figure 16 will also help you create an overall picture of the global process and its possibilities.

20 What Does the Future Hold?

What Direction Will the Internet Network and Its Services Take in the Coming Years?

In order to know what to expect in the future, one needs to analyze what has happened in the past, to see how the Internet has evolved.

From Early On...

Up to the early 1980s, the Internet was mainly used for exchanging computer files. This exchange took place mainly between universities, private research centers and the U.S. Department of Defense.

The early to mid 1980s witnessed the emergence of an exchange of information. With it came the capacity to communicate more efficiently through electronic messages.

From the mid 1980s to the early 1990s, the Internet was used to store information for consultation purposes. This is what brought about the early search tools. The World Wide Web was being developed and introduced at the end of this period.

The early to mid 1990s saw the development of passive interrogation. The early Yahoo! was among the first tools for such a purpose. At that time, it was still a simple directory of World Wide Web pages.

From the mid 1990s to the year 2000, the interrogation becomes active. Search engines with new features allow a search to be refined by using keywords.

What Is Next?

What will follow all this? It can safely be projected that the next step will be intelligent interrogation. Artificial intelligence is nothing new. The main obstacle to its success during the last decade was probably the human factor. Using artificial intelligence efficiently required heavy investments in human resources, which the structure of our society neither permitted nor encouraged for economic reasons. The Internet now offers new avenues and opportunities for profitability. For the first time, we are starting to see a new motivation as well as new opportunities for new applications of artificial intelligence.

The future will probably lead toward an intuitive interrogation, closely followed by an integration of virtual experience. For instance, if you were looking for travel information, you could experience a virtual visit to a specific region or location, based on your tastes and preferences. Virtual participation will be an increasing trend as people seek new experiences but want to spend less time and money living them. Figure 17 summarizes this.

Notice that the forecast at the beginning of this chapter is made in five-year increments. In reality, there is an opportunity for faster availability and implementation. However, widespread use will be limited by acceptance and the speed at which the general population can assimilate new technologies and start using them effectively on a regular basis. The youngest generation will probably allow the process to take place at an increasing pace, as they do not have the same hang-ups about computers that some of their parents have.

Concretely, What Does It Mean?

In the next five to ten years, the two main uses of the Internet — individual/personal use and work/business use — will evolve in a parallel direction, for maximum efficiency.

Work/Business Use

Business applications will expand in order to fulfill educational, training, communication and commercial requirements and objectives. Each sector will be developed according to specific and evolving industry

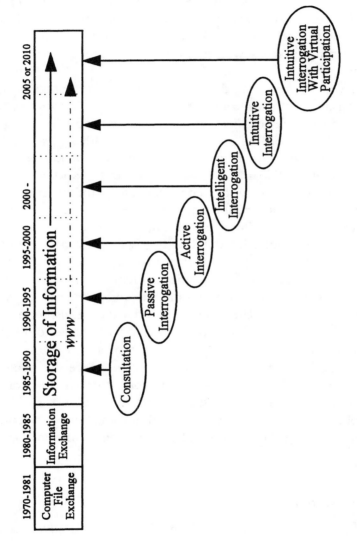

Figure 17 The evolution of the Internet over the years.

needs. For instance, as machinery is increasingly computerized, specific training needs will attain a very refined state. We will also see equipment operated from a distance by remote access. Heavy equipment operation, miniaturized precise tasks and medical interventions are but a few examples. Robots will occupy an important place in both heavy work and precision tasks. Applications for the Internet will cover earthly tasks as well as increasing space exploration and applications.

Training will take on new dimensions as it further evolves toward specialization and individualization, while becoming intertwined with virtual experience. Individualization and customization of training will have a direct impact on the speed at which individuals assimilate it. There will be a revolution in education as more individuals choose to be self-taught and learn their specialties faster and in a more customized manner, refusing to accept mandatory and often outdated training and courses. One could argue that the new breed of specialists will lack a general cultural education, but the new options and vast information provided by the Internet will offer more attractive and stimulating ways to acquire it, motivating people in new ways. It is already apparent that rigid education structures will have to adapt to a completely new training environment, and that may represent their biggest challenge to date. Traditional educational institutions will definitely have very strong competition and will have to reinvent themselves. What is coming is nothing short of a revolution.

For a while, this new way of learning will produce the necessary pioneers, some of whom are already at work, to pave the way for emerging new specialties. For instance, Internet business specialists, virtual experience design specialists and information and content specialists are among those who will play a greater role in the near future.

Individual/Personal Use

On a more personal level, users will benefit from more advanced and specialized services. A new type of user will emerge, one who is not intimidated by individual use of computers and advanced telecommunications, as a lot of people of previous generations were. Although seniors are getting involved with the Internet in increasing numbers, many of them, as well as their children's generation, are still hesitant when it comes to computers. This is similar to what happened historically with the automobile, telephone, airplane and fax. Internet communities, which have started to emerge, will take on new importance, and new types of organizations will expand their reach far beyond what now exists.

New forms of entertainment will result from merging various technologies. For instance, the convergence of television, telecommunications and the Internet will provide individual users with more interactive entertainment, where the user also becomes a producer. Interactivity will foster the development of new devices that add movement to participation, which will lead to an enhanced virtual experience. Content will become richer and more vast in quantity.

Self-teaching will also play an important role, but with a dual purpose: for entertainment as much as for professional development. Users will be able to access extensive instructional material before actually engaging in a recreational activity, whether it is golf, water skiing, parasailing and so on.

How Will All This Be Possible?

Technologically, this will be made possible by structuring information with the help of information storage devices of various levels, capacities and capabilities, as well as with an important investment in specialized content.

Users will have access, through the Internet and through a first level of servers used for storage of information, at the Internet service provider (ISP) level, to larger remote mainframe computers that warehouse relational databases. In turn, those computers will be able to, on a more regular basis and in a more accessible manner than they do now, communicate with parallel servers that will manage and process information and communication and that also will communicate, on an as-needed basis, with supercomputers such as Cray and IBM. We will see an increasing use of inference. Inference is the process of deriving logical consequences from a series of premises. Inference search tools present results that include some data derived from initial searches that possess some degree of probability in relation to the search. We are just now seeing the initial stage of inference search on the World Wide Web. This process on a wider scale will make searches more efficient and will allow users to personalize their searches in a more intelligent and refined way.

Although costly, this can already be done, and as time goes by, it will become more affordable. We will see the emergence of "super ISPs" that will implement and use that technology on a wider scale. By doing so, the technology will be applied more locally and specifically, thus expanding the possibilities in an incredible manner. The real challenge will be to provide important quantities of quality content by type of information, specialty, location (country, state, region, city, etc.) and organization (large corporations, small and medium-size businesses, governments, nonprofit organizations, clubs, schools and colleges, etc.).

Conclusion

As has been demonstrated in this book, when it comes to the Internet, we are limited mainly by our imagination and our vision of all the positive options that are laid before us as consumers and business-people.

It is important to note that as the technical aspects are simplified, the risk that inaccuracies will be introduced increases. Simplifying complex technical matters is never an easy task. This is not a technical manual; if you are seriously interested in the technical aspects of the Internet, do not hesitate to research the matter further, especially because new developments appear every week.

At this point, it is important for the businessperson to keep a global picture while determining a precise Internet direction for his or her business. The Internet is accessible to businesses at a very low cost, from about $25 or $50 a month all the way up to an investment of over $1 million. The cost depends on what you want to do, how you want to do it and your budget.

Details are important, and you can take care of quite a few yourself, especially at the beginning of the process. Soon after, they can be assigned to technicians or specialists. Getting lost in too many details only prevents a business manager from ensuring a profitable process. This book could easily have contained at least two or three times the information and technical details as it does. However, its purpose is to make understanding the Internet and implementing it in a business simple and efficient. If you need more information than is contained here, you can find it easily on the World Wide Web, and you will know what to look for.

The most successful companies on the Internet are those which have transposed their existing business into an electronic format while adding extra services or features that are exclusive to the Internet. Understanding the very nature of this medium, along with the impact it has now and will have in the future, is the secret to being successful in the new emerging electronic economy. We have seen only a shadow of it so far, and it is continually transforming itself.

As a final note, some of the Uniform Resource Locator addresses included in this book may not be functional when you try to access them. While great care has been taken to provide up-to-date addresses as of the time of this writing and resources that are the most likely to be perennial, there is no guarantee of permanence attached to the World Wide Web. Because it is a growing and constantly evolving entity, much like a living organism, things appear, change and disappear. Remember that much of what is available on the World Wide Web is prepared on a voluntary basis; although this may at first glance seem like a downside, it is in reality the Internet's greatest asset.

May you have the greatest success on the World Wide Web!

Glossary

ADSL: Asymmetrical Digital Subscriber Line.

Aggregator: A device that concentrates transmissions.

Animated GIF: GIF image that contains several versions of an image in the same file and shows those images in a timed sequence for the effect of motion.

Applet: Small application software designed to work within a Web page.

Bandwidth: On the Internet, it commonly designates the amount of data that can be sent through a circuit and, by extension, the physical capacity and space available to transmit data.

Bit: Smallest unit of data. It designates a binary digit (i.e., a 1 or 0; 8 bits = 1 byte). The symbol for bit is lower case b, and the symbol for byte is upper case B.

bps: Bits per second.

Bps: Bytes per second.

Browser: Also called a Web browser or World Wide Web browser, it is software that plays the role of a graphical interface and displays HTML files in the form of Web pages. It allows users to navigate or surf the World Wide Web.

CGI: Common Gateway Interface.

Coaxial cable: Type of cable that contains one type of conductor in the center, surrounded by insulation and then by another type of conductor. It is the type of cable used for cable television.

Cookie: Piece of information in the form of a small file that is stored on a user's computer following instructions built into a Web page and that can be retrieved by specific Web sites for a certain level of interaction.

Cracker: Criminal hacker.

Crawler: Software that acts as a spider and explores the Internet, collecting Web page addresses and content. Can also refer users to FTP sites.

Cryptography: The science of encrypting.

CSS: Cascading style sheets.

Cyberworld: The world contained within the Internet.

DHTML: Dynamic HTML. More powerful HTML.

DNS: Domain Name System. System for identifying Web sites and their locations. DNS is managed by DNS servers.

DOS: Disk operating system.

Download: Transfer a file from another system to the user's system.

DSL: Digital Subscriber Line. Often referred to as xDSL.

EDI: Electronic data interchange.

e-mail: Electronic mail.

Encryption: Process of scrambling information for security purposes (i.e., to prevent it from being read by unauthorized parties).

Extranet: Outside network linked to an intranet through the Internet using the Internet Protocol.

Firewall: Hardware and/or software that is a security interface of a closed network and is designed to limit access from the outside as well as manage communication both ways for security purposes.

Freeware: Software available for free to the public.

FTP: File Transfer Protocol.

Gateway: Point of entrance to another network, which can be a company's intranet.

GIF: Graphical Interchange Format. Designates an image format that is compatible with the World Wide Web. GIF is limited to 256 colors and is particularly appropriate for images with solid colors with distinct lines or borders between them. GIF files use the .gif extension.

GIF89a: Animated GIF format.

Hacker: Someone who breaks into computer systems with the intent of doing damage, in the form of either data theft or destruction.

Hit: Request made by a user or Web surfer to a Web site for one of its pages.

HTML: HyperText Markup Language.

HTTP: HyperText Transfer Protocol. Set of rules for exchanging files on the World Wide Web and linking them with one another.

Hub: Point of convergence of data that is equipped with some kind of device that will redirect the data toward its destination.

Hyperlink: Element of text, image or other graphic that is linked with another element, Web page or Web site by an HTML reference.

HyperText: Text that is tagged with a link to Web pages or to elements in Web pages.

Hz: Hertz; cycles per second. Can be used with a prefix, such as KHz for kilohertz, MHz for megahertz and GHz for gigahertz.

Imagemap: Graphic element of which various portions are hyperlinked to various other elements or Web pages.

Inference: The process of deriving logical consequences from a series of premises.

Internet: Worldwide network of computer networks and computers that interconnect with one another and use the Internet Protocol.

InterNIC: The registration service for (second-level) World Wide Web domain names.

Interstitial: In the Internet context and more precisely the Web advertising context, it designates a commercial message that is displayed in the middle of another action, usually after a banner has been clicked on.

IP: Internet Protocol.

ISDN: Integrated Services Digital Network.

ISP: Internet service provider.

Java: Programming language based on C++ and developed by Sun Microsystems.

JavaScript: Scripting language developed by Netscape and read by one of the engines running in a browser.

JPEG: Joint Photographic Experts Group. Image format compatible with the World Wide Web.

Kbps: Kilobits per second.

Kbps: Kilobytes per second.

Keyword: Word used to find documents when using a search tool or engine.

LAN: Local area network.

Linux: Version of UNIX adapted to personal computers.

LISTSERV: Electronic mailing list that allows a public discussion. It is one of the earliest mailing lists and is still popular.

Mbps: Megabits per second.

Mbps: Megabytes per second.

META data: Information contained within META tags.

META tag: On a Web page, it is a special tag in HTML format that provides invisible information as to the author of the Web page, keywords and description of content, as well as other specialized information.

MIDI: Musical Instrument Data Interface. Protocol for recording sound and playing it back on computers with sound cards and on digital synthesizers. It is also used to designate sound files, as in "MIDI file."

Mirror site: An exact replica that reflects the content of the original Web site on another server.

Modem: Modulator/demodulator.

NAP: Network access point.

Network: A netlike combination of elements. In the case of the Internet, it is a group of computers and related hardware interconnected with telecommunication links.

Newsgroup: Commonly designates Usenet.

NSP: Network service provider.

Operating system: Program that manages all the other programs on a computer.

Packet: Unit of data in the form of a self-contained bundle, usually less than 1,500 bytes in size.

PCS: Personal communication services.

PDF: Portable Document Format.

Platform: Designates various mainframe, server or client station operating systems. Among the variety of platforms are types of mainframes (VM, MVS, VMS), types of servers (NT, Novell, UNIX, Sun Solaris, HP-UX, AIX, SCO, Linux) and types of client stations (Macintosh, Windows, NT Station, DOS, UNIX).

Plug-in: On the World Wide Web, a small software program that adds a specific function to a browser.

POP: Point of presence.

Portal: The Web site of a search engine that offers extended content and/or capabilities.

Protocol: A code or a standard for transferring data and exchanging information.

Proxy server: A server linked to an intranet that acts as an intermediary between the "inside" and the "outside" of a business. It manages communications to allow only authorized communications with the rest of the Internet, as part of or in association with a firewall/firewall server and gateway/gateway server.

Push: Technology that sends preselected Web content directly to a user's browser without the user having to access the specific Web site.

RAM: Random access memory.

RDBM: Relational database management.

Router: A device (or software) that connects networks together and routes packets (units of data) to their final destination.

Search engine: On the World Wide Web, a search engine is a site that offers some kind of search tool utility to search through the millions of pages on the World Wide Web. It can also designate a local utility contained on a particular Web site or intranet that will limit its search to that particular Web site or intranet.

SGML: Standard Graphic Markup Language. It is the forerunner of HTML and XML.

Shareware: Software that is widely distributed and for which the author asks for a voluntary contribution.

SMB: Small and medium business.

Spam: Unsolicited message in the form of private e-mail or e-mail sent to newsgroups or mailing lists. Usually designates advertisements, chain letters and other similar types of messages.

SQL: Structured Query Language.

Streaming: Technology that allows a user to listen to or view an audio or video file as it is downloaded on his or her computer.

T1 carrier: Type of transmission line that can carry a digital signal at a speed of 1.544 to 3.152 Mbps.

T3: Type of transmission line that can carry a digital signal at a speed of 44.736 Mbps.

Telnet: Protocol that allows users to access a remote computer and use programs and data as if they were using the actual computer that contains the data.

Transparent GIF: Type of GIF image in which one of the colors has been rendered transparent. Often used for the GIF background color, to make a picture appear integrated into the background of a Web page and give it a shaped look instead of the usual rectangle that appears around it.

Trojan horse: Small destructive program often disguised as another useful program or an Internet Relay Chat script.

UNIX: Type of computer operating system.

URL: Uniform Resource Locator. Address of a World Wide Web site.

Usenet: A separate network that is carried by Internet connections but is not actually part of the Internet. It carries newsgroups, which are discussion groups about specific topics.

Virus: Destructive program that has the ability to reproduce and widely infect files, programs and disks.

VPN: Virtual private network.

VRML: Virtual Reality Modeling Language.

WAN: Wide area network.

Web surfing: Navigating on the World Wide Web with the help of a browser.

WWW: World Wide Web. A graphical interface that provides access to documents and includes all resources and users that use the HyperText Transport Protocol.

WWW site: Document in HTML format that possesses a URL address and may or may not be linked to other documents. The HTML document is stored in the form of a Web file on an Internet server.

xDSL: An undetermined type (in a general sense) of Digital Subscriber Line.

XML: Acronym for Extensible Markup Language. It is a subset of SGML. It is forecasted that it will eventually replace HTML on the Web.

XSL: Acronym for Extensible Stylesheet Language.

For more information about the Internet and other related terms, go to:

http://www.whatis.com
http://www.zdwebopedia.com
http://www.delphi.com/navnet/glossary

Index